NEWCOMERS

NEWCOMERS

IMMIGRANTS AND THEIR DESCENDANTS IN THE NETHERLANDS 1550-1995

JAN LUCASSEN & RINUS PENNINX

HET SPINHUIS 1997

Orig. title: Nieuwkomers, nakomelingen, Nederlanders. Immigranten in Nederland 1550-1993.
© 1994 Amsterdam: Het Spinhuis. Revised edition
© Translation by Michael Wintle.

ISBN 90-73052-093-6

Coverdesign: Jos Hendrix
Typesetting: René de Ree

Het Spinhuis Publishers, Oudezijds Achterburgwal 185, 1012 DK Amsterdam

List of contents

Introduction

All over Western Europe, the problems of immigration and the integration of new arrivals are firmly fixed at the centre of the political debate. They dominate the national agendas of Europe, and also that of the emerging collective political unit, the European Union.[1] And in the wake of new migrations, anti-immigrant reactions and xenophobia gain momentum.

A common denominator in the public and political debate seems to be the opinion that we are dealing with something new, and previously unheard of. These supposedly new phenomena are associated with internationalization and globalization in the economic domains of finance, production and markets, but also in cultural exchange and communication. Such developments, especially their intensity and their increasingly global character, have certainly had an impact on the conditions governing international migration and its composition. But at the same time, these phenomena are by no means completely new. Over-emphasis on the novelty of the situation can easily lead to a distortion of our picture of the past, to the extent that it might almost be believed that Europe has only experienced in recent decades what the United States has known for the last century.

Remarkably, it is not only the public and political debate which betrays a kind of moral panic about new developments in international migration and their supposed consequences, and which presents a distorted picture of Western Europe's past experience. Scholars of migration also contribute on occasion to the misconception of a static Europe in the past. For example, Potts's discussion of Europe's migration history concentrates almost exclusively – apart from a mention of forced migrations in Nazi Germany – on the 'guest worker' issue since the 1960s.[2] There is every reason to doubt this picture of a Europe undisturbed until recently by great migration flows. One has only to think of France, which alone in the inter-war years took in more immigrants than did the United States, the immigration country *par excellence.*

Over recent decades, historians have conducted an impressive exercise which has gradually resulted in an entirely new picture of European migration history. The results of this research leave no room for doubt. For many centuries, European history has been fundamentally affected by major migration flows, making it in this respect not nearly as divergent from the history of the Americas as many historians of an earlier generation may have thought.[3] Charles Tilly has aptly expressed the meaning of this for the rewriting of the social history of Western Europe in stating, 'The history of European migration is the history of social life.'[4]

In recent years, national surveys of immigration history have been published in a significant number of Western European countries. Prominent amongst the examples are those by Lequin, Noiriel and Green for France,[5] Bade, Herbert, Hoerder and others for Germany,[6] Holmes and Lunn for Britain,[7] Caestecker, Deslé and Morelli for Belgium,[8] and Gallo for Luxembourg.[9]

This book follows suit in its own particular way. It depicts the rich immigration history of the Netherlands, and examines in detail the process of settlement of the various immigrant groups over a period of roughly four and a half centuries. It was originally published in Dutch in 1985 and appeared in a revised edition in 1994.[10] For this English edition it has been revised once again in the course of 1995 and early 1996.

We feel that our monograph on Dutch immigration and its history will contribute in the first place to a more balanced historical picture of immigration and the settlement process of immigrants. Secondly, it is our intention that monographs of this kind will lead to a systematic categorization or taxonomy of national developments and traditions; they must be grounded in meticulous historical and sociological data, and – even more importantly – on clearly defined concepts and theory.[11] A systematic, taxonomic exercise along these lines should ultimately lead to theoretical propositions which transcend the limitations of specific dates and locations.

On a rather more modest and practical level of aspiration, a thorough study of the different national trajectories may prove a basis for discussion not only of European migration history,[12] but also of migration policies and the actual position of immigrants in an increasingly united Europe. One of the essential questions is whether there are converging tendencies in the various countries. And which (if any) of the national traditions will become the predominant European standard?

There are varying and sometimes mutually contradictory images and opinions about the history of the Netherlands as an immigration country. On the one hand the idea is regularly put forward, with a degree of restrained pride, that the Dutch nation has traditionally always been an island of tolerance. It was therefore a refuge for those in trouble elsewhere for political or religious reasons. On the other hand the opinion is often expressed in the post-war Netherlands that the country seems to be faced with immigration flows which have no historical precedent. The comparison with the past implicit in this assertion is, however, never substantiated, and seems only to serve to accentuate the anxiety and disapproval contained in the assertion. The two views, of a tradition of tolerance and of the alleged uniqueness of the extent of post-war immigration, are hardly ever advanced together.

Such historical images seem only to be employed when they serve the purposes of their users, who select those images which underline their convictions. In this way the images, which in themselves often have some historical grounding, become 'stylized' into a caricature, a kind of half-truth. In fact the two images outlined in the previous paragraph indeed have some historical foundation. As will be related in the subsequent chapters, there has indeed been a degree of toleration in the areas of religion and politics in the Netherlands since the early seventeenth century, but at the same time this toleration needs to be qualified in various ways: tolerant in comparison with neighbouring countries, tolerant of a large number of groups but not of all, and tolerant within a specific interpretation of tolerance. Similarly, the idea that the flow of post-war immigration is unique in its extent is not entirely divorced from the truth, if this immigration is compared with that of the preceding hundred years from 1850 to 1950. If, however, earlier periods are included in the comparison, then the extent of post-war immigration has been relatively limited.

In this book we attempt, albeit in broad terms, to reconstruct as complete a picture as possible of the arrival of foreigners in the Netherlands from the middle of the sixteenth century onwards, and to describe how they acquired a place in Dutch society. But we turn our attention not only to these foreigners themselves, and their place in society; the question of how their descendants have fared is of much greater importance in the long-term perspective chosen for this study. The deliberate choice to examine the arrival of newcomers and the process of the reception of immigrants and their descendants in the Netherlands over a lengthy period covering more than four centuries has important consequences for the nature of this study.

In the first place the long timescale, and therefore the large number of immigrants and immigrant groups, means that this book cannot attempt to give a full description, or make any pretensions to be one. Our object is not encyclopedic comprehensiveness, but the considered analysis of immigration and settlement processes, of the causes and the consequences associated with them, and of the constantly recurring elements which can be identified in each immigration flow and in each process of the settlement of a group of newcomers and their descendants. To achieve this analysis, we must examine the phenomena in a thorough and consistent way. This means that the book consists alternately of chapters which explicitly set out the methods of studying the phenomena and their associated concepts, followed by chapters giving a selection of historical data and descriptions, and chapters devoted predominantly to discussion.

In the second place the long-term view means that we look mainly at immigrant groups as a whole and over a long period. The often dramatic vicissitudes experienced by individual immigrants, or by their descendants, are seldom featured; even the fact that the migration itself and the process of settlement is in almost all cases an energy-draining, often painful and sometimes traumatic process for newcomers and their descendants is assumed to be common knowledge. The long-term perspective, and the restriction of discussion to the level of the group, leads to a detached analysis, which may sometimes appear even clinical, particularly if compared with the often strongly committed positions taken in current Dutch literature on newcomers.

In the third place, it follows from our central objectives as well as from the long-term perspective, that attention must also be directed to Dutch society. In the discussion about the settlement process of newcomers and their descendants, one of our basic assumptions is that the host society, and the way in which it influences the settlement process, needs to receive at least as much attention as the newcomers themselves and their descendants. And this means that in the long-term view we must examine the various successive Dutch societies over the course of time, which have reacted to newcomers in different ways. The Netherlands of the Republic of the Seven Provinces treated both its subjects and newcomers differently from the nation-state after 1815, and from the welfare state of the period after the Second World War.

The way in which all this material is presented in this book can be envisaged as a triptych with two wide side-panels and a narrow central panel. On the left is hinged a picture portraying the arrival in the Netherlands of a great number of people over the course of four centuries. The central panel shows the country to which they have come, the diversified and constantly changing Netherlands. On the right is an image depicting the relationships between the newcomers and the Dutch, and the process of settlement of newcomers and of their descendants.

The design of the panels on the left and right is identical. Both analyses start with an explanation of how the facts will be approached and with definitions of the concepts which will be involved. In each case there follows a summary of the historical experience in the Netherlands of the arrival and settlement of newcomers and their descendants. Finally follows a general discussion of what has been presented earlier, in order to provide the reader with a clearer view of the material.

The central panel shows the host society, its political structure and social divisions. This society changed in the course of four centuries, and the social differences within it acquired new significance, not only for indigenous people, but also for newcomers.

The way in which the total picture is arrived at is rather unconventional. To maintain the artistic metaphor, the painters are not of the same school. An attempt has been made in this book to combine and integrate the sociological approach with the historical one.

Chapter 1

Looking at newcomers
Differing approaches and concepts

Newcomers to the Netherlands and their descendants are subjected to a confusing number of labels. Some people use the terms 'foreigners' or 'aliens', without much concern about the different meanings these words can have. Others prefer 'immigrants' or 'allochthons',[1] emphasizing in so doing that they are referring to people who have come from outside the country. Yet others want to lay the stress less on their different legal position or on the fact that they come from outside, but rather on their special position in the Netherlands; they therefore use terms such as 'cultural' or 'ethnic minorities', or just 'minorities'.[2]

This assortment of rapidly changing and often poorly defined concepts and designations can be explained in several ways. The first and simplest explanation is that over a period of time, real changes occur which require a suitable designation. It is, for instance, clearly demonstrable that migration from the Mediterranean area to the Netherlands was quite different in character in the 1960s from what occurred in the late 1970s. The original temporary labour migration of young males, denoted by the term *gastarbeiders* (guest workers), adopted from the German *Gastarbeiter*, changed into a migration flow of immigrants' families, settling for longer, if not permanently. These kinds of changes rightly led to the use of other, more appropriate, terms. However, some time inevitably elapses before such changes are generally recognized and accepted.[3]

The reverse phenomenon produces further occasion for a confusion of concepts: this is when there is no change in reality, but the terminology used to describe and designate it is continually changing, because in heated political and social arguments the terms employed soon become tainted and therefore unusable. In the debate about newcomers in the Netherlands this kind of sensitivity has been particularly evident since 1970. Concepts such as 'assimilation' and 'integration', derived from sociology and reasonably well defined in that discipline, became so controversial in the discussions about policy to do with newcomers that their use became quite scarce in government documents and academic debate. In the frequently bitter arguments about government policy they seem to have acquired the status of terms of abuse.

Such a rapid change in concepts is awkward and causes continual confusion. But perhaps this phenomenon need not be regarded as entirely negative; it can also be seen as a mark of sensitivity for the problem. It suggests that some attention is paid to the groups of newcomers themselves, or at least shows a desire not to offend these groups by using unfortunate terminology.

The most important reason for the present confusion of tongues is probably lack of clarity about the questions which are implicitly posed when a particular term is used, together with uncertainty about what concepts best suit which questions. Those with an interest in the legal aspects should exclusively use the legal term 'alien', and should not, for example, switch to the concept of 'immigrant'. For instance, an immigrant from the Netherlands Antilles is not an alien; on the other hand, there are many Turkish children born in the Netherlands who are still aliens, but not immigrants. The different terms result from completely different approaches and different sets of questions.

We tried to avoid this linguistic confusion of terms in 1985 – in the first edition of this book – by introducing a new and hitherto untainted term: *newcomers.* By this no more was meant than the word implies: people or groups who had not previously been inside the current national frontiers. Under more detailed scrutiny this designation will have to make way for more specific terms. We cannot therefore avoid devising some ranking of the current terminology in use and defining the various concepts.

Newcomers as migrants

A first method of approach to newcomers is that of the sociology of migration in a strict sense, sometimes also referred to as the sociology of geographical mobility. Important questions in this approach are: why do people leave at a specific moment? Who moves away?

What determines the direction of the migration flow? Who, in due course, comes back, and why? In short, these are questions about the conditions under which migration originates, takes place, and ceases, the different types of migration, and the selection of migrants and those who return.[4]

The concepts involved here are strictly defined and have a clear relationship to each other. *Migration* can be briefly characterized as a change of domicile on the part of a person or household for a sustained period. If the change occurs across national frontiers, it is called *international migration*.

By this definition the term *migrant* is a neutral one: it says nothing about what the person involved will or would like to do in the future. Nor does it say anything about the countries of origin or destination. The related concepts of *emigrant, immigrant,* and *remigrant* do express this and are therefore more specific. Seen from the Netherlands, an *emigrant* is a person born in the Netherlands who settles abroad for a period of time.[5] In common speech in the Netherlands the notion has been added that an emigrant settles somewhere else with the intention of staying there permanently. The post-war emigrants to Australia, Canada, New Zealand and certain other destinations have apparently come to define the concept. It will also be used here in this sense: persons born in the Netherlands who move abroad with the aim of staying there permanently.

If migrants who had settled in the Netherlands go back to their country of origin, we call them *remigrants, returning migrants* or *returnees.* The same terms will be used for emigrants who, after a stay abroad, move back to the Netherlands.

These concepts provide relatively few problems: the emigrant and the immigrant who subsequently remigrates go away. They therefore disappear from the field of view and so are not the subject of this study. That is also the case with Dutch-born remigrants from, for instance, Australia, because they merge back into Dutch society and are no longer identifiable. A surprising consequence of this terminology is that migrants' children born in the Netherlands who finally settle in, for example, Turkey, are not remigrants, but emigrants. The number in this category grows in proportion to the increase in the average length of stay of immigrants and therefore with the increase in the number of children they have in the Netherlands.[6] As early as 1984, of all the Turks who left the Netherlands, 1,283 were born in the Netherlands. These young emigrants then made up 20 per cent of all Turks leaving the country.[7]

Turkish children born in the Netherlands may not be immigrants, but they are aliens. The term 'alien' (vreemdeling) is a legal one, and is unaffected by whether they are regarded as non-Dutch by society. (Photo Hannes Wallrafen)

A newcomer can also stay on in the country where he has settled, in this case the Netherlands; he then becomes an *immigrant*. It makes sense only to speak of immigrants when there are sufficient indications that the stay of individuals or groups will be permanent, or of significant duration. To be born elsewhere, and the expectation of a long stay, are therefore the most important elements of the definition.

It is striking that the concepts of 'migrant' and 'immigrant' have been so little used in the Netherlands since the Second World War. On the other hand, the term 'emigrant', referring in this case to the intended permanent migration of indigenous Dutchmen to specific countries of destination, has been used all the more. This selective usage is linked with the general assumption after the war that the Netherlands was overpopulated. Immigrants could and should not come and emigration was to be encouraged. More than half a million Dutch citizens left with the help of a specially organized Emigration

Service.[8] The immigrants who arrived all the same in this period were designated in other terms: *repatriates* for those who could not or would not stay in a now independent Indonesia; most of them, however, had never been in the 'patria' (fatherland) before, or had in any case not been born there. Immigrants from Surinam and the Dutch Antilles (West Indies) were called '*rijksgenoten*' ('fellow citizens' of the overseas parts of the Kingdom of the Netherlands), as if it were a matter of internal migration. And some were called *guest workers*, as if to stress the fact that they were only here for a short time.

To see newcomers as migrants or immigrants, and to use the associated terminology consistently, has the advantage of increased clarity. But there are also limitations. For example, these terms say nothing about the citizenship of the immigrant, and therefore also nothing about his legal position after immigration. Repatriates and 'fellow citizens' are just as much immigrants as adopted children from

Like many Americans, the Japanese belong to a fairly prosperous group of aliens. They are much less dependent on Dutch social provisions than, for instance, Turks or Moroccans. The Japanese have their own schools, their own clubs, and normally have little contact with Dutch families. (Photo Hannes Wallrafen)

abroad and Turkish or German long-stay families. The definitions also avoid the question of whether the immigrant is regarded by society as a foreigner, in the sense of 'not one of us', or as an ordinary Dutchman. Neither do the terms do anything to clarify the position of the immigrant in his new society. Perhaps the most important limitation is that the approach from the point of view of migration in the strict sense says nothing about how the children of immigrants are affected. They are beyond its scope, if they are born in the country where their parents have settled. The second generation, defined as the children born to immigrants in their country of settlement, remains invisible according to this approach.

Newcomers and citizenship

The second approach, already mentioned in passing, is the legal one. As the ideal of the nation-state grew stronger in the course of the nineteenth century, citizenship gained in significance. Boundaries between states, and particularly between the citizens of states, became more distinct. Every individual is considered to be a citizen of a single state. In that state, but only there, he enjoys his full rights as a citizen. Outside his own country he is an alien and another system of law applies to him. This definition of 'alien' and the situation outlined here has applied to the Netherlands at least since its first Aliens Act of 1849.[9]

The concept of *nationality* is important for two reasons. In the first place citizenship plays a crucial role in admittance and in possible expulsion: an alien can easily be denied entry to the country, and he can be expelled if he does not keep to the rules. A country's own nationals cannot as a rule be refused entry or expelled; at the most they can be imprisoned. In the second place citizenship determines a person's position in law: in general an alien has fewer rights and more obligations, and this can appreciably influence his social position and opportunities. In this sense the legal approach also has a sociological significance. Over the last century the most plentiful and most comprehensive statistical data have been based on this legal criterion, which also reflects the social importance that has become attached to it since the middle of the nineteenth century. In earlier periods the award of rights in the Netherlands was much more at the level of local governments of towns and provinces.

There are limitations on the legal approach too. First of all this approach does not necessarily coincide with newcomers or immigrants: at the present time about 13,500 aliens are born in the Netherlands every year; on the other hand, every year 33,000 aliens are naturalized (awarded Dutch citizenship).[10] The figures for immigrants and aliens match each other best when there is a new extensive wave of immigration exclusively of aliens. This was, for instance, more or less the case in the period between 1976 and 1981. If the wave of immigration continues for longer, or ceases, the two criteria grow steadily further apart.[11]

One perhaps rather obvious qualification is that not all aliens are the same, in the first place because there are different kinds of aliens with unequal positions under the law. For example, since 1968 subjects of countries in the European Community/European Union can, normally speaking, not be denied entry to the Netherlands, and they can look for work without a special permit. Citizens of non-EC/EU states, on the other hand, must apply for residence and work permits before entering the Netherlands.[12]

But a more fundamental qualification is that, apart from this kind of difference between aliens, legal status appears to have no predictive value for the social position of the newcomer. Not everyone with an unusual legal position suffers from restricted opportunities, as is clear from research done among American citizens in The Hague.[13] This group of generally prosperous aliens appears to experience relatively little trouble on account of their distinct legal position. Few of these Americans speak much Dutch or have many contacts with Dutch families. They rarely join Dutch organizations but, on the other hand, are able to support their own organizations, clubs, schools, and other facilities. In short, as a group they lead a socially segregated but generally prosperous existence within Dutch society.

If this only slightly caricatured sketch of the position of American aliens is compared with that of, for instance, Turkish aliens, then the differences are plain to see. For the less well-off Turkish aliens their anomalous position under the law has a quite different significance. To acquire an income and to educate their children they must rely on whatever social provisions are available. The legal status of an alien seems to work as a constraint especially when it is in combination with disadvantageous socio-economic circumstances.

The distinction between nationals and aliens is therefore closely connected with the ideal of the nation-state, which holds in short that the inhabitants of a state's territory form a single nation, with the same culture, language, and if possible, the same religion too. There is also a historic link implied, whether or not expressly stated, between the people and the state. The distinction between nationals and aliens can be seen as the legal expression of the idea of the nation-state. This concept, this ideal, in this way becomes an ideology. The national or citizen is, in a manner of speaking, 'at home'; the alien is a subject of another state or nation-state and has no self-evident rights, as does the citizen. He should have permission to stay, for instance, and he has no automatic right to services and facilities, let alone to exercise political rights.

The consequence is that, in this ideology of the nation-state, migration across national frontiers produces an exceptional situation that really ought not to exist. It is as it were the exception to the rule. This is all the more remarkable since international migration appears to be increasing in scale the world over.[14] Nation-states with a long tradition of immigration, or which take in substantial groups of aliens, eventually see themselves forced to make special regulations for these foreign immigrants. We will return to this later.

Since the 1980s the traditional distinction between nationals and aliens has been complicated in Western Europe by an additional factor: the economic and political unification within the European Community. Citizens of countries of what is now the European Union have increasingly also acquired rights – such as the right to seek work – in the other EU member-states. The result is that a new category has been inserted into the original divide between 'own nationals' and aliens, consisting of nationals of the other EU member-states. From this arises a hierarchy with three categories of rights and obligations, and also of entry: a country's own citizens, EU subjects, and the 'citizens of third-party or other countries'. Another consequence of the development of the European Union, particularly of the removal in practice of internal frontiers between the countries of the Union, is that the autonomy of the separate states as regards entry and immigration policy has diminished. There is strong pressure to reach a common policy on these issues, so that controls are moved away to the external frontiers of the European Union (including, in practice, the airports).

Newcomers as 'others'

In addition to the two ways of looking at newcomers described above there is a third, the sociological point of view. Here it is not so much a matter of formal criteria, such as whether someone has moved across a national frontier, or whether they hold some other nationality. The key question in this approach is in the first place the extent to which newcomers are seen by the established society as 'different', as belonging to another group, and as a consequence of this are treated as 'different' and perhaps as 'outsiders' in a large number of aspects.

The ways in which this 'being different' is labelled can vary. One way is to consider newcomers as 'culturally deviant', laying great stress on the different language, religion and culture which the newcomers bring with them. There is often an implicit assumption that the Dutch society in which they have arrived is homogeneous and uniform in cultural terms. Such a definition of newcomers as 'cultural minorities' itself begs the question of how these cultural differences should be resolved. In the process of thought outlined this can only be achieved in one way: society must aim for the cultural adaptation of the newcomers, who will then be assimilated in the long run. In this process the established society undergoes no essential change: it is perceived as a given, or as axiomatic. The alternative to this one-sided approach is for society to choose to become 'multicultural'. In this case a number of aspects of society will change; to a certain extent it allows newcomers to retain and continue the development of the language, religion and culture they have brought with them. This demands adaptation from both sides, and cultural differentiation remains possible in principle.

A second way in which this 'being different' of newcomers can be labelled goes much further: they are then considered primarily as belonging to another race or people, with unalterable cultural differences. These kinds of racist ideologies are based on the irreconcilability of the nation-state with the phenomenon of immigration by other 'races' or 'peoples'. For supporters of this view of newcomers (or certain groups of them), the measures which should be taken by the state are plain: immigration of such newcomers should be restricted as much as possible. If immigration is unavoidable the position of these newcomers should be defined as far as possible as temporary and in subordinate roles. The possibility of deportation or even expulsion should be kept open.

A third form of labelling newcomers as 'being different' is to regard them primarily as 'socially deprived' or 'disadvantaged groups'. The core of this is not a matter of cultural differences or of belonging to a different 'race' or 'people', but the low social position which they occupy in the society they have joined. In the Netherlands this last form of labelling, particularly in government policy, has exercised a steadily increasing influence with the advancing development of the welfare state. After all, in the welfare state equality and equal opportunities for all inhabitants (that is to say, regardless of nationality) are important values. It admits of no second and third-class inhabitants. It therefore goes on to define certain groups of newcomers (who occupy a low social position) as disadvantaged groups, and promotes special policies directed at their emancipation.

These three ways of labelling newcomers as different, based on the core sociological concepts of culture, race, and class, can indeed be distinguished in analysis, but in practice they are often combined and intermixed. Arguments are borrowed from more than one form of labelling at once. For example, Dutch 'minorities policy' since 1981 has been officially founded on elements from the first form of labelling (moving towards a multicultural society) and in a negative sense on the second (the fight against discrimination and racism), but primarily on the third form of labelling (combating disadvantage); only those newcomers who are in a disadvantaged position are counted among the groups targeted by the government's minorities policy.

Newcomers in figures

The various ways of looking at newcomers and the various characteristics of these groups have far-reaching consequences, not least on the figures with which the number of newcomers is calculated. A few examples from the most recent statistics will illustrate this.

Take first the approach of migration sociology:[15] in 1994 the number of migrants entering the Netherlands totalled 99,000. In the same year 62,000 people left the country. The net figure for migration, or migration surplus, was therefore positive: 37,000.

If we now look at the same figures from the second point of view, and distinguish between nationals and aliens (and within that, between EU subjects and others), then the figures look quite different. In 1994 a total of 39,000 Dutch nationals left the Netherlands and 31,000 of the same category entered the Netherlands from abroad. The net migration of Dutch nationals was therefore negative. In the same year 68,000 aliens entered the Netherlands (16,000 of whom were EU nationals) and 23,000 left (of whom 10,000 were EU nationals). The migration surplus of aliens was therefore 45,000.

If we turn our attention to the newcomers settled in the Netherlands, than the figures are even more contradictory. If we look at nationality alone, then 774,000 aliens appear to have been living in the Netherlands on 1 January 1995: 5.0 per cent of the population. If, however, we were to keep to the government definition of 'ethnic minorities', then 865,000 people were covered by it in 1994; about 5.7 per cent of the total population. But if we take yet another definition, as is done in certain political debates, that of *allochthons* (defined in the broadest sense as all people of non-Dutch nationality and/or born outside the Netherlands, plus all those who have at least one parent born outside the Netherlands), then on 1 January 1992 there appear in total to have been 2.4 million people of non-Dutch origin: 15.7 per cent of the total population! Depending upon the definition, the totals show enormous discrepancies. It will become apparent that the social characteristics of these statistical categories also show marked differences.

Chapter 2

Newcomers in the Netherlands since the sixteenth century

For centuries large numbers of newcomers have been arriving in the Netherlands, probably more than in any other country in north-western Europe. That the Netherlands has apparently been an attractive land to come to for so long is the consequence mainly of its relative wealth and its relative religious and political tolerance. By 'relative' is meant that it was often in great contrast to the regions from which the newcomers came. What then did this relative wealth and this relative toleration involve?

The economic foundations

In Dutch history the period from about 1585 to 1670 is justifiably known as the Golden Age. But even before that time the country could hardly be called poor and backward, although it still lagged behind its southern neighbours.[1] In the Dutch Golden Age our first thoughts are usually of the flowering of the arts, with painters such as Rembrandt van Rijn, Frans Hals and Jan Vermeer, and writers such as Hooft and Vondel. This cultural blossoming was, however, rooted in a healthy economy. The successes of the merchant fleet appeal most to the imagination: the Dutch East India Company (VOC), founded in 1602 and for a long time ruler of the waves from the Cape of Good Hope to Japan, and the West India Company, which counted amongst its exploits Piet Hein's capture of the Spanish silver fleet off Cuba in 1628. Less spectacular, but more important in volume and in value, was the trade in grain, fish and timber southwards from the Baltic and Norway, and the trade in wine and salt northwards from the Mediterranean and the Atlantic coast. These flows of trade formed the basis of Dutch commerce, and indeed they were called the 'mother-trade'.

The size, reputation and success of the merchant navy went more
or less hand in hand with that of the battle fleet. Its best known
exploit was Michiel de Ruyter's Chatham expedition in 1667. There,
in the Thames estuary just short of London, he succeeded in
attacking and partly destroying the English fleet.

Extensive processing industries developed in direct association
with the trade. Spanish wool was woven into cloth in Leiden, and
imported linens were bleached in the dunes round Haarlem. The
windmills on the River Zaan, north of Amsterdam – at their peak
about six hundred of them – produced oil and dyestuffs, sawed
Norwegian and German timber, crushed lead, and also milled basic
and luxury foodstuffs such as grain, cocoa and mustard. Almost
every port had a number of these 'traffics', or industries based on
trade.

The gold of the Golden Age was not earned only by trade and
industry. Particularly in the coastal provinces, agriculture was prosperous, thanks to extensive specialization, for example in the many
polders newly reclaimed from the sea. Farmers no longer concentrated primarily on production for their own family or for the local
market, but increasingly cultivated specialist crops for industry and
for the international market such as flax, hemp, madder (for dying
textiles red) and tobacco. Cattle farmers engaged in the large-scale
commercial production of cheese and butter. There was a well
developed fishing industry along the coast.

In the rural areas peat-digging was also expanding. Peat was more
important as a source of energy than the windmills of the time, and
as important as gas and oil are now. If one adds to all this a superb
– for the period – communications network in the coastal areas in
the form of punctual and frequent barge services, and well developed
financial institutions such as banks and exchanges, then the economic boom and the associated flowering of culture in this period
becomes easier to understand.

Naturally not all was gold that glittered. The wealth was concentrated in the coastal regions and among the highest social classes.[2]
But rather than questions of distribution, it is the relative wealth of
the Republic and its successor, the Kingdom of the Netherlands,
which is our present concern. To establish whether it was economically attractive for newcomers to settle there, particularly in the
coastal regions, we must compare Dutch prosperity with that
abroad.[3] The standard of living in the province of Holland and the

adjacent areas developed favourably during the sixteenth century, if in fits and starts, which was much less or not at all the case in the surrounding countries. In the seventeenth century the Republic reached a level of prosperity that made it the richest country in north-western Europe. The absence of growth in the eighteenth century and the regression particularly of the towns in the coastal areas during the 'French period' (1795-1813) forced the Netherlands to yield its prominence to England in the first half of the nineteenth century. But even then the Netherlands by no means brought up the rear: it remained one of the front runners in Europe, although the difference between the Netherlands and industrializing Belgium and Germany gradually diminished after about 1850.

In the Netherlands industrialization started in the late nineteenth century, and this led to a new period of prosperity, though a short one. The growth was retarded, particularly during and between the two World Wars. Only with the period of reconstruction after 1945 and the tempestuous economic growth in the slipstream of the German 'economic miracle' has the Netherlands again become one of the wealthiest countries in Western Europe. Until the end of the

View of the River IJ. Painting by Willem van de Velde the Younger, 1686. In the seventeenth century the Republic reached a level of prosperity that made it one of the wealthiest countries of Europe. This prosperity attracted hundreds of thousands of hopeful job-seekers. In Amsterdam thousands of foreigners, particularly Germans and Scandinavians, signed on to crew the VOC (East India Company) fleet. In the left background of the picture is the VOC wharf and warehouse; on the right the Schreierstoren (Weepers' tower) and the South Church. (Amsterdam Historical Museum)

1950s, this did not mean much of an increase in the purchasing power of the man in the street, but from the 1960s, backed up by social security, it grew rapidly.[4]

For four centuries therefore the Netherlands has been one of the richest countries in the world. That this fact alone should exercise a great attraction for newcomers arouses no surprise, even bearing in mind the uneven distribution of wealth and income. This, after all, also applies to most other countries. The link between the Republic and newcomers can also be viewed from a different perspective: the mobilization of labour from elsewhere was one of the conditions for economic growth and its continuation. In the coastal regions of the Republic, as we shall see, constant in-migration produced a doubling of the labour supply. In any event, the link was a mutually beneficial one.[5]

The political foundations

The statement that the Netherlands has traditionally been relatively tolerant needs some closer consideration. From the early sixteenth century onwards criticism of the Catholic Church, to which practically everyone in Western Europe belonged, became steadily more vociferous. Erasmus of Rotterdam played an important part in articulating that criticism. It was not directed exclusively at contemporary Catholic practices; he also stated the need for rationality and for mutual tolerance. This was anything but an empty platitude at the time: both the Catholics and the schismatic Protestant groups often fought each other with fire and sword. The Inquisition, which pronounced 877 death sentences in the Netherlands, especially on Anabaptists, was the embodiment of Catholic intolerance. Protestant intolerance in the Netherlands was evidenced by the iconoclastic riots of 1566 and the murder of the 'Gorcum martyrs' – nineteen Catholic priests – in 1572. They were, in spite of William of Orange's orders to let them go free, tortured and hanged by Protestant rebels.

The supporters of the Reformation faced the fundamental question of whether they were prepared for the freedom of religion, which they demanded for themselves, also to be allowed to those who wished to remain Catholic. During the course of the Eighty Years War the answer was increasingly often in the negative. Although William of Orange still proposed a religious truce in 1578, when this failed the 'True Reformed Religion' became in fact the only official religion of the Republic. Moreover, during the Twelve Year Truce (the armistice between the Republic and Spain from 1609 to 1621) a bitter dispute broke out within the Reformed Church itself. The National Synod of Dordrecht (1618-1619) condemned one of the two rival theological factions, the Remonstrants. More than two hundred Remonstrant preachers were dismissed and well over eighty exiled. The execution of the best-known Remonstrant, Johan van Oldenbarnevelt, at The Hague in 1619 in front of what is now the Dutch parliament, shows how fiercely religious and political feelings had flared up, even if these were not the primary reasons for his death sentence.

The idea of tolerance, introduced by Erasmus, and after him espoused by many others, including Dirk Coornhert, William of Orange, and Oldenbarnevelt, therefore still seemed very remote at the start of the Golden Age. But there were also powerful forces against the centrifugal and divisive tendencies. The Regents, who held political power in the Republic, and who in the main were important merchants from the coastal regions, often inclined towards a humanist attitude to life. They saw little profit in religious and political hairsplitting, which could well have international political ramifications likely to harm trade. Their efforts, not entirely divorced from their own interests, were therefore directed towards combating extremism of whatever kind, and in this they were usually reasonably successful. The Republic only actually recognized Counter-Remonstrants (they would be called Dutch Reformed Church nowadays) as full citizens, but in practice dissenters were tolerated provided they did not act provocatively and – in a number of cases – they could afford to pay for their beliefs.

At that time most other countries in Europe followed a completely different line on the toleration of religious dissidents. In the German Empire the principle of *cuius regio, eius religio* applied, which meant that each prince imposed his religion on his subjects. So, for instance, Bavaria, Austria and Paderborn stayed Catholic, while Brandenburg (which later became Prussia) and Saxony became Lutheran, and Lippe, East Friesland and Bentheim 'reformed', or Calvinist.

Catholic countries like France, Spain, the Italian states, and the Southern Netherlands experienced the triumphalism of the

Counter-Reformation, which persecuted heretics with all vigour. The established Anglican Church founded by King Henry VIII, energetically oppressed its non-conformist subjects, particularly the Roman Catholic Irish. The Republic became a refuge for many who were persecuted elsewhere because of their beliefs. Among them were famous scholars such as the French philosopher René Descartes, who lived in the Netherlands from 1628 to 1649, and the English philosopher John Locke, who settled in the Republic from 1683 to 1689.[6] Freedom of the press made it possible for the collected works of the Englishman Thomas Hobbes to appear in Amsterdam in 1668; the same went for Jean-Jacques Rousseau's *Du Contrat Social* and *Emile* in 1762.

In assessing the nature of this sense of intellectual freedom and toleration at its proper value it is useful to examine both the theoretical basis of the idea of tolerance and the practical conditions under which it was realized. For the philosophical groundwork we return to John Locke. During his stay in the Netherlands he engaged in numerous discussions with the Remonstrant theologian Philip van Limborch. The result of these discussions, the *Epistola de tolerantia,* was published in Latin by Van Limborch in Gouda in 1689, before the appearance of the English edition. In this work Locke maintained that the civil authorities should neither defend nor attack any religious beliefs, so long as the adherents of those beliefs tolerate each other and are loyal to the same authorities.

So it was a theory of religious tolerance, in which the word 'tolerance' should be taken literally as putting up with dissidents, in this case with the minority by the majority. To quote the Dutch historian E.H. Kossmann: 'Dutch tolerance at that time was undogmatic, pragmatic, and only to a limited extent a matter of principle.' This narrow interpretation of the concept of 'tolerance' was recognized and sharply condemned during the American and French revolutions in the late eighteenth century. For instance Thomas Paine, the English radical involved in both revolutions, wrote in his *Rights of Man* of 1791-1792: 'Toleration is not the *opposite* of Intolerance, but is the counterfeit of it. Both are despotisms. The one assumes to itself the right of with-holding Liberty of Conscience, and the other of granting it.'[7]

Such revolutionary ideas found their own Dutch expression during the Batavian Revolution of 1795 and the various constitutional measures resulting from it. The most important outcome was the proclamation of freedom of religion and political equality for all in 1796. From that time Catholics, Jews, Baptists, Remonstrants and others, even those who wished to cast doubt on or actually deny the existence of God, were no longer excluded on those grounds from political rights and obligations. On paper this meant the realization of the idea of tolerance, but that it did not lead directly to tolerant relations between the various religious parties is clear from such things as the difficulties still experienced by the Catholics in the course of the nineteenth century.[8] For instance, as a consequence of the new 1848 Constitution the restoration of the Dutch Catholic episcopal hierarchy, which had been dragging on for half a century, seemed inevitable. This Constitution recognized the complete freedom of the adherents of any religious faith to organize themselves as they thought fit. The Catholics therefore appealed to the pope to appoint bishops again in the Netherlands for the first time since the Reformation. When in March 1853, after consultation in general terms with the Dutch government, the pope created the archdiocese of Utrecht, and the dioceses of Haarlem, 's-Hertogenbosch, Breda and Roermond, he was therefore fully within his rights. It was done, however, with extremely tactless phrasing. The Protestants were referred to by the pope as 'the weeds of Calvinism which were sown in God's fields three centuries ago'. He labelled the Old Catholics (a Jansenist sect of some significance in the Netherlands) as 'a monster and a plague'. Utterances of this kind were naturally not taken kindly, and there was an unparalleled Protestant reaction: the 1853 April Movement. A massive petition against the restoration of the Catholic hierarchy was organized, and reached its culmination when it was submitted to King William III in Utrecht by the poet and church minister Bernhard ter Haar. This petition was signed by two hundred thousand Dutchmen, a high response in a total population of three million. The king could not, however, negate the Constitution, and although the cabinet led by the Liberal J.R. Thorbecke fell, the principle survived. The bishops were installed, even in Utrecht, where there was so much Protestant feeling. The survival of the principle in this latest trial of strength meant in fact that there was no longer a religious majority in the Netherlands, but only minorities.

Less than a generation after the April Movement the Catholics and orthodox Protestants combined their forces to form a counter-weight against liberal policies, particularly where these promoted secular education. It was not that the orthodox Protestants had forgotten their anti-papism so quickly, or that the Catholics had given up their opinion of the 'weeds of Calvinism'. The simple fact that this seemed to be the only effective way to achieve the emancipation of both, brought these two old enemies to a pragmatic collaboration. The leader of the orthodox Protestants, Abraham Kuyper, and of the Catholics, H.J.A.M. Schaepman, started to co-operate in parliament in their fight against liberalism, and soon also against socialism: in 1888 the first 'coalition cabinet' made up of Catholics and of members of the Calvinist Anti-Revolutionary Party was formed, and was to be followed by many more in an almost uninterrupted sequence.

From the early twentieth century the recognition of religious minorities started to take the typically Dutch form of a 'pillarized' or 'plural' society.[9] Catholics and Protestants built up their own organizations in all the domains of public life, and non-religious segments of the population, such as the socialists and the liberals, found themselves forced to organize in more or less the same way. This society divided into 'pillars' was governed by an elite at the top, and because none of the parties formed a majority, the state's politics was a matter of coalition. Consultation and compromise were always necessary; what is known as the 'consociational society' arose. In practice an extensive system of legislation and regulation was developed, within which the finances and services of government were distributed among the different pillars, and the implementation of policy was carried out by organizations within the pillars.

This pillarized society was still fully operational in the 1950s. From then on deconfessionalization and secularization increased rapidly: fewer and fewer Dutchmen claimed to belong to a specific church, and if they did do so, felt less obliged than before to make exclusive use of the organizations and facilities of their own pillar. Thus the sociological basis for pillarization rapidly disappeared, but its structure, established in legislation and regulations, institutions and organizations, proved to be more enduring. We shall see later that the surviving structure of pillarization also became important for the institutionalization of religions like Islam and Hinduism which were brought by migrants to the Netherlands after the Second World War.

Another political circumstance has also been of great importance in the post-war context: the antagonism between the 'free world' of liberal-democratic states and the 'communist' world, in Europe often reduced to the contrast between East and West. This political situation had important consequences for migration. On the one hand, many countries of the communist world systematically limited or even entirely forbade their subjects' emigration, while at the same time the 'free West' tended automatically to regard people who nevertheless managed to escape from these régimes as political refugees. On the other hand, labour migration and recruitment occurred virtually exclusively between non-communist countries, since the frontiers of communist countries were closed. The fall of the Berlin Wall in 1989, and the disintegration of the Soviet Union soon afterwards, signalled the end of this period, and also implied a drastic revision of the attitude of Western countries to migrants from the former communist countries.

Finally, another recent change in the political environment is the 'unification of Europe'. Its early history lay in the economic co-operation which the West European countries launched quite soon after the Second World War. Initially it was in the form of limited co-operation in a few sectors (the European Steel and Coal Community), and later expanded steadily to cover more sectors and more countries: the European Economic Community of the Six (1958) became the Nine in 1972, which in the course of the 1980s became the Twelve with the entry of Greece, Spain and Portugal, and which finally totalled fifteen members in 1995 with the accession of Austria, Finland and Sweden.

For migration it was particularly important that from 1968 free movement not only of capital and goods, but also of labour, was created within the European Economic Community: subjects of EEC countries acquired the right to look for work in all the other countries of the Community, and if they found it they were free to work there. In this way there arose a large geographical area within which EEC subjects could migrate and work without hindrance.

From the mid-1980s a new situation arose as a result of two developments. In the first place the concept of a free economic area had progressed to the stage of abolishing many of the internal frontiers between EC states.[10] In the second place the discussion about unification gradually shifted from economic to political unification: the European Economic Community became the European Union. A combination of both these factors led to the issue of a common immigration or entry policy for subjects from 'third countries' outside the EU being put high on the agenda of the Union, where it still remains. The consequences of this are discussed later.

Who came and why?

Now that we have seen that for four centuries Dutch society has been characterized by great prosperity and by toleration, in comparison with the surrounding countries, the question can be asked whether newcomers were attracted by one of these two characteristics or – as was frequently the case – by both of them. But first some attention needs to be paid to the population of the Netherlands at the time of the transition from the Middle Ages to the modern era, and about earlier migratory movements.

It would be a mistake to describe the Dutch population at that time as 'racially pure', culturally homogeneous, and not influenced by migration.[11] In the first place the concept of 'race' has been shown to be scientifically completely untenable. But even if one still wished to retain it, then in the case of the Netherlands account would have to be taken of the complicated history of the origins of the population during the innumerable movements of peoples from prehistory up to and including the early Middle Ages. Although there appears to have been some stabilization after the year 1000, a great many groups of immigrants are known to us in the period 1100 to 1500. There were merchants from many countries, such as the Lombards from northern Italy, to whom the Dutch language owes the word *lommerd* (pawnshop). There were also heathen Balts, Dravants from the East, and gypsies, to give just a few examples. However, it is reasonable to accept that these were not large-scale immigrations, and so the great waves of immigration from the sixteenth century onwards seem to form a good starting point for a more detailed examination.

From the late sixteenth century one can indeed speak of the Netherlands' great power of attraction. Figure 1 gives a reconstruction of the number of newcomers from the second quarter of the sixteenth century until now, shown as percentages of the total population. This is more useful than absolute numbers, as the Dutch population grew in this period from about one and a half to fourteen million, so that ten thousand immigrants in 1600 means something quite different from the same figure now.

Figure 1: Newcomers as a percentage of the Dutch population, 1531-1995: statistical data and estimates

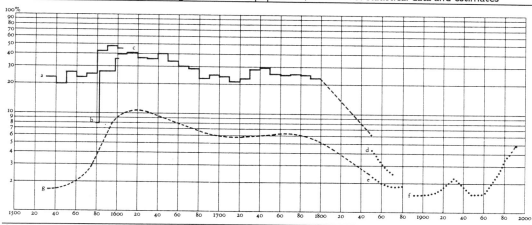

Source: Lucassen and Penninx 1985:28; Central Bureau for Statistics

Up to the middle of the nineteenth century the percentage share of foreigners in the total population appears to have developed roughly in parallel with the relative wealth of the Netherlands. In the eighteenth century, but particularly in the nineteenth, economic stagnation or decline appears to have gone hand in hand with much lower percentages of newcomers. While there are many problems in the calculation of these data, one conclusion is quite clear: although the current percentage is thought by many to be very high, it was appreciably higher throughout almost the whole of the seventeenth and eighteenth centuries.

The percentages shown in the graph are estimates of national averages. In reality there can be wide local variations. In general towns attract more immigrants than rural areas, but there are and were also striking differences between the various towns. The large towns in the West have always been strong magnets in comparison with the rest of the country. That applied in the seventeenth century too, as will be clear later from the accounts of the immigration of people from the Southern Netherlands and of Huguenots.

Based on their motives for coming to the Netherlands, four categories of newcomers are distinguished in the following historical summary: the first were influenced primarily by the relative toleration, the second, third and fourth were mainly attracted by the relative prosperity. However, neither motive should be seen in isolation; anyone fleeing for reasons of conscience will choose if he

a. Percentage of new freemen of Amsterdam born abroad, 1531-1606.
b. Percentage born abroad of men publishing banns of marriage in Amsterdam, 1578-1601.
c. Percentage born abroad of persons publishing their first banns of marriage in Amsterdam, 1601-1800, and percentage born abroad of persons married in Amsterdam, 1850.
d. Percentage of Amsterdam residents born abroad, 1849, 1859, 1869.
e. Percentage of residents in the Netherlands born abroad, 1849, 1859, 1869, 1879.
f. Percentage of aliens in the Netherlands in various years in the period 1889-1995.
g. Estimated percentage of residents of the Netherlands born abroad 1531-1849.

can a country where he can earn his living. And the reverse is true: if someone wants to earn a living elsewhere, he rarely does so in a country where he expects to find problems of conscience.

The four categories can be defined as follows:

a. Those who saw themselves forced to travel to the Netherlands because of shifts in religious and/or political power in their own country; in the case of these *refugees* it is usually a question of immigration in groups, which is completed within a short period of time.

b. Those who stayed in the Netherlands for a period of a few years. This category is mainly made up of young adults wanting to save up enough money to set up in business later on, and get married. These *labour migrants* consist for the most part of seamen, soldiers and domestic servants, and in the second half of the twentieth century the 'guest workers' can also be included among them. Then there are also other temporary migrants such as students, academics, and representatives of foreign industry and commerce, who can be gathered under the label of *transients.*

c. Those who regularly (in past centuries usually every year), according to the cycle of the seasons, came to offer their labour in the Netherlands. The length of stay of these *migrant labourers* was usually seasonally determined, and varied from a minimum of a few weeks to almost a year.

d. Those who, attracted by the opportunity of earning a good living, travelled to the Netherlands to settle there; this mainly consists of immigration by individuals or families.

We will examine each of these categories more closely.

Religious and political refugees

In the second half of the sixteenth century the changing fortunes of the Eighty Years War caused a great flow of people from the *Southern Netherlands* to the Northern Provinces.[12] Under Charles V and his son Philip II (1556-1598) almost the whole of the Low Countries, both north and south, were united under one ruler. In other words, at that time roughly the present-day Benelux, with the modern *départements* of Pas-de-Calais and Nord in north-western France, were a single political unit. The fact that all these regions were subject to the same prince meant that they could also combine their discontents about that prince. And discontent there was to an increasing degree, particularly under Philip II: taxation, increased in the context of his global policies, was thought to be too high; the independence of the provinces – jealously guarded for centuries – was too little respected; voices critical of the Catholic Church were suppressed, to mention only some of the most important grievances.

Particularly in the south-west, in Flanders, Artois, Hainault, Tournai and parts of Brabant, this discontent grew. This is where the first Calvinist congregations were founded. There, too, textile workers demanded better wages and working conditions, while nobility and burghers gave voice to their own – mainly political – protests. The discontent spread throughout all the provinces and resulted in a formal revolt, the Eighty Years War, traditionally dated from 1568 to 1648. Of principal interest to us is that Philip II with the aid of his Spanish troops finally succeeded in defeating the rebels in the southern part of the Low Countries. On the other hand the North gained its independence: the Republic of the Seven United Provinces was firmly established by the end of the sixteenth century, and was officially recognized by Spain in 1648. The Spanish reconquest of the Southern Netherlands had considerable significance for the inhabitants of those provinces, particularly for those who had been actively involved in the Revolt. The Catholic Church, supported by the authorities in Brussels, implemented an extensive campaign for the conversion of backsliders and for the restoration of religious observance, which became known as the Counter-Reformation. Economic development in the South, particularly trade, was frustrated because from 1585 to 1795 the Republic was able to control access to the port of Antwerp.

The result of these events and of the many military operations associated with them was a mass flight of people from the Southern Netherlands – particularly of Flemings – whether from Lille in the south or from Bruges and Ghent in the north. They fled to England and to the Protestant principalities of Germany, but mostly to the Republic. A large proportion of those who had originally sought refuge in England and Germany also made the Republic their final destination. By a conservative estimate there were at least 100,000 Southern Netherlanders living there around 1600, in other words about seven per cent of the total population.

It should not be forgotten that there were great differences between the people of the North and the South, even if they had both started the Revolt together. Their dialects were so different that they could often hardly understand each other. Moreover, many Southern Netherlanders only spoke French, particularly those coming from French Flanders (Lille and the surrounding area) and the inhabitants of Hainault and Artois. In the eyes of those actually involved, these and other differences were certainly greater at the time than the term 'Southern Netherlanders' would suggest.

Many textile workers from the Southern Netherlands settled in Leiden where they were responsible for a new boom in the industry. Many labourers and artisans from the Southern Netherlands chose the towns of Holland and Zeeland as their new abode. Among the newcomers were important merchants and entrepreneurs, who were to exercise considerable influence on the development of the Dutch economy: Balthasar de Moucheron from Tournai was, for instance, the driving force behind the trade expeditions from Zeeland to the White Sea. One of the explorers travelling in his service was Olivier Brunel from Louvain in the South, who sailed from Enkhuizen in the North. Willem Usselincx from Antwerp settled in Middelburg in Zeeland and was involved in a major land reclamation project in the Beemster lake or polder, north of Amsterdam, as well as in the West India Company and in Swedish-Dutch trade. When the East India Company was floated more than a third of the capital raised in Amsterdam came from Southern Netherlands immigrants. In 1599 Isaac Le Maire from Tournai had a stake in the Brabant Company trading with the East, and in 1602 was a co-founder, the most important shareholder, and one of the 'Gentlemen XVII' (the Board) of the Dutch East India Company. Many of these enterprises and expeditions would not have been possible without renowned cartographers such as Petrus Plancius, an Amsterdammer originally from West Flanders.

The intellectual achievements of many Southern Netherlands immigrants are no less impressive. The young University of Leiden, founded in 1575, had several immigrants among its professors: the classicists Justus Lipsius from Louvain and Daniel Heinsius from Ghent, the French historian and classicist Scaliger, and the theologian Franciscus Gomarus from Bruges, who became famous as the champion of the strict Calvinism of the Counter-Remonstrants, the doctrine that was blessed by the Synod of Dordrecht. The southern clergy were often extremely orthodox in their doctrine, and it is remarkable how their religious pressure group determined both the course of the Synod and the translation of the Bible authorized by the Dordrecht Synod. This meant that they had a profound influence not only on the idiosyncrasies of Dutch Calvinism, but also on those of the official Dutch language, which is to a large degree based on the language of the authorized version or States Bible, the Dordrecht translation.

If we add to this list the famous names of so many southern painters and graphic artists, it is safe to conclude that this wave of immigration was not only one of quantity but also of quality, and was of inestimable value for the economic, social and cultural flowering of the Netherlands in the Golden Age.

Almost a century later there was a second wave of Protestant refugees, the *Huguenots*.[13] In the sixteenth century the Protestant minority in France had long been living in suspense over the recognition of their rights by the king, who was Catholic. A number of them had already left for the Netherlands in that period. Although their rights had been guaranteed in 1598 by the Edict of Nantes, these guarantees were gradually undermined, as for instance by the Edict of Nîmes in 1629. From 1680 troops were billeted on Protestant families, and a further flight began, this time on a large scale. This became a flood when Louis XIV, the Sun King, finally revoked the Edict of Nantes in 1685 and annulled their guaranteed rights. An estimated 200,000 people fled abroad between 1680 and the first decades of the eighteenth century: more than a quarter of them, some 50,000 to 60,000, to the Republic.

In the early years they were welcomed by the towns with open arms. Amsterdam in this way received an additional 12,000 inhabitants in a short period, 2,243 of whom were given citizen's rights without payment, three years freedom from taxes, and other privileges. An important reason for this welcome and generosity was that the first groups consisted mainly of townspeople, specialized in trade and industry, such as textile manufacture and hat-making. When many more and much poorer partners in adversity arrived, the exceptional advantages granted to newcomers were withdrawn after a few years.

The economic and religious significance of the Huguenots was very similar to that of the Southern Netherlanders a century beforehand. That there was also some degree of spiritual connection between the two groups is shown by the fact that the Huguenots became members of the Walloon or French-speaking Calvinist

French Huguenots flee the country. A Dutch artist's impression of their flight. Detail of a print by Jan Luiken, c. 1685. (Amsterdam Historical Museum)

congregations already founded by their predecessors. In number they were, however, fewer in both absolute and relative terms; they made up about three per cent of the total population, still a respectable percentage. They, too, brought with them successful businessmen and great scholars. The philosopher Pierre Bayle is an example of the latter; he settled in Rotterdam and was one of the most important precursors of the Enlightenment.

Not only Protestant, but also *Jewish* refugees settled in the Netherlands. As a result of the reconquest of 'Moorish Spain' and Portugal by Catholic princes during the late Middle Ages, Muslims and Jews were driven back ever further to the south. After the fall of Granada – the last Moorish foothold in Spain – in 1492, the Jews could no longer practise their religion freely. Two roads were open to them: flight abroad, particularly across the Straits of Gibraltar to Morocco, or conversion to Catholicism. Those who chose this last solution were known as 'new Christians' or *conversos* (converts).[14] However, the position of these converts remained extremely fragile under the Spanish – and after 1540 the Portuguese – Inquisition, which accused many of them of 'crypto-judaism', practising the Jewish religion in secret. In this atmosphere of suspicion many found themselves on trial. Particularly after 1580, when both countries were united under one crown, that of Philip II, the persecution of real and alleged *conversos* became unbearable. Countless Portuguese, rightly or not, were accused of being descendants of the *conversos*, and of the 'crimes' which were almost inextricably associated with them. Many of those persecuted fled and settled abroad. In this way several thousand Portuguese found their way to the Republic in the early seventeenth century. These refugees, accused of Jewish sympathies, but officially and probably for the most part actually Catholic, ended up in an extremely anomalous position.[15] In spite of all the toleration, very little esteem was shown in the Netherlands for these Catholics, even if they were victims of the Inquisition.

These newcomers must also have had their own doubts about their place in the religious spectrum. Trapped in a spiritual no-man's-land, they chose to revert to Judaism.[16] This was, however, easier said then done; they knew neither the Jewish religious observances, nor Hebrew. It was far from clear where they were to get this knowledge from, as there were at that time hardly any Jews living in the Republic. The story goes that a German rabbi and, of all people and by a twist of fate, the Moroccan ambassador in the Republic provided this knowledge. Both the Republic and Morocco were at that time at war with Spain. The Moroccan ambassador was a learned Sephardic Jew, descended from those who had decided around 1500 to flee the Iberian peninsula for North Africa. In this way there arose in Amsterdam, where most of these 'Portuguese' or 'Sephardic' Jews had ended up, a relatively small new Jewish community with, after some time, its own synagogues.

The persecution of Jews in Central and Eastern Europe caused new flows of refugees after 1635. These were known as 'High German' or 'Ashkenazic' Jews, who spoke Yiddish and who fled the anti-Semitism in the Germany of the Thirty Years War and in Poland and later on also in Russia. These Central and East European Jews also settled in the Netherlands, by preference in Amsterdam, and set up their own congregations, distinct from the Sephardic Jews. This Ashkenazic group was much poorer than the Sephardic one and also much larger. Before 1750 about 10,000 of them had settled in the Republic and in the next half century the same number again.

The census of 1796 held in the Netherlands (by then known as the Batavian Republic) counted about 30,000 Jewish residents, including both Sephardim and Ashkenazim. They then formed 1.5 per cent of the population, the result of two centuries of immigration and natural increase.[17]

Apart from these larger groups, a great many smaller groups of refugees also made their way to the Netherlands, the country dubbed by Pierre Bayle, not without cause, *la grande arche des fugitifs* – the great ark for fugitives.[18] In the seventeenth century these included Polish Socinians, English Puritans and Quakers and, led by Comenius, Bohemian and Moravian Brothers from the Czech lands. In the first half of the eighteenth century Baptists arrived from Berne in Switzerland, from Poland and from Prussia, Lutherans from Salzburg in Austria,[19] and German Hernhutters or Moravian Brothers, who in 1745 established their centre in the 'Slot' or Castle at Zeist.

With the exception of the persecution of the Jews in Central and Eastern Europe, the phenomenon of refugees fleeing for their religious convictions was, up to that point, a mainly Western European one lasting from the sixteenth to the first half of the eighteenth century.

In the nineteenth century the Netherlands received few refugees. The exodus of East European Jews almost completely by-passed the Netherlands. The major flow of the years 1880-1900 settled in England and particularly in America. Only in the twentieth century did this change with the arrival of large numbers of Belgian refugees. During the First World War the Netherlands managed to remain neutral, but Belgium was defeated by the Germans and subsequently almost completely occupied. When Antwerp was bombarded in October 1914 nearly 900,000 Belgians fled across the northern frontier. Most soon went back, but towards the end of the first year of the war there were still between 200,000 and 300,000 Belgians in the Netherlands. These numbers stabilized at a lower level towards the end of 1915. At the end of the war, three years later, there were still 50,000 to 100,000 civilian refugees and another 35,000 interned soldiers in the Netherlands. After the war they almost all went back to Belgium.

As a consequence of the First World War and the revolutions that followed it, many people, particularly in Eastern Europe, were displaced. The Netherlands received many Austro-Hungarian orphans, and a small number of Russian refugees.[20] The continuing

anti-Semitism in Eastern Europe brought some 10,000 Jewish refugees to the Netherlands in the 1920s.[21]

The settlement of refugees from Germany arriving in the 1930s was, like that of the Belgians before them, temporary, but had a more tragic outcome. The persecution of the Jews in Germany from 1933 and from 1938 onwards in Austria forced 20,000 Jewish refugees to head for the Netherlands, primarily because of the fact that they had been classified by the Nazis as Jews. And alongside the anti-Semitism, many of them also had fundamental political objections to the regime in their country.

In addition many other political refugees arrived, estimated at 7,000. These were mostly persecuted socialists, communists and

Registration of Belgian refugees in the Amsterdam Stock Exchange. Painting by Herman Lugt, 1914. In order to forestall the threatening chaos, the flood of Belgian refugees entering the Netherlands in 1914 was distributed across the country. In Amsterdam they first had to register at the Stock Exchange to be allocated accommodation. The largest influx was temporarily housed in sheds along the River IJ. (AHM)

Jewish refugees from Germany arriving in Amsterdam. Drawing by Martin Monnickendam, 1936. (Jewish Historical Museum, Amsterdam)

Trotskyists, but they also included Catholic opponents of the Nazi regime, and persecuted intellectuals and artists. For this last group Nazi ideas about art were yet another reason to leave their country. When the Bauhaus was closed down in 1933 many German artists fled across the frontiers, a flow which further increased when in 1937 Hitler opened the exhibition of *Entartete Kunst* (Degenerate Art).[22]

By the German invasion of May 1940 there were about 20,000 German and Austrian refugees in the Netherlands, of whom about 16,000 were classed by the Nazis as Jewish. Finding themselves trapped after all, most of them were killed in the concentration camps over the next few years. No more than 5,000 of these refugees survived the war.

After the Second World War the Netherlands was confronted with two kinds of immigrants, coming from various political backgrounds. First there was the immigration resulting from decolonization: the repatriates from the former Netherlands Indies, New Guinea and Surinam. In addition, there were numerous political refugees.

The first immigration generated by the colonial heritage was from Indonesia. Indonesian independence came about in fits and starts, and therefore the migration to the Netherlands took on the same character.[23] In a period of thirty years, from 1945 to 1975, 273,000 more people from Indonesia settled in the Netherlands than left the Netherlands for Indonesia. To follow the course of these events since 1945, a brief account of the colonial history of Indonesia is needed here.

The East India Company's trading empire was taken over by the Dutch state in 1796, and after the ravages of the French occupation and the Napoleonic Wars had been reduced to not much more than the former Dutch East Indies, now Indonesia. In the last decades of the nineteenth century the government allowed Dutch entrepreneurs to go and settle there. Plantations were developed where tobacco, sugar, tea and such products were cultivated on a large scale. Oil was found in Sumatra and mining expanded. At the same time the government had to see that it exercised effective authority throughout the vast island kingdom. This resulted in a series of colonial wars, of which the Atjeh or Achinese War, on the northern tip of Sumatra, is probably the most notorious.

The colonial society which had developed over three centuries was made up of a wide bottom layer of Indonesians, for the most part Moslem; they formed the majority. The 'Indos' or Eurasians (people acknowledged to be of mixed Dutch and Indonesian descent) occupied a middle position between this bottom layer and the top of the pyramid, the Dutch. Before the war, in 1930, there were sixty million Indonesians and about 200,000 Dutch citizens, of whom 150,000 were born in the Dutch East Indies – most of them Eurasian – and 50,000 were born in the Netherlands.

In the course of the twentieth century, just when the 'pacification' seemed to have been completed, a drive for independence began among the Indonesians. The colonial government was unable to find an adequate response, and external influences accelerated the movement towards independence. The Japanese, who occupied Indonesia from early 1942 until August 1945, promoted anti-Dutch feeling. They supported a number of nationalists to a limited extent, prohibited the use of Dutch, and interned all the Dutch in concentration camps.

The Dutch were only able to leave their camps some months after the Japanese capitulation on 15 August 1945; most of them had been held prisoner there for more than three years. The reason for the delayed release was that there was an authority vacuum after the capitulation; the Netherlands had nothing like enough troops to take over the former colony from the defeated Japanese. Consequently this was done mainly by their allies, the Australians, the British and particularly British Indian Army troops. At the same time the nationalists had declared a republic and the allies took this new situation into account.

After the hardships suffered during the war, and after their delayed liberation, the Dutch found themselves in an uncertain political situation: the Netherlands refused to recognize the Republic of Indonesia, but nevertheless was not in a position to put a stop to it. Many of them therefore left for the Netherlands almost as soon as they were released. Meanwhile the Dutch government recruited more and more troops and the struggle with the nationalists intensified. Atrocities on both sides did not improve the atmosphere for the Dutch population. Whenever the struggle seemed likely to end to the Republic's advantage, more people decided to move. On 27 December 1949 Queen Juliana handed over sovereignty. Because of

Repatriates from Indonesia disembarking, March 1958. Drawing by G. Hens, 1958. (Atlas van Stolk, Rotterdam)

this, and particularly the rapidly worsening relations between the two countries, yet more groups left for the Netherlands: Dutch nationals, some entirely Dutch in origin and some of mixed Dutch-Indonesian descent. But there was also a group of wholly Indonesian origin who had committed themselves to the Dutch cause, the Moluccans.

For those of wholly Dutch descent the choice was usually clear and inevitable. For the Eurasians, whose descent from a Dutch parent was acknowledged and who therefore held Dutch citizenship, it was more complicated. They could opt for Indonesian nationality, and were encouraged to do so from all sides, including that of the Dutch government. Yet only 31,000 of them took this step and many – about 25,000 – changed their minds after a few years; they wanted to become Dutch after all and they travelled to the Netherlands. They were christened *spijtoptanten* – those who regretted their choice.[24]

Eventually the great majority of Dutch nationals in Indonesia and their direct descendants moved to the Netherlands between 1945 and 1965: a total of some 300,000 people, of whom about 180,000 were Eurasians. Small numbers went to Australia, South Africa, the United States or other destinations.[25]

The position of the Moluccans, who until the late 1950s were known as Ambonese, was very complicated.[26] For centuries the Moluccas, at the eastern end of the Indonesian archipelago, had been intensively colonized and partly converted to Christianity. Many Moluccans were in the service of the colonial government, for the most part as soldiers in the Royal Netherlands Indian Army (KNIL), formed in 1832.

The establishment of the Moluccans as a military caste, and so as a social group, dated from 1870, influenced among other things by the collapse of the Moluccan clove market, since when many of them had enlisted in the KNIL. Particularly in the last years of the Atjeh War, from 1894 onwards, this development led to the emergence of a specific Ambonese military and Christian identity, embedded in what was known as '*tangsi*' (cantonment) culture and encouraged by the Dutch.[27] Those serving in the KNIL and their families mainly lived outside their native Moluccas. When the KNIL was disbanded as a result of Indonesian independence, 4,000 Moluccans, who were then serving in Java, refused to be transferred into the Indonesian army. Their refusal was caused not only by the difficult step of becoming comrades-in-arms with their former enemies, but also by political developments in the Moluccan island group from which they came. These Moluccans supported the struggle for the formation of an independent Republic of the South Moluccas, and wanted to be demobilized in the Moluccas, not in Java. The Indonesians would not allow this. The Republic of the South Moluccas proved to be no match for the unitary state of Indonesia. The Moluccans serving in Java had nowhere to turn; they refused to be either transferred to the Indonesian army or to be demobilized from the KNIL. And they were not allowed to go to the Moluccas. This impasse was only broken in 1951, when the Dutch government was forced by a judicial decision to accept this group of 3,578 soldiers with their families, around 12,500 people in total, 'temporarily' into the Netherlands. The number of Moluccans (the original group and their descendants) in the Netherlands in the early 1990s has been estimated at about 40,000.

The western part of the island of New Guinea was excluded from the transfer of sovereignty to Indonesia 1949. However, President Sukarno demanded this last fragment of the Dutch possessions in Asia in increasingly strident tones. This was also the period when the *spijtoptanten*, mentioned above, were quitting Indonesia. In 1962 the Netherlands was forced to abandon West New Guinea. The United Nations took over power temporarily, and in 1963 it recognized Indonesian sovereignty. The Dutch residents of New Guinea – including many who had left Indonesia ten years earlier, but also Papuans who had opposed this course of events – took refuge in the Netherlands.

Although the independence of Surinam (Dutch Guyana) in 1975 produced problems which were smaller in size, they were still substantial. Surinam's society is deeply divided on account of the historical development of the population. From the seventeenth century the Dutch colonizers imported African slaves, because the native Indians were not thought suited to work on the plantations. After the abolition of slavery in 1863 many former slaves refused to remain on the hated plantations, and first of all coolies, Hindu contract labour from British India, were brought in from 1873 onwards. Later, after 1890, they were also brought in from Java. The friction between these racial groups, particularly between the largest, the Creoles (those of African origin), and the Hindustanis, caused many of them to view the prospect of independence in 1975 with fear and anxiety.

Surinamese arriving at Schiphol Airport, 1975. Surinamese migration to the Netherlands increased sharply between 1973 and 1975. Many of them had little faith in the forthcoming independence of Surinam. (Photo Kors van Bennekom)

The sharpening of the existing differences between the various racial groups in the run-up to independence certainly contributed to the steep increase in the migration of Surinamese to the Netherlands between 1973 and 1975. But other factors were also at work in the Surinamese (and also Antillean) migration. According to the Charter for the Kingdom of the Netherlands of 1954 Surinam formed part of that Kingdom of the Netherlands. There was freedom of movement between its constituent parts and all inhabitants were Dutch citizens with equal rights. These provisions took on great importance when in the 1960s the demand for labour in the

Netherlands was increasing and the standard of living was rising. Opportunities for travel were better and cheaper than they ever had been before. From the mid-1960s, so before the issue of Surinam's independence arose, migration from Surinam was already increasing. In particular, members of the middle and lower income groups of Surinamese society came to the Netherlands at that time. There were great waves of migrants from 1973 to 1975 and in 1979-80, directly related to Surinam's independence in 1975, and to the expiry in 1980 of an agreement to allow settlement reciprocally for five years. These waves might well be ascribed to a lack of faith in the political stability of an independent Surinam, but for many of the migrants the lack of faith in its economic development probably played as important a role as any direct political threat.[28]

After 1980, independent Surinam slid steadily towards a military dictatorship. Particularly after the dramatic 'December massacre' of opposition leaders in 1982, a number of Surinamese requested the

- - - **Immigration**
• • • **Emigration**
—— **Net migration**

Figure 2: Migration between Surinam and the Netherlands (country of origin and destination) 1960-1995

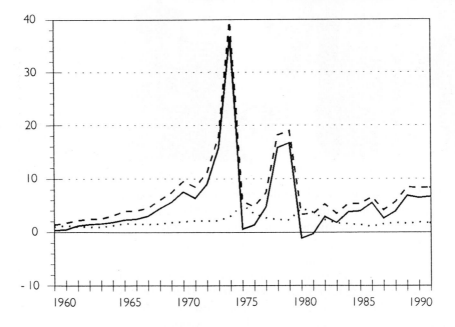

Figures obtained from J. Schoorl, Central Bureau for Statistics

right of asylum in the Netherlands. In addition, even since the restoration of democracy, immigration from Surinam has continued on the basis of family reunion and of bringing over marriage partners. In the early 1990s the migration surplus was at about the same level as in the early 1970s, around 6,000 per year.

From the point of view of Surinam there has been large-scale emigration: a third of the population has left for the Netherlands. In November 1995, twenty years after independence, there were about 296,000 people of Surinamese origin in the Netherlands.[29] Only a few of these have Surinamese nationality; about 38 per cent were born in the Netherlands.

In Dutch eyes, migration from the Netherlands Antilles and Aruba[30] is often lumped together with that from Surinam. It is therefore also mentioned briefly here, but it should be borne in mind that it is neither an ex-colonial, nor a political migration, and therefore does not strictly belong in this section. Because the

- - - **Immigration**
• • • **Emigration**
_____ **Net migration**

Figure 3: Migration between the Netherl. Antilles and the Netherlands (country of origin and destination) 1960-1995

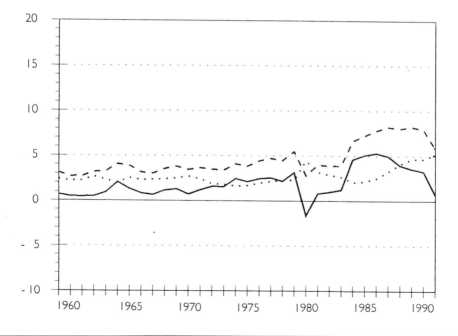

Figures obtained from J. Schoorl, Central Bureau for Statistics

Netherlands Antilles and Aruba form part of the Kingdom of the Netherlands under the terms of the 1954 Charter, Antilleans and Arubans have Dutch nationality, and there are no bars to their migration. In practice migration from the Antilles to the Netherlands is largely determined by shifts in the economic circumstances of the islands; moreover, return migration from the Netherlands to the Antilles is fairly high, so that it is really a matter of a floating immigrant population in the Netherlands. From 1984 up to the early 1990s, this immigration was significantly higher than previously, but has returned to low levels in recent years. On 1 January 1994 the number of people of Antillean origin in the Netherlands was about 82,000.[31]

To close this summary of the many and varied flows of migration of a significantly religious or political nature, which often reached very large proportions, reference must also be made to the many political refugees in the period after the Second World War, who had nothing to do with the Dutch withdrawal from their colonies. The end of the Second World War in the Netherlands was achieved not only by British, American and Canadian troops, but also by Polish ones. Because of the political upheaval in their own country many of them decided not to return, and some of them wanted to stay in the Netherlands. In all 2,350 Polish soldiers remained, mainly in Breda and Flushing. For much the same reasons several hundred Hungarians, Czechs, Balts and Russians also stayed on in the Netherlands.[32]

After the failure of the Hungarian rising in 1956 several thousand Hungarians were added to these numbers. In 1968, after the unhappy ending of the Prague Spring, a group of Czech refugees followed. In the 1980s migratory movements from Eastern Europe again brought several thousand Polish refugees and asylum seekers, members or sympathizers of the Solidarity movement.[33]

However, the post-war refugees and asylum seekers who found a home in the Netherlands, or who at least sought one, were by no means all from Eastern Europe. In 1972-1973 about 300 Ugandan refugees of Asiatic origin arrived, expelled by Idi Amin. Between 1973 and 1979 a total of 1,070 Chilean refugees were invited to the Netherlands; an unknown number also came seeking asylum. The Portuguese colonial wars in the early 1960s not only caused their colonial subjects to flee, but also gave rise to extensive 'draft dodging' by young Portuguese,[34] of whom a significant number ended up in the Netherlands. The Colonels' regime in Greece and the dictatorships of Franco and Salazar also contributed to a number of their subjects settling abroad, some of them in the Netherlands. They did not all necessarily come under the official category of refugees; some came as 'guest workers'.

Looking back at the period from 1945 to 1975, it can be said that both the number of movements of refugees reaching the Netherlands and the number of refugees involved were relatively few. The largest group was from Hungary, some 3,300. The other groups of refugees could be counted in hundreds rather than in thousands.[35]

This, however, changed from the mid-1970s. Table 1 below, showing annual totals of invited refugees and asylum seekers, illustrates this.

Table 1	Invited refugees and requests for asylum in the Netherlands, 1977-1995				
	Invited refugees				
		Requests for asylum			
Year			**Most common countries of origin**		
1977	291	452	1 Pakistan	2 Chile	3 Ethiopia	4 Turkey
1978	324	964	1 Turkey	2 Ethiopia	3 Pakistan	4 Chile
1979	2458	816	1 Turkey	2 Ethiopia	3 Pakistan	4 Chile
1980	1625	976	1 Turkey	2 Ethiopia	3 Chile	4 Iran/ Pakistan
1981	1179	832	1 Ethiopia	2 Pakistan	3 Iraq	4 Turkey
1982	513	840	1 Pakistan	2 Turkey	3 Iraq	4 Ethiopia
1983	406	1400	1 Suriname	2 Turkey	3 Pakistan	4 Sri Lanka
1984	481	2304	1 Sri Lanka	2 Turkey	3 Iran	4 Surinam
1985	440	4522	1 Sri Lanka	2 Turkey	3 Iran	4 Surinam
1986	371	3650	1 Turkey	2 India	3 Afghanistan	4 Iran
1987	532	13460	1 Ghana	2 India	3 Turkey	4 Zaïre
1988	782	7486	1 Ghana	2 Ethiopia	3 Iran	4 India
1989	596	13898	1 Somalia	2 Lebanon	3 Poland	4 Ethiopia
1990	701	21208	1 Sri Lanka	2 Rumania	3 Iran	4 Somalia
1991	589	21615	1 Yugoslavia	2 Sri Lanka	3 Iran	4 Somalia
1992	643	20346	1 Yugoslavia*	2 Somalia	3 Iran	4 Sri Lanka
1993	659	35399	1 Bosnia-H.	2 Yugoslavia	3 Somalia	4 Iraq
1994	493	52576	1 Bosnia-H.	2 Iran	3 Somalia	4 Iraq
1995		29258	1 Bosnia-H.	2 Somalia	3 Iran	4 Iraq

Source: 1977-1986: Gooszen 1988:7
1987-1991: Brink/Pasariboe 1993
1992-1995: *Maandstatistiek van de Bevolking* (CBS) (Feb. 1996): 46; and
Muus 1996: 62.
* From 1992 onwards: the former Yugoslav Republics of Serbia and Montenegro.

Two different reasons can account for this steep increase. The first lies in the actions of the host society and the rules it applies for admission. We have already remarked that before their recruitment was stopped in 1974, refugees could enter the Netherlands as 'guest workers'. If they found work in the Netherlands they were given a work permit, and provided they had a work permit they could acquire a residence permit. After 1974 this option was ended by a more restrictive admission policy. From then on only an appeal for asylum made entry into the country possible. This meant not only that refugees became more visible than before, but also that the pressure for asylum increased, because other immigrants, such as economic ones, found that access was blocked, with the result that some of them also appealed for asylum.

The second reason for the increase lies in the source of the refugee migrations. There we see that the number of political flashpoints has been large in recent decades and the number of people in flight from them substantial.[36] But there have also been some important changes which have contributed to refugees reaching the Netherlands (and the wealthier countries in general) in larger numbers. First there have been great changes in the distribution of knowledge: in recent decades radio, television and the telephone have found their way into the Third World on a grand scale, which has led to wider knowledge of possible and desirable destinations. Secondly, there has been a great increase in transport facilities, particularly in air and motor transport, and the cost of a mile's travel has fallen in relative terms. These two factors have enormously increased the geographical reach of refugees and asylum seekers.

From 1978 to 1982 the number of requests for asylum was certainly higher than in the previous period, but it still retained a certain stability. In this period the largest group was made up of Turkish Christians; between 1976 and 1982 they accounted for some 3,200 requests for asylum.[37] Ethiopians, Pakistanis and Chileans were the most important groups of asylum seekers after the Turkish Christians. The invited refugees were dominated by Chileans (in 1977-1978) and the much larger group of some 6,000 Vietnamese (1979-1982).[38]

From 1983 onwards the number of requests for asylum shows a strongly rising trend, with 1994 producing a peak of 53,000 applications. The origin of the asylum seekers has been subject to violent fluctuations since 1983: the largest groups to appeal for asylum in the Netherlands are Surinamese (1983), Pakistanis (1984 and 1985), Turks (1986), Ghanaians (1987 and 1988), Somalis (1989), Rumanians (1990), refugees from Sri Lanka (1990), and from the former Yugoslavia (1991, 1992, 1993, 1994, and 1995).

Finally two glosses must be added to this general account of the way the flow of refugees developed. The first is that the number of invited refugees[39] has remained fairly constant except from 1979 to 1981; this was a result of deliberate policy. On the other hand the number of asylum seekers has grown explosively: something which was definitely not the object of policy. There is no question therefore of greater generosity on the part of the Netherlands, but of heavier pressure for asylum from outside.

The second gloss is that an appeal for asylum does not necessarily mean admission.[40] If the number of asylum seekers is compared with the number of positive decisions on their appeals, then a substantial increase in the number of rejections can be observed: of all the asylum decisions taken in the period 1988-1994 (163,000), 67 per cent (109,000) were negative. 25,000 were granted asylum (A-status); 25,000 received B-status, which means that their appeals were rejected, but that they were given residence permits because the risks attendant upon repatriation were thought to be too high; and 3,500 were given temporary provisional status. Thus rejection does not necessarily always mean that the asylum seeker leaves the country or is expelled: in practice expulsion is often not possible, because the person involved has disappeared, or simply because expulsion is not a police priority.

It is extremely difficult to provide reliable figures for the number of refugees and asylum seekers in the Netherlands, but by 1 January 1995 the number of legally admitted refugees and asylum seekers since the war had certainly reached a total of at least 100,000.[41]

Labour migrants and transients during the Republic

Although it is difficult to exaggerate their importance for the Dutch economy, it is only possible to devote a modicum of attention to this second category of newcomers, which we have defined as people who remain in the Netherlands only for a number of years. Attention must be limited precisely because of the temporary nature of their stay, implying that their contact with the Dutch population was generally of a different kind; their point of view was coloured primarily by the prospect of return to their county of origin. In contrast to the next category, that of the migrant labourers, there was no question of regular trips back and forth between their place of regular residence and their place of work in the Netherlands.

Numerically the labour migrants far outnumbered the transients. Hundreds of thousands of young men and women tried to amass savings as servants or in the armed forces in the Netherlands and its colonies. Servants were attracted from abroad in large numbers. At first this was mainly for specific positions with prosperous citizens, for instance, as English butlers, French valets, Swiss nannies and tutors, and even sometimes negro servants for retired colonials in the late nineteenth century. Particularly between the wars it became more common to have a maid, and there was a remarkably large supply of German girls entering service. In the years just after the First World War, when Germany was rapidly impoverished by runaway inflation, they came looking for employment on a massive scale.[42]

Foreign soldiers and sailors came in still greater numbers.[43] Before compulsory military service was introduced during the French period in 1810-1813, and in a few cases even afterwards, the Dutch

German servant girl. Detail of an eighteenth-century penny print about the adventures of a German maid in Holland. (Gemeentelijke Archiefdienst, Amsterdam)

army and navy relied on volunteers, often called 'mercenaries'. These mercenaries normally came from abroad because pay and opportunities for employment in this sector of the labour market were so bad that Dutchmen only came forward when forced to do so.

The armies deployed on behalf of the Dutch cause – which happened on the occasions when the Netherlands, particularly under the Stadtholder-King William III, helped to determine the course of European politics – consisted mainly of foreign soldiers: Germans, Swiss, Scots, and French too, tens of thousands of them at a time. Much the same applied to the navy as for the army, except in times of crisis, when Dutch merchant seamen had to help out.

The colonial empire in the East, first under the East India Company and later under the state, also employed many soldiers and sailors. Service as an ordinary soldier or sailor for the East India Company was perhaps the worst paid and most dangerous job that could be found in the Republic, and only a proportion of them ever returned to Europe alive. Tropical diseases and sickness on board ship both took a particularly high toll. The East India Company therefore recruited foreigners *en masse* as well as large numbers of Dutchmen, and its successor, the Dutch state, continued to make use of the services of foreigners. For instance, until the turn of this century the KNIL had a colonial recruiting depot at Harderwijk, a barracks where anyone could enlist for this Dutch 'foreign legion'. Many foreigners, particularly Germans, did so.

In the merchant navy the number of foreigners was generally greater the farther and longer the ships were away from home. The intercontinental merchant fleet had a particular tradition of hiring foreign sailors. Even nowadays crews still include Chinese, Indonesians, Philippinos and Cape Verde islanders.

Among the transients there were extremely varied social groups. A few examples will have to suffice here. The larger Dutch towns already had trading colonies of foreign merchants in the Middle Ages, and of course this phenomenon underwent a significant increase during the Golden Age. Often these merchants formed their own communities or enclaves, outwardly symbolized by their church buildings.[44] For example, we find Walloon and Scottish, even Armenian and Greek churches. Many of the merchants only stayed a few years in a Dutch town. In the nineteenth and twentieth centuries this stay often became shorter still, when the merchants

TWEEDE DEEL.

Monkelbaens – Tooren;

Company troops embarking from the jetty near the Montelbaan tower in Amsterdam. From there they were transshipped to the East Indiamen waiting near the island of Texel. On the right the West Indies Company warehouse, built in 1642. Print by Reinier Nooms, 1650. (Gemeentelijke Archiefdienst, Amsterdam)

were succeeded by their modern equivalents, commercial travellers, agency employees and the like.

Although less closely related to the economy, embassy personnel and intellectuals can also usually be considered as transients. The wealthy Republic could afford to attract famous scholars from abroad. Evidently this was such a success that it spurred the English to follow suit, and so John Hall in his *Advance of Learning* of 1649 suggested that England, too, should import scholars from abroad, as the Dutch did, 'having in a manner monopolized all the sparkling wits of Europe'.[45] From the second half of the nineteenth century, a great many German professors were invited to take up Dutch posts, especially in the exact sciences.

Artisans and craftsmen also stayed temporarily in the Netherlands, both to earn money and to gain experience in their trade. A well known example were the German 'journeymen', who were obliged to travel for years through different towns and countries before they could settle anywhere as master craftsmen.

The entertainment industry inevitably attracts foreigners: bear baiters from Eastern Europe, clowns and camera obscura operators from Italy, musicians from Germany, and prostitutes from everywhere: the run-of-the-mill from Germany, the high-class ones from Switzerland, France and other countries, sometimes imaginary and sometimes not. Theatrical, ballet and operatic companies from abroad also come under the heading of transients in the entertainment industry.

All these groups have had temporary and irregular contact with the Netherlands and its people. This does not apply, however, to the third category, the migrant labourers.

Migrant labourers

From the seventeenth to the late nineteenth century tens of thousands of workers travelled annually from Westphalia, from the east and south of the present-day Netherlands, from the Eifel and Hunsrück on the left bank of the Rhine, from parts of Belgium, and from Picardy, to the North Sea coasts, to carry out seasonal work. This extended pull-area of coast, only a few dozen kilometres wide, stretched from Bremen to the north of France.[46] For the provinces of Zeeland, Holland, the western parts of Utrecht and the sea-clay and peat areas of the northern provinces, this meant that some 20,000 labourers travelled back and forth in a regular system between the poor interior and the rich coastal region. These migratory labourers earned a living by combining a smallholding at home with seasonal work on the North Sea coast, usually during spring, summer or autumn. In many cases cottage industry during the winter months completed this cycle of activity and earnings.

The migratory labourers primarily found agricultural work. In the spring there was an opportunity for some in weeding and thinning out flax, for instance, and later also sugar beet. In June many found work in hay making, like the *hannekemaaiers* ('*hanneke*', derived from the common name 'Johannes', referred to their German origin, and '*maaiers*' to their occupation, mowing), and from July in reaping and harvesting grain and autumn crops such as madder and potatoes. Secondly, particularly in spring, infrastructural works, such as constructing dykes, canals and other excavations, large building projects and also peat cutting offered many opportunities for employment to migratory labourers. Other industries which depended partly or wholly on them were the bleaching works round Haarlem, the brickworks in Groningen, and timber rafting on the major rivers. Because of the more or less permanent link which existed particularly with the agricultural activities, there was fairly intensive contact between the migratory labourers and the farmers for whom they worked; for the most part they stayed in rural areas, unlike most of the other groups discussed in this chapter.

After 1870 there was a change in the character of seasonal work in the Netherlands. The rise of industry in the vicinity of the traditional push areas for migratory labourers increasingly offered them the opportunity of permanent rather than seasonal employment. In the case of the Netherlands the rise of the Ruhr in Germany was especially important. Not only did it now attract the Westphalians who had earlier been in the habit of going to the Netherlands for seasonal work, but it also drew in Dutch workers in large numbers. The direction of travel, which for centuries had been from east to west, was reversed.

Labour migrants in the twentieth century; guest workers

The development of the Dutch mining industry in South Limburg coincided with these developments in Germany. After 1900 it escalated rapidly, and because sufficient labour could not be found locally, management had to attract workers from elsewhere. Many German and – following the example of the Ruhr – also thousands of Italian, Polish and Slovene miners went to work in Limburg. A large proportion of them were laid off again in the 1930s and expelled from the country, but some settled there permanently.[47] The transition which occurred on a wide scale around 1900 from seasonal migratory work, mainly in agriculture or on infrastructure projects, to more permanent employment mainly in industry, had many consequences both for the migrants and for society. To reflect this situation we will continue to use the term 'labour migrant' for this last category of migrants.

Only after the Second World War did the phenomenon of modern industrial labour migration really get under way, and again it started in the Limburg mines, which by 1949 were again recruiting Italian labour. The rapid economic growth which, particularly in the 1960s, led to structural shortages on the labour market, caused industrial firms throughout the country to recruit foreign labour. At first personnel departments looked for workers in Italy and Spain, later in Yugoslavia and Greece, and from the mid-1960s they set their sights on Turkey, Morocco and Tunisia. The Dutch

Group of migrant workers in a hostel, early 1960s. (Photo Spaarnestad)

government signed labour agreements and acted as mediator in recruitment. From 1968 the same government made such mediation services not only available, but also mandatory: the flow of migration, which had reached massive proportions in the interim, needed to be kept under control, according to the requirements of the economic climate.[48]

There are various similarities between the pre-1870 migratory labourers described above and the post-war labour migrants. For many of the latter, just as for the earlier seasonal migrants, the object was to amass savings in order to expand or to set up a business at home, usually a farm, workshop or a small shop. Here, too, it was generally a matter of combining two sources of income, one in the Netherlands and one at home, where the wife and children or other relatives remained to keep the business going.[49]

A second way in which many of the twentieth-century labour migrants resemble their predecessors of earlier centuries is that the major part of the family's consumption took place in the country of origin, at low prices, while at the same time just one or a few wage-earners tried to earn most of the family income in a high-wage country, in this case the Netherlands. The cheap home-produced smoked bacon the German *hannekemaaiers* brought with them had the same object as the couscous or bulgur brought along by later migrants; it kept their expenses down and so maximized their earnings. Their attempts to find the cheapest possible accommodation, at that time in huts on the building site, or in a farmer's hay barns, and in the 1960s in cheap pensions, sometimes even doubling up in beds, fits the same pattern. It is a question of taking as much advantage as possible of the differences in wage and price levels between the place where the family lives and the place where the migratory labourers earn their living.

In the early 1970s a clear change emerged in labour migration from the Mediterranean countries: the temporary nature of the labour migration, which had always been the aim both of the migrants and of the government, and which had by and large been achieved in the 1960s, disappeared within a very short period. The return percentages (that is the number of returnees in one year as a percentage of the total number of migrants at the start of that year) fell dramatically, particularly for labour migrants from Turkey and Morocco. Family reunion started. This marked an automatic switch from labour migrants to the last category of newcomers: economic immigrants.

Economic immigrants

For this fourth category, permanent immigrants with a primarily economic motivation, we return once more to the Dutch Golden Age. The great wealth and expanding economy of the Republic naturally attracted many newcomers from poorer countries. Reference has already been made to the fact that political and religious refugees were also driven by economic motives, that many foreigners temporarily filled the lower ranks of the army and the navy, and that much seasonal work was carried out by foreigners. Apart from these temporary newcomers, there was continual permanent settlement by immigrants who came for economic reasons. Among them were many small businessmen, merchants, shopkeepers and craftsmen.[50] It was said of Amsterdam that almost all the bakers and confectioners were German.

Research into place of birth and nationality in the Amsterdam registers of the publication of banns of marriage has shown how overwhelming the presence of these immigrants must have been. During the seventeenth and eighteenth centuries on average no

The Tofani family's ice cream factory in Amsterdam, c. 1930. (Photo copyright IJs-salon Peppino)

fewer than 28 per cent of all brides and grooms in Amsterdam came from abroad. In the first half of the seventeenth century the figure was as high as 39 per cent, dropping to 25 per cent in the eighteenth century. Even a town such as Hoorn managed a figure of 23 per cent in the first half of the seventeenth century.[51] It must therefore be accepted that immigration at least into the province of Holland was very heavy during the Republic, even if the groups of refugees mentioned earlier are not included.

If for the period of the Republic we have to work with indirect evidence, since the second half of the nineteenth century country-wide census information on nationality has been available.[52] We have observed that hardly any refugees arrived between 1815 and the First World War, and so the count of aliens during this period can be interpreted as an indicator of economic immigration.

From the early nineteenth century this immigration shows a sharp drop in a number of places. This is plain to see in the first censuses in which place of birth was recorded. The low point of the presence of foreigners in the Netherlands was probably reached around 1870, in both relative and absolute terms.

After 1870 the number of registered aliens is observed to rise, from about 50,000 in the years 1890-1900, or one per cent of the population, to 175,000 or more than two per cent in 1930. After a dip during the war and in the period of reconstruction, the number of aliens rose rapidly again after 1960. The percentage figures also rose, but more slowly. In 1960 just 118,000 non-Dutch were counted, at that time one per cent of the Dutch population. On 1 January 1994 there were 780,000 aliens living in the Netherlands, 5.1 per cent of the total population.

The rise during the interwar years is partly explained by the stream of servant girls and refugees. There are no indications that at that time the Netherlands was generally a popular destination for economically motivated immigrants. Exceptions to this rule were those domestic servants and the miners mentioned earlier, and in addition technical staff for the Philips works in Eindhoven and the industrial area around Dordrecht; from Italy there were ice cream vendors, sculpture sellers and terazzo layers, and there was a first wave of Chinese immigrants.[53]

The increase after 1960 can be largely explained by the arrival of labour migrants. The change in the character of this labour migration around 1970-1975 means that from 1970 onwards it might be better simply to speak of immigrants. Several factors are at play in this shift. Among the labour migrants, some had already been in the country for an extended period. Certain of these, mostly those of urban origin, had already brought their families to the Netherlands. With the cessation of industrial recruitment after the 1973 oil crisis, these long-term labour migrants became much more visible. The large numbers of returnees in earlier years had seemed to be closely connected with the large numbers of workers recruited previously: the likelihood of returning was statistically highest in the first years after arrival. Whereas up till then the long-term labour migrants had been concealed behind the general picture of large numbers returning, in both absolute and relative terms, after 1973 they became much more visible.

In addition a shift had taken place in terms of nationality: the original large groups of Italians and Spaniards had made way, numerically, for large numbers of Turks and Moroccans. In the second half of the 1970s there was a substantial return flow of the two first groups (see figures 4 and 5) and an absolute reduction in the number of remaining residents from these groups. On the other hand only small and decreasing percentages of Turks and Moroccans went back, and there was amongst these groups a strong tendency towards family reunion, which reached a peak in 1980.

Very soon the Turks and Moroccans exceeded the other groups of labour migrants in numbers. There is no special policy explanation for this phenomenon, because the policy for both groups was officially the same. Rather we should look to differences in economic development in the countries of origin: the level of prosperity was rising in Italy, Spain, Greece and Portugal, and they were themselves becoming immigration countries. Economic backwardness and demographic pressure in Turkey and the North African countries on the other hand continued for a longer period, and even increased.[54]

If one examines the geographical origin of Turkish and Moroccan immigrants within their own countries, it is striking that recruitment underwent a shift from the towns in the most developed parts of the country to the less developed rural districts. This shift meant in practice that more and more labour migrants came to the Netherlands from regions and countries where the economic prospects for the less well endowed were virtually non-existent if they were later to return for good. Research into the consequences of labour migration in the districts of origin in Turkey, Morocco and Tunisia in 1974-1976 demonstrated this.[55] It is even more apparent from the experiences of returnees, to the effect that only in exceptional cases could they really support themselves after their return. At the very least this led to a longer stay abroad in order to save more, and sometimes to a more or less deliberate decision to settle permanently. In both cases, however, those staying elected where possible to bring their families over, whether for social or economic reasons (more breadwinners). And, particularly because of their children, that step appears to increase substantially the likelihood of a longer stay and eventual permanent settlement.[56]

A third factor lies in the aliens policy as it developed in the Netherlands, particularly after 1968. It became steadily more restrictive. Entry to the Netherlands was only possible after prior approval, and more importantly for the purposes of this discussion, departure led to the loss of the right to a residence permit, and so return to the Netherlands became impossible. For a migrant with doubts about his prospects after returning home, this meant that he chose to be on the safe side (staying in the Netherlands as long as he retained rights) rather than uncertainty (going home, with the possibility of failure, and no possibility of returning).

After 1985 the migration of Turks and Moroccans entered a new phase: family reunion declined because the families available to be

Figure 4: International migration between eight recruitment countries and the Netherlands 1960-1995

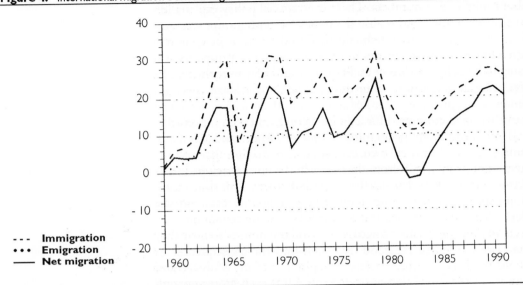

- - - **Immigration**
• • • **Emigration**
—— **Net migration**

Greece, Italy, Portugal, Spain, Turkey, Morocco, Tunisia, (former) Yugoslavia
Source: Central Bureau for Statistics

Figure 5: International migration between the southern countries of the EU and the Netherlands 1960-1995

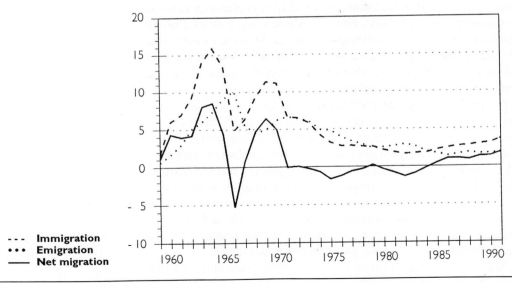

- - - **Immigration**
• • • **Emigration**
—— **Net migration**

Greece, Italy, Portugal, Spain
Source: Central Bureau for Statistics

reunited were running out, whereas family formation increased, meaning that legal immigrants brought spouses over to the Netherlands. In the early 1990s this family-forming migration was estimated at 40 per cent of Turkish and Moroccan immigration;[57] this type of migration had passed its peak by 1992.[58] In 1992 the Turks and Moroccans constituted the largest groups of immigrants in the Netherlands (250,000 and 195,000 respectively)[59] after the Surinamese.

Although this metamorphosis of labour migrants and their families into permanent immigrants explains the largest part of the increase in the number of aliens, the number of immigrants from other countries also makes up a by no means negligible figure. Economic development has also attracted many 'ordinary' immigrants since the 1960s. To list some of the largest groups: the number of EU nationals grew from 61,000 in 1960 to 188,000 in 1994. In the same period the number of citizens of industrialized countries like the USA and Japan (respectively 13,000 and 5,000 in 1994) also increased. But the number of immigrants from the Third World rose relatively faster, mainly on account of the recent migrations of refugees. Among the last category there is also a large group of immigrants of Chinese origin, estimated at between 40,000 and 50,000.[60]

Finally, attention should be drawn to a very special category of newcomers: adopted children from abroad, who number some 20,000 for the post-war period. Without underestimating the motives of the adopting parents, it can be said that they are able to care for an adopted child from abroad because of their relative wealth, and that the countries from which the children came allowed their departure because of their relative poverty.

Chapter 3

Coming, going and staying on
Some considerations on selection, migrant behaviour, and the role of government

The previous chapter with its catalogue of movements reads almost like the description of a colourful procession. Who came from where, when and why: these were the questions posed. It focused on the long-term consequences of all imaginable migration flows, set out in figures, with some famous names, and sometimes dramatic events.

Those migrants who stay on are, however, usually the result of a lengthy and complicated process of selection. The process starts well before actual arrival: who decides, or is forced to decide, to leave the country of their birth? Who is able to do so? The process continues with the crossing of frontiers: who is allowed in and who not? And even after immigration there is selection: who decides to go back after a while, or to move on, and who stays? Selectivity of migration, or the way in which migrants assess their own situation and on the basis of that take their decisions, and the role of government at various points are therefore important subjects for consideration.

This chapter discusses only the first generation of immigrants: those who were born elsewhere and who have taken up residence in the Netherlands. The various destinies of their descendants born in the Netherlands are discussed in later chapters.

Selectivity of migration

A distinction has already been made in Chapter 2 between two motives for coming to the Netherlands: the mainly political and/or religious motives, and the mainly economic ones. This dichotomy is of great importance here, too. Migratory movements based on political and/or religious grounds are of their nature connected with political events. They are therefore, from a historical point of view, often quite spectacular, and so are less quickly forgotten than the ordinary waves of migration. Their patterns are also less fixed. Because they depend upon political developments they are less predictable than the regular migratory movements, which sociologists of migration have tried to study in an attempt to discover the conditions governing their genesis and cessation.[1] The timing and the ways in which selection for these two types of migration operates can also differ sharply. Some comments on selectivity for both types are given below.

Migration flows on political and religious grounds

With migratory movements caused by a religious or political situation, it is often assumed that 'enforced' migration is involved. The migrants, so goes the assumption, are refugees forced to flee because of their political or religious convictions. Without wishing to play down the seriousness of certain persecutions, one should not lose sight of the fact that in this kind of situation there is almost always an element of selection. Among the refugees who came to the Netherlands from Hungary in 1956 and Czechoslovakia in 1968, there was a strong over-representation of young single males with a fair or high level of education.[2] Yet no-one would want to maintain that there were not just as many female, older, or less educated people who abhorred the Russian occupation of their respective countries.

Of the approximately seven thousand Vietnamese refugees who arrived in the Netherlands in 1985, half were less than thirty years old, and almost all were young, single men. The same categories make up the largest group among Tamils from Sri Lanka. Demographic analysis of the refugees and asylum seekers who came to the Netherlands in the period from 1977 to 1987 indicates the same selectivity: appreciably more men than women and many individuals aged between twenty and thirty-five. For certain groups a relatively high level of education also applies, though the Turkish Christians form an exception.[3] Among the Hungarians in 1956 it also appears that by no means all of them were equally motivated to flee by their political convictions; in some cases it appears that political problems were not the only ones they were fleeing.[4]

To clarify the criteria and the reasons for selection taking place among refugees, a series of questions needs to be asked. Who thinks they have good reason to flee? Who in theory is capable, or has the opportunity, of escaping? Who seizes this opportunity or can take advantage of it? Who is accepted for entry elsewhere? And after arrival, who stays, who returns, and who leaves for another destination?

The French Protestants in the seventeenth and eighteenth centuries can serve as an example. Of the estimated one million Protestants in France, about a quarter fled the country in the late seventeenth and early eighteenth century. The Huguenots who came to the Dutch Republic made up in their turn a quarter of that quarter. Those who remained behind converted under duress and without any enthusiasm to Catholicism; occasionally, however, they renewed their rebellion and were again persecuted, until the French Revolution finally brought equality for the handful of faithful left.[5]

So what factors determined who stayed and who left? And where to? And what factors decided whether the Huguenots coming to the Netherlands joined the rather exclusive Walloon congregations (which still had only eight thousand members a century after the arrival of the Huguenots), or ended up in the Dutch Reformed Church? A pointer to the answer can be found in the particular characteristics we observed earlier of the first Huguenots to arrive; they were both a socio-economic and intellectual elite, in contrast to the groups who came later. To quote Cruson on the first group of Protestant refugees from France: 'If we look at some of the characteristics of the group, it is clear that for the most part it is made up of members of the urban middle class, with the specific skills, knowledge, networks and mentality which enabled them to flee and reconstruct an existence elsewhere. The Republic drew them not only because of its freedom of religion, though that was an important reason, but above all because they could build up a new life there.'[6]

The sorry tale of the Portuguese Jews, outlined briefly in Chapter 2, is equally an example of a succession of selections: first the flight from the Iberian peninsula or conversion; next whether or not they were accused of being a false convert; then the choice of whether or not to flee; and, dependent on their destination, the question of whether or not to revert to Judaism.

Sometimes the selection appears to depend entirely on coincidence. For instance, the arrival in 1951 of the 3,578 KNIL soldiers of

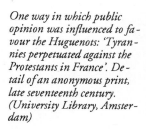

One way in which public opinion was influenced to favour the Huguenots: 'Tyrannies perpetuated against the Protestants in France'. Detail of an anonymous print, late seventeenth century. (University Library, Amsterdam)

Moluccan origin, with their families, was the result of an extraordinary series of political developments and complications beforehand. In many respects this group was essentially no different from all the other KNIL soldiers of Moluccan origin who, stationed elsewhere and in different circumstances, were not able to insist on being transferred to the Netherlands.

In the examples given so far the emphasis has been primarily on selection based on the motivation and decisions of the refugees themselves, and on the availability of the physical possibility or opportunity to escape, with or without the consent of the government of the country they were escaping from. However, attitudes in the chosen country of destination can also be very important. This becomes immediately apparent if the virtually closed frontier encountered by refugees from Nazi Germany, most of them Jewish, in the Netherlands in the late 1930s, is compared with the rapturous welcome with which the first French Protestant co-religionists were received in the late seventeenth century.

Selection on the basis of which refugees are admitted and which are not (or admitted after long delays or only in small numbers) is almost always directly dependent on whether an important section of the host society, in this case the Netherlands, can be mobilized in favour of the refugees. This tends to be easier when it is clear that the refugees are viable and desirable economically.[7]

Since the rise of the nation-state from the early nineteenth century onwards, the criterion for admission has primarily been the question of whether potential immigrants can claim intrinsically or legally to be members of the nation or people of the country into which they want to immigrate.[8] Particularly for migrants from former colonies this has been shown to be of great importance. For example, Eurasians of mixed origin were admitted to the Netherlands if they had been acknowledged by their Dutch parent (usually the father), on which grounds they were granted Dutch nationality. But even when this kind of formal link in the form of citizenship does not exist, or no longer exists, political refugees tend to receive more support for their asylum or refugee status in the mother country of the original colony. The Surinamese refugees after the military coup and the so-called 'December massacre' of 1982 are an example of this.[9]

In cases where political refugees are regarded as aliens, the next question is: for which aliens can support for their case most easily be gained? Admission on humanitarian grounds is usually listed first, but these are rarely unequivocal. For instance, in the Netherlands Turks appear to be considered eligible for asylum more easily on religious than on ethnic grounds: Christian Turks could count on more support from Dutch society than, for example, Kurdish (Muslim) Turks. Polish refugees can count on a humanitarian reception sooner than Cambodian refugees. In the ideological climate of East-West confrontation before the 1990s, anyone who managed to break through the Iron Curtain had to be accepted as a refugee by definition. Granting asylum to American draft-dodgers who did not want to go to Vietnam was on the other hand much more difficult; it could be interpreted as an insult to a friendly state.

Selection also takes place among refugees after arrival. First of all, even in cases where return to the country of origin appears to be ruled out, there is always some possibility of return. In the cases of the Southern Netherlanders, the Huguenots, the Hungarians and the Moluccans it is known that some of each of these groups returned after a while to the country they had fled; they preferred return to an extended or permanent stay in the Netherlands.[10]

In cases where there is a change for the better in the political situation in the country of origin not long after their flight, a

Gelderland Post and the Jews Savannah in Surinam. Print by G.B.C. Voorduin, c. 1875. Part of an immigrant group may move on after a period of time. In the seventeenth century there was already a Jewish settlement in Surinam. (Jewish Historical Museum)

virtually wholesale return may be possible for the refugees. This happened with the Belgian refugees during the First World War, but also, for example, with the Chilean and Argentine refugees who came to the Netherlands in the 1970s, most of whom have now gone back. In such cases the only refugees who stay on are those who have forged strong links with the Netherlands in the interim, for instance by marrying a Dutch partner.

A group of immigrants can also decline substantially in numbers when some of them move on after a period of time to another destination. For instance, a number of Huguenots went on to South Africa via the Netherlands, and Jews re-established themselves in the Dutch colonies. It is known that a group of Indonesian Dutch and some Moluccan families settled in California in the USA, in search of a climate more suited to their experience and desires than the Dutch one.[11]

Looking in summary at the characteristics from which it is evident that refugees are often a select group, then it stands out that those who are socio-economically stronger and better educated are the most likely to take flight. This is in addition to the demographic criteria: refugees are mostly men, often unmarried, and below the age of thirty-five, particularly when it is a matter of unexpected flight for which it has not been possible to make preparations.

Migration for economic reasons

When it comes to flows of migration which occur on economic grounds, there are appreciably more theoretical considerations and explanations available to us.[12] The mainstream of migration theory starts with fairly simple models: there are regions or countries – the 'pull areas' – with a relatively strong economic structure, with relatively good employment opportunities and a high standard of living, which act as a magnetic pole attracting people living in regions or countries where the economy is weaker, unemployment higher, the level of wages lower, and the standard of living of a substantial part of the population low – the 'push areas'. If the attraction factors in one place and the push factors in the other were free to operate without interference, one could assume perfect communication between the two extremes, but this is not the case. There are 'intervening obstacles', such as the geographical distance to be crossed, or familiarity with the other region. In short, as well as the 'necessary conditions' for migration one must also look for the 'sufficient conditions' which actually lead to migration itself.

Such models make the directions of migration flows comprehensible in terms of the economic development of a specific region.[13] The massive influx of foreigners to the Low Countries in the Golden Age and other periods of economic prosperity can be explained on a macro level in this way: employment opportunities grew much faster in times of economic expansion than the much slower demographic growth could provide a labour force.

The migration flows emerging in this way are in principle selective: they attract especially and in the first instance *workers*: men – and for some kinds of work also women and sometimes even children – in the prime of life, healthy and, where possible, with experience in the kind of work that needs to be done. These are the most desirable labour migrants. In earlier times it was not necessary to state the required qualities expressly, because selection was 'automatic': waged labour on the basis of work performed at piece rates

demanded a healthy and fast worker for the migration to be viable.
In the post-war years there were age limits set (between eighteen and
thirty-five for unskilled, and eighteen and forty-five for skilled
workers); these, and medical examinations, were among the conditions for official recruitment in Mediterranean countries.

The question of the rigour of further selection, based on the
requirements of the labour market, after the initial settlement of a
group of migrants, depends heavily on economic development in
the country of settlement. The foreign miners in South Limburg
before the Second World War illustrate the point. Employment of
foreigners in the mines reached its peak shortly before the great crisis
of 1929. The crisis was immediately followed by the introduction of
a strict selection process. The government demanded selective lay-
offs by the mining companies, to the effect that foreigners generally
had to be the first to go. And being laid off meant leaving the
country. In six years the number of foreigners declined by nearly
two thirds. This was not a random reduction: '... particularly those
foreigners survived who adapted easily and were also more easily
accepted; those who had lived in Limburg for some time, who were
married (to Dutch women), spoke Dutch, German or the local
dialect of the province of Limburg as a result of having been here
longer; those who worked hard and occupied positions which were
hard to fill with Limburgers; and those who were not disruptive of
authority [i.e. socialists or communists].'[14]

When a period of recruitment is followed soon afterwards by a
recession, an increase in the rate of return is generally seen, even
without government intervention.[15] The extent to which this occurs
is understandable when one takes into account the assessment which
the individual migrant makes of his situation. Migrants who think
that by returning home they have at least some opportunity of
making a living, or that they can create such an opportunity, will
assess these opportunities (plus the associated expenses) against
continuing their stay in the country where they have settled. And
here, too, there is selection: those who have left most resources
behind on which to fall back, will be the first to return, and those
who have nothing to fall back on will be least inclined to return.
Regulations imposed by the government in the country of settlement nearly always operate selectively here too: those who have been
there longest have built up a relatively stronger legal position; those

who have contracted a marriage with a partner from the country of settlement have more rights because of it, and so on.[16]

The reverse side of this is that measures aimed at encouraging return are particularly attractive to those who have formed the fewest links with the new society: loners, who even after a long stay have not brought their families over; and also those who can add the extra income from departure-inducements to their possessions and savings in their country of origin, and so build up a life there after going back. In general these kinds of measures are particularly attractive to older migrants of the first generation.[17]

The migrant, society's definition, and the reality

So far we have looked only at facts. The motives, desires, hopes, and behaviour of individual migrants have been outside our purview. It is important now to examine them, if only because with hindsight intentions and desires can sometimes be in sharp contrast with actual behaviour. Below is an example in which emigration, earlier defined as a permanent change of country by Dutch nationals, is compared with 'temporary labour migration' by nationals of Mediterranean countries.

This table shows the fallacy of the distinction generally used and accepted between permanent emigration by Dutchmen and temporary migration by Mediterranean workers, at least for the 1970s. A far larger proportion of the Dutch emigrants leaving in 1970 and

Table 2 Comparison of the number of returning Dutch emigrants (emigrants to Australia, Canada and New Zealand) and temporary migrant workers (Spanish, Moroccan and Turkish 'guest workers') in the Netherlands for 1970 and 1975, measured 10 and 5 years later respectively.[18]

Nationality	Year of departure/arrival	Percentage returned by 1980
Turks	1970	30.5
Moroccans	1970	16.3
Spaniards	1970	74.1
Dutch emigrants	1970	34.0
Turks	1975	15.8
Moroccans	1975	6.2
Spaniards	1975	46.9
Dutch emigrants	1975	28.0

*Accommodation for tempo-
rary migrant workers in a
hostel, early 1960s. (Photo
Robert de Hartogh)*

1975 seem by 1980 to have returned to their home base than was the
case with temporary labour migrants from Turkey and Morocco. In
the 1970s only the Spaniards matched their own and society's
expectations reasonably well.

We have not been able to find any good comparative material for
periods before the 1970s. Generally the figures for returnees were
less at variance with society's expectations or with the migrants' own
intentions, but that does not mean that they corresponded with
them completely. The percentages of return migration amongst the
Turks and Moroccans who had arrived in 1966 were indeed higher
than those of later cohorts: 51.4 per cent of Turks who arrived in
1966, and 38.4 per cent of Moroccans in the same year, appeared in
1980 to have gone back. But the number who stayed on is still so
large that it is an exaggeration to insist on calling them 'temporary
labour migrants'.

The motives, opinions, desires and hopes of the migrants themselves, and their view of their own situation, are fairly well documented, particularly for the last century; some practitioners of the

sociology of migration go so far as to regard the utterances of the migrants as almost the only source of knowledge about migration. However, this can be highly misleading, as J.H. Kraak, a student of the repatriation process of the Indonesian Dutch, makes clear: 'The reasons for repatriation can be briefly summarized as the complex of consequences of the ending of a colonial situation, which meant, among other things, that the continued existence in Indonesia of such a relatively large group of former colonials had in principle been rendered impossible. In the subjective opinion of the repatriates, however, the reasons for their repatriation were very varied, while a whole range of rationalizations were put forward as reasons for their departure from Indonesia. These rationalizations are a consequence of the inability – in the midst of actual manifestations of what was going on – to take in the social shifts resulting from the end of a colonial government, and to judge their significance.'[19]

Without wishing to fall into this trap, it is still necessary to direct some attention to a few important characteristics of the opinions and motives of migrants. A first observation involves the fact that for the migrant, raised and reaching maturity in the society from which he has migrated, that society will remain his implicit frame of reference for the whole of his life. This has far-reaching consequences: reared as he has been in the culture of his country of origin, he may be able to adapt at an instrumental level in the land of settlement, but this will be much less the case when it comes to norms and values, to matters involving appreciation or approval: taste in the broad sense of the word. If this starting point is not sufficiently recognized, it is easy to demand too high a level of adaptation from the immigrant.

By the same token it is much easier to explain the fact that migrants sometimes seem happy to put up with unacceptable working conditions, if one knows what the work situation and living conditions of these migrants were before. They themselves can regard a poor situation – from the Dutch point of view – as a relatively good one, certainly in the early stages of their stay. What the Dutch call discrimination can for newly arrived immigrants be an understandable differential treatment.

In this connection many migrants in a strange country undergo a psychological process in which their country of origin, usually also the country where they spent their youth, becomes idealized in their memory. This becomes even more strongly manifested as the new

A migrant often lives in two worlds. A Turkish woman is preparing the traditional Turkish yufka bread, while the Dutch Prime Minister of the time, J. den Uyl, ad-dresses the nation on television. (Photo Ad van Denderen)

circumstances are accompanied by problems such as hostility, offensive treatment and discrimination, of which the migrants gradually become more conscious, and when they have relatively few opportunities of regular visits to their country of origin.

The idea of returning home and the expression of the desire to do so can take strong forms among certain groups. Among many Turkish and Moroccan migrants in the Netherlands, most of whom had intended to return from the moment they first began their migration, this is expressed in the obstinate retention of a belief in their eventual return, even in situations in which by objective standards it is no longer a likely option.[20]

Among migrants from Surinam, of whom it was never certain whether they originally regarded their stay as temporary or permanent, this was expressed, at least in the second half of the 1970s and actually right up to the 'December massacre' of 1982, in a kind of 'return home ideology'. Every right-minded Surinamese ought to go home, even when there was almost no sign of actual return.[21]

Among the Dutch emigrants to Australia, Canada and New Zealand, who intended to stay there for good, this feeling sometimes takes the form of wanting to be buried in the Netherlands, or of wanting to visit the Netherlands at least once more before they die, while in the country where they have settled they make arrangements for their old age which recreate a Dutch atmosphere. One striking example is '*Ons Dorp*' [our village], founded in the early 1980s for elderly ex-Dutch people in Auckland in New Zealand.

This ambivalence, which is encountered among many migrants, also has another side to it, that of someone who seems incapable of making choices, always determined to keep all opportunities and options open. This common human characteristic acquires a new dimension in the case of a migrant: by leaving he may put at risk his status, position and rights in his country of origin, while he well understands that as a newcomer in the new society he will be at the back of the queue. In such a situation it is of great importance to the migrant that he does not burn his boats either before him or behind. This can be well illustrated by the following observation: it concerns Dutchmen in Australia, but it seems to apply equally well to Turkish or other migrants in the Netherlands: 'Among the Dutch there is, in comparison with other nationalities, little interest in naturalization. The reason given is to have a kind of "safety net": if anything happens, as Dutch citizens they can always return to the Netherlands and generally enjoy all their rights as Dutch nationals.'[22]

These considerations also apply to immigrants into the Netherlands. The consequences now attendant on definitive remigration, namely, loss of residence permit and the absence of any right of re-entry into the Netherlands if the remigration goes wrong, tips the balance for many migrants towards staying. Recently the introduction of the possibility of dual nationality for particular groups of aliens has added a new element to the assessments the migrant has to make. It is consequently hardly surprising that the number of naturalizations, including those of Turks and Moroccans, has increased steeply in recent years.[23] They now acquire the same 'safety net' as the Dutchman we have just quoted: access to the Netherlands remains open even after remigration, temporary or otherwise.[24]

The role of government

Migration flows can never be separated from the context of the role of government in the countries of origin and destination. The nature of government in the immigrants' new homeland, in this case the Netherlands, has changed in the course of time. During the Republic, that is until 1795, most important decisions were taken at the town or provincial level. Later these were transferred to the central government with its larger and more effective instruments of power.

How did the Dutch government define newcomers, and where appropriate their descendants, and what was its policy on admitting or expelling them?

Despite the wide spectrum of variety which existed during the Republic, the common denominator in all provincial and local regulations was the distinction in principle between 'native-born' (those born within the territory in question), and aliens (born outside it, even if the family was previously settled within it).[25] This therefore meant that all newcomers were aliens. This approach also meant that the second generation of immigrants always acquired the rights of the native-born, simply by the fact that they were born in the country to which their parents had immigrated. Newcomers could only acquire rights equal to those of the native-born by means of naturalization.[26] It was mainly people in high official posts who wanted these rights, and in practice therefore only a very small number of newcomers had themselves naturalized.

The federal structure of the Republic also allowed natives of one province to be naturalized in another. In this connection the requirements concerning the place of birth of the town pensionaries of Holland are instructive.[27] A town pensionary was the highest official in a town; he issued legal and policy pronouncements and represented the town externally, for instance, in the Provincial Estates (or States). After the mass immigration of highly qualified Southern Netherlanders at the beginning of the Revolt, several of them were appointed town pensionaries, such as Josse de Menyn from West Flanders in Dordrecht, Nicasius de Sille from Mechelen in Amsterdam, and Leonard de Voocht from Flanders in Delft. After 1585 the States of the Province of Holland began to oppose appointments of this kind, and in 1589 they decided that their assembly would only be open to those born in Holland, Zeeland,

West-Friesland and Utrecht, 'as being under a single government'. In 1658 a further restriction was imposed, when access was barred to all except those born in Holland.

These and similar decisions led to naturalizations, showing clearly the way in which citizenship was perceived. For instance, the town of Gorcum went to a great deal of trouble in 1727 to get Jacobus van Vechoven accepted as town pensionary. He had been born in Tiel, thirty kilometres away in Gelderland, where his father was a minister of religion. However, he could only become town pensionary of Gorcum after he had been naturalized as a Hollander, a citizen of the province of Holland.[28]

Furthermore, children born abroad or in the colonies to citizens did not count as citizens because of their birth elsewhere. For instance, Jacob de Hochepied, born in Constantinople, and his brother Elbert, born in Smyrna in Turkey, the two sons of the Dutch consul in the Ottoman Empire, had to be naturalized as Hollanders. Various children of Dutch parents in the East Indies also applied to the States of Holland for naturalization, just to be on the safe side.[29]

Even membership of a privileged class could not supersede the importance of the place of birth, as is shown by the case of the well known politician Joan Derk van der Capellen tot den Pol, a nobleman from Tiel in Gelderland. He married a noblewoman from Overijssel and settled in that province. When, however, he wished to be admitted there to the *Ridderschap*, or Estate of Nobility, it took him more than two years. Although he met all the requirements, the fact that he was not native-born appeared to be an almost insuperable obstacle.[30]

With the Batavian Revolution of 1795, the national state maintained the same line of thinking with respect to the native-born and aliens. The Kingdom of the Netherlands, too, on its foundation in 1815, at first continued the distinction. This meant that several of King William I's ministers and senior officials had to be naturalized.[31]

The residents of the kingdom did not have equal rights for a variety of reasons, which included the difference between residents who were native-born and residents who were not. However, this inequality under the law had no bearing on their right of residence: newcomers, once admitted, were considered to be full residents, and normally speaking ran no risk of expulsion.

That there should be a more or less fixed population in a national state, a community of the nation, whose make-up is not determined by the settlement or departure of individuals alone, is an idea that only gradually gained acceptance in the nineteenth century.[32] In the 1838 Civil Code the definition of a citizen of the Netherlands was not determined by domicile, but by a combination of the principles of ancestry and of territoriality; in other words, what counts is partly the nationality of the parents and partly the place of birth.

Although in the 1848 Constitution attempts were made to separate residence and Dutch nationality, and this process was quite advanced by the constitutional revision of 1887, it was only the law on Dutch nationality and residence in 1892 which finally accomplished this separation. 'Much more clearly than before, Dutch nationality consisted of membership of a community, whose members were linked with each other by factors such as a common language, culture and tradition, and a feeling of belonging to a nation.'[33] The principle of descent is the most important: anyone born to a Dutch citizen is Dutch. The territorial principle has a complementary role, partly to avoid the occurrence of incongruous situations. Subsequent legislation only altered these precepts as late as 1985.

How did the Dutch government regulate the entry and, if necessary, expulsion of foreigners? During the Republic everyone was welcome in theory, subject to two conditions: the newcomer had to be capable of maintaining himself and his dependants, and moreover he should not cause any trouble of any kind.

As far as the first condition goes, the countless measures for the suppression of vagrants and beggars offer eloquent examples. Every town and district, as well as the central government, were terrified of admitting persons thought to be economically unproductive, or 'low foreign people' as they put it in Utrecht.[34] They were therefore kept out by the threat of severe punishments.

The difference between poor and rich newcomers is also demonstrated in the legislation against the Jews in the provinces of Utrecht and Gelderland. In 1713 the States of Utrecht banned the entry of all German Jews to the province, which did not, of course, apply to the Sephardim who were known to be more prosperous. At about the same time the city of Utrecht decreed that no 'foreign High-German Jews or Smouches, their wives or children, should be allowed to come into this town, not even during the free markets, or hawk their merchandise around the houses, let alone spend the night there, on pain of being arrested, of being confined in this town's house of correction, or otherwise appropriately punished according to the nature of the circumstances'. When this anti-Jewish legislation in Utrecht was moderated in 1789, they could gain entry if they could prove that their behaviour was beyond reproach, and provided they were capable of earning an honest living. In Gelderland it was decreed in 1726 that no German Jews (Ashkenazim) should settle in the countryside on pain of a flogging on the first offence, of being flogged and branded on the second, and of death on the third. Wealthy merchants were expressly excepted from this ruling.

As for the second condition: an attempt was made to bar criminals, and the rare expulsions which took place in the Republic always involved them. In addition persons were barred who might be expected to cause political or religious complications. The exiled English king, Charles II, was consequently denied entry to the Republic in 1653. Members of Catholic religious orders were also taboo in the Republic; numerous bans were promulgated against the Jesuits in particular.

Within the general context of this policy on admission, exclusion and expulsion, the government carried on a policy of actively recruiting and inviting newcomers, subject to certain conditions. This was the case with the Southern Netherlanders and Huguenots, particularly in the early stages of both these immigrations, and for smaller groups of Protestant refugees, such as those from the Palatinate and from Salzburg, or for foreigners with special skills, such as professors and students.[35]

At first the Protestants from the Southern Netherlands, and particularly the Huguenot co-religionists, were received with open arms. At the time of the exodus of the Southern Netherlanders only a minority of the population of the rebellious north were Calvinists. Most were still Catholic, which does not, of course, mean that they were necessarily pro-Spanish. Yet it can be assumed that the Calvinist minority in the Northern Netherlands were pleased to see their membership strengthened by their co-religionists from the south. It is estimated that by about 1615 some three hundred ministers from congregations in the Southern Netherlands had settled in the north. They found immediate employment.

The governments of many towns welcomed the immigrants not only for their religious convictions, but also for their knowledge and skills. Middelburg in Zeeland even arranged for their transport from Antwerp by ship. Leiden offered them extensive facilities to get them to bring in their textile industry. Other towns like Delft tried in their turn to lure the immigrants away from Leiden with attractive settlement premiums. In 1596 the town authorities of Delft offered prospective newcomers the convent of St Ursula, to be developed with streets and housing.

This competition between Dutch towns and districts for the favours of immigrants was repeated with the arrival of the Huguenots.[36] Amsterdam demonstrated its superiority in this contest. In 1681 the Amsterdam city fathers granted three special privileges to incoming Huguenots: citizenship, exemption from local taxes for three years, and the right to practise their profession without having to become members of a guild. In 1688 and 1689 special local taxes were even raised for the benefit of the refugees.

One of the consequences of the Batavian Revolution of 1795 was the first national Dutch constitutions. Article 50 of the 1798 Constitution has this to say about foreigners: 'society accepts into its midst all foreigners who wish to enjoy the benefits of liberty in peace, granting them every security and protection.'

Article 11 of the same Constitution even laid down that newcomers, after having lived in the country for ten years, were enfranchised; in 1801 this period was reduced to six years. Although these advantageous provisions with respect to newcomers' right to vote were discontinued later, the principle of hospitality survived.[37]

At the same time, anyone not thought to be economically useful, or suspected trouble-makers, were banned, or if possible, expelled. Expulsion does not seem to have been too easy at first, since article 4 of the 1815 Constitution ruled: 'all those abiding in the territory of the realm, whether native or foreign, have an equal right to protection of their person and goods.' Some were of the opinion that this implied that foreigners who, after their settlement, were thought to be a threat to the country's stability, could no longer be expelled. Attempts were therefore made in the constitutional revision proposed in 1844 – though at that time in vain – to make it possible to deport alien criminals, subject to specific provisions.

This change of attitude was probably not based simply on these practical legal considerations, but was also – and perhaps predominantly – informed by the rise of nationalism in the Netherlands. This was particularly engendered by the Belgian Revolution of 1830, which resulted in the south of the kingdom separating off into the modern Belgium, causing a good deal of nationalist frustration in the north.

The immediate cause of the adoption of the 1849 Aliens Act, the first to address these particular problems, should, however, be sought not so much in the Belgian Revolution, but in the general atmosphere of revolution in the Europe of 1848.[38] The revolutions in France and several states of Germany found their echoes elsewhere, and led to tighter supervision of aliens. In March 1848 two thousand Belgian workers, with arms provided by France, invaded Belgium near a hamlet later called 'Risquons-Tout' after them, near Moeskroen. Although this attempt to export revolution from France was a failure, it led to tight supervision of suspicious aliens in Belgium. There was less of a threat in the Netherlands. The only riots were in the same month of March on the Dam in Amsterdam, when the fact that German 'communists' were involved must have increased the general mood of panic.

The 1849 Aliens Act in theory brought into force a watertight system for controlling the entry of aliens, 'in theory' because in practice it soon became clear that this act was only being applied very selectively. Just as suddenly as the danger of revolution had arisen in 1848, it seemed to have gone away again. Although as an organic law the 1849 Aliens Act stemmed from the new 1848 Constitution, it should not therefore be seen as confirmation of a practice or concept that had been growing for a long time. It was an act informed by external circumstances, introduced on the spur of the moment, and it therefore soon lost any significance, at least for most aliens. Its most frequent application was to bar foreigners who were not considered economically productive. Itinerant musicians had already been refused travel and residence permits in 1851, and in 1852 this ban was widened to cover all travelling fairground people.[39]

Although Dutch nationalism increased in the second half of the nineteenth century, no new aliens legislation was introduced, unlike such countries as Great Britain, probably because of the absence of large, sudden waves of immigration.[40] Only the First World War, with its massive refugee problems and resulting political changes, led to new legislation, such as the 1918 Act on the Control of Aliens and the 1920 Act on Frontier Controls.[41] There is no doubt that fear of revolution played a role at the time, just as it had in 1848.

Particularly the German political revolution of 1918-1919, and the ultimately unsuccessful social upheaval, were echoed in the Netherlands in the abortive attempt at revolution by Pieter Jelles Troelstra, the socialist leader. Perhaps it was not so much this purely oratorical attempt at revolution in November 1918, as the almost hysterical nationalist and Orangist reaction to it, which created the atmosphere for new legislation.

The main effect of this legislation was to make it very difficult for refugees to enter the Netherlands, particularly in the 1930s.[42] In 1934 Van Schaik, the Catholic Minister of Justice, admitted that the position of the Jews in Germany was deplorable, but judged that 'for rights of asylum ... more is needed'. The fact that unemployment was rising fast in the Netherlands, because of the world-wide economic crisis, was put forward as one obstacle to taking in so many refugees. In addition, the government coalition between the Protestant Anti-Revolutionaries and the Catholic Party viewed the immigration of quite large numbers of left-wing refugees with some suspicion, and also deployed the argument that a 'friendly head of state' might be offended.

On 7 May 1938 the government published additional restrictive measures, because an increasing flow of refugees was starting to arrive as a consequence of the *Anschluss* of Austria into the Third Reich the previous March. However, these restrictions had to be partially revoked when it became impossible to ignore German anti-Semitism any longer after the *Kristallnacht* of November that year. Seven thousand Jews were admitted legally to the Netherlands, and a further fifteen hundred managed to enter illegally. Illegal Jewish refugees, meaning those without valid passports, were henceforth no longer driven straight back into the arms of the Nazis, but housed in specially erected camps. Among these was the notorious Westerbork camp (which was actually financed by Jewish organizations and not by the government), where the first refugees arrived in October 1939, and which was later to be used by the Germans for their own ends. It was from there that the Dutch Jews and gypsies were sent to the extermination camps.[43]

Two overriding requirements can be distinguished in this brief description of the admission of German and Austrian refugees in the 1930s: immigrants should not cause any undesirable international political complications, and they should also fit into the economic context of the Netherlands, particularly to the demands of its labour market. Looking at admission policy over a longer period, two other requirements can be added. Immigrants had to be loyal to the Dutch authorities and tolerant of the rest of the population.

After the Second World War we find in fact the same quartet of requirements, but within an even stricter framework of government policy and control. In the first instance this revolves round the criterion of 'nationality'. Böhning has encapsulated its controlling role in admission as follows: 'The modern states draw a border line around them over which foreigners may not step without explicit or tacit consent.'[44] In practice this can mean that entry is tacitly allowed, or even encouraged, when it coincides with national interests. The recruitment agreements and enrolment offices of the Dutch government put in place to ensure the smooth and rapid attraction of workers from Mediterranean countries demonstrate that. But this tacit agreement or assisted recruitment can, if it is thought necessary, be replaced by controls on admission or even refusal of entry without acquiring a visa first, or for more than short tourist visits.

The sequence described here applies, for instance, to the arrival of Mediterranean workers, who until 1968 came to the Netherlands on the off-chance, and if they found work here, could obtain a work permit and then a residence permit. After 1968 they could only enter the Netherlands and seek employment after obtaining prior agreement, and since 1973 this has only been granted in very exceptional cases.[45]

For a subject of a non-EU country, entry has only been possible since the mid-1970s if no-one qualified to do the work intended can be found in the Netherlands. Otherwise access is only available to family members in the context of family reunion and family formation (marriage partners),[46] which once again clearly implies a fairly strict selection by sex, marital status and age. For aliens who cannot satisfy these criteria and who do not come under the privileged category of nationals of countries of the EU, there can be no question of freedom of settlement in the Netherlands. For some of them even a short stay as a tourist is problematic because of the need for a visa. This has started to apply to an increasing number of nationalities, among them Turks and Surinamese since 1980, and North Africans since 1983. The closing of the Dutch frontiers in the 1980s is symbolized *par excellence* by the denial of entry to foreign gypsies, and even their expulsion.[47]

One subject which from the mid-1980s has come to dominate political discussion about immigration and entry policy is the rapid growth in the number of asylum seekers. The rise of this new wave of migration coincided with the move towards a European Community/Union in which it gradually became possible to envisage a Europe (or at least a Western Europe) without internal frontiers. The spectre of uncontrollable migration, both within the Union and coming from outside it, not only led to panic political reactions,[48] but also contributed to the emergence of a transnational policy on immigration.[49]

The increasing flow of asylum seekers led to a number of measures to debar them categorically. These measures have been introduced at the national and international level, and are based on certain principles. At the national level the policy consists of the following main components:

a. measures aimed at making the land of settlement less attractive: a more austere reception regime (bread, bed and bath), and no access to the labour market or educational facilities until the request for asylum is granted;
b. measures aimed at preventing people being able to come and claim asylum: 'high-risk' countries are subjected to visa requirements; carriers, including airlines, are held responsible for bringing in people without valid documentation and are obliged to bear the expense of their return;
c. tighter criteria for granting asylum (there must be a demonstrable political threat to the individual – a general threat to a group is not sufficient) and the separation of 'economic' from 'political' refugees. Since then the percentage of rejections of appeals for asylum has risen significantly.

On the international level of the 'Schengen countries'[50] and the European Union, these kinds of measures are integrated and supplemented by instruments and agreements (some still to be negotiated, some already in force) such as harmonization of policy on visas, tighter controls at external frontiers, the agreement that within a united Europe asylum seekers should only have one opportunity of making their application, and the automatic exchange of information about undesirable migrants or those wanted by the authorities.[51]

In practice, however, the implementation of the policy on asylum comes up against several problems. In the first place the procedures for dealing with applications can become very extended, a result of the authorities responsible becoming overwhelmed with work, but also of the system of legal protection developed in the welfare state countries where, of course, judicial rights and appeal procedures are taken advantage of to the full.[52] And if there has been a long delay before a negative decision on an appeal for asylum, expulsion is often no longer considered acceptable. As a result new statuses have evolved, lodged between acceptance and rejection of a request for asylum: first that of 'tolerated', when the application for asylum has indeed been rejected, but the risk involved in deporting the person is considered too great, at least for the moment. Secondly there is the equally ambivalent status of the temporarily 'displaced' (introduced in 1992 for refugees from former Yugoslavia). People with this status make no application for asylum, but temporary residence is granted them as long as the situation in their country of origin makes it necessary. Thirdly, in 1994 a comparable status was introduced for those asylum applicants who failed to acquire either A or B-status, but who could not be sent home: the provisional status for temporary protection.

A very anomalous situation has arisen, not only in the Netherlands, but in almost all West European countries (and particularly in Germany), with thousands of asylum seekers pitched into a political and social no-man's-land. The extent of the problem has become so great that reactions from within society have begun to occur. A political climate threatens to arise in which drastic measures to impose control on this migration flow gain majority support. Policies to prevent and slow down the flow of arrivals, often developed at an international level, and divorced from any estimate of the seriousness of the situation of the prospective asylum seekers, consequently have an increasing likelihood of being adopted. It cannot be denied that national policy in the Netherlands in recent years has been influenced by this European climate, and that it is continually being forced along the road of this policy of unqualified exclusion.

The role of government in the admission of workers and of refugees as described here is common knowledge. Less familiar perhaps is the role of government in the strict control of the post-war flows of migration of their own nationals or fellow citizens. For instance, the Dutch government made a sustained effort to limit the arrival of Eurasians or Indonesian Dutch from Indonesia. In particular the government tried to prevent the arrival of those who had

never previously been in the Netherlands 'by the pressure exercised
to opt for Indonesian citizenship, by making it difficult to obtain
the necessary travel documents, and by the way in which applications for travel loans were processed.'[53] An equally restrictive policy
on entry was later applied to the *spijtoptanten*, who regretted their
initial choice of Indonesian nationality.[54]

Restrictions could not officially be applied to the immigration
from Surinam, which began to increase from 1966 and changed
from being an elite migration into a migratory flow of ordinary
Surinamese. The relatively small but nonetheless gradually increasing flow of migrants gave the Netherlands reason after 1970 to look
for ways to call a halt to this migration. However, migration control
of this kind could not be introduced without the agreement of the
overseas territory of Surinam, and it was plain that Surinam would
never co-operate in it. The attempt was in vain.[55]

The immigration of Dutch citizens from Surinam so obsessed
Dutch politicians, that it must certainly have encouraged their efforts
to end the statutory relationship. The coincidence of internal political events in Surinam made it possible to achieve this in 1975. During
the negotiations on Surinam's independence, the Dutch tried for the
last time to prevent Surinamese from coming to the Netherlands by
means of a strict ruling on nationality, and to remove Dutch nationality from all those already settled there, turning them into aliens.
When in preliminary discussions this proposal was clearly quite
unacceptable, the Dutch delegation withdrew it and even agreed to
allow free passage to continue between the Netherlands and Surinam
until 1980: a transitional period of five years.

This Dutch policy established the impression – first at the time
of independence in 1975 and later when the transitional period was
coming to an end in 1980 – that there would be virtually no further
possibility of going to the Netherlands. This led to an enormous
flow of 'last minute' migrants, first in 1974-1975, and then in
1979-1980. The policy appeared to have evoked exactly the reaction
it had been designed to avoid.[56]

It can be demonstrated for every group in the post-war period
that allowing the entry of immigrants was accompanied by control
and often restrictions on the part of the government. Periods of
lenience in allowing entry coincided with periods of an over-
stretched labour market and economic expansion. This applies in
particular to the periods 1960 to 1966 and 1967 to 1973. In times

when unemployment is relatively high and it is difficult to absorb newcomers straight into the labour market, attempts are made to keep the inflow as small as possible. If this is not always successful, it is mainly because of the legal rights immigrants have acquired, and the resulting impossibility of denying them entry. Most recently this applied to the reunion of Mediterranean workers' families at a time when the labour market was depressed (1976-1981), and to the family-forming migration from the mid-1980s onwards.

Looking back on government policies on immigration and admission over a long period of more than four centuries, three clear phases can be distinguished. In the first phase – from the seventeenth century to the end of the Republic – the Netherlands was an immigration country *par excellence*. As a political entity it consisted of a fairly loose association of towns and provinces. Country or place of birth was the most important criterion by which newcomers were distinguished from the native-born. The descendants of immigrants were native-born and therefore in principle no distinction applied to them. Policy towards these newcomers was mainly a matter for individual towns.

In the second phase – from the early nineteenth century until about 1970 – there were important changes. The number of immigrants gradually declined until 1870 and then remained at a relatively low level until the Second World War, apart from some refugee migration. Since the creation of the Kingdom of the Netherlands in 1815, the political entity has acquired much more the legal and political structure of a nation-state, with nationality as its legal expression; this nationality was now based primarily on the hereditary principle. The distinction between native-born and newcomers born elsewhere, which had applied during the Republic, was replaced by that between Dutch citizens by descent and foreign subjects. The state now expressly articulated the right to decide on allowing entry to its territory and on expulsion from it of foreign citizens. Actual policy based on these new principles really only took on concrete form in the early twentieth century, when properly worked-out legislation and executive agencies came into being. These became operative when political and economic developments required it.

From the mid-1980s we enter the third phase, the internationalization of immigration policy in the context of the European Union.

For immigration policy this has meant in the first place that a new status has been created between nationals and aliens: that of the EU subject, who has the right to migrate relatively freely within the area of the EU; in addition this phase is characterized by a common effort towards a – restrictive – policy on the admission of the subjects of 'third countries' (non-EU). This puts increasing pressure on the autonomous and relatively open tradition of Dutch policy on immigration.

Chapter 4

The host country
The Netherlands and the Dutch

Before discussing the nature of the contacts between the Dutch and newcomers and their descendants, and how the latter were received into the community, it makes sense to examine in this chapter the various divergent interests in the Netherlands and how the Dutch have coped with them from the time they gained their independence until now.[1]

The Dutch harbour many internal differences – and always have done. These differences are by no means always the result of individual characteristics, for in the course of history the inhabitants of the Netherlands have never all shared equal rights and opportunities. This inequality, moreover, has changed over time. We shall illustrate this by examining two particular aspects of this set of circumstances.

First, very often inequality was quite divorced from any distinction between natives and newcomers, and this was something which the newcomers had to be aware of. They were not dealing with a single monolithic society, but with sub-groups all with differing interests, of different social classes, and with diverging cultural and religious orientations.

Secondly, the sectional interests within Dutch society clashed to such an extent that it became necessary to develop special techniques of conflict-resolution in order for people to be able to live together in the same country. These measures to regulate conflict might also have a role to play in any incidents of friction between newcomers or their descendants and the Dutch.

Inequality and differences

A brief and necessarily very simplified review of the development of
the rights of a Dutch citizen seems a good way to clarify the
inequality of opportunities and rights between the various sections
of the Dutch population. The award of these rights, particularly the
franchise, is a reflection of changing views on the subject of social
differences.

During the Republic, the period up to 1795, there was no franchise in the modern sense of the word. The structure of the Dutch
state was a decentralized one which, if we exclude the rural areas, in
the more densely populated provinces was made up of three layers:
the towns, above them the regions or provinces and, superimposed
upon the provinces, the Union. The towns, assembled in the
Regional or Provincial States, to a large extent determined the policy
of the provinces, and the provinces, assembled in the States General,
determined the policy of the Union. At provincial and national
level, decision-making was in principle by majority vote, though in
practice the views of those who bore the highest financial contribution often weighed very heavily.

Throughout the seventeenth and eighteenth centuries the unity
of the Netherlands remained a problem; this unity was also elusive
in a formal sense, existing as it was meant to between the full
members of the Seven Provinces (Holland, Zeeland, Utrecht,
Gelderland, Overijssel, Friesland and Groningen), the 'territory' of
Drenthe, which was not represented in the States General, and the
'Generalities', seen rather as conquered provinces consisting of
Zeeland-Flanders, most of North Brabant, and parts of Limburg.

At the town level, decisions were made by a group of wealthy
citizens, sometimes divided among themselves in rival families. In
this sense, practically all the inhabitants were therefore excluded
from civil rights. There was, however, a citizenship of the towns,
called *poorterschap* (the freedom of the town), the significance of
which was economic rather than political. This 'freedom' was
accompanied by privileges: freedom from tolls, the right to be
recognized by a guild as a master craftsman, the right to be appointed to most official positions, and the right to be heard before
the local town courts.

A town considered the granting of its freedom to be a privilege
and was certainly not prepared to award it to all comers. The most

HAERLEMMER POORT. *1617.*

important criterion for its award or removal was that the freeman must be able to provide for himself without difficulty. Although this economic condition was the most important, in a number of cases there were also others. For instance, in 1655 a number of Catholics in Utrecht were refused the freedom of the city unless 'for some significant reason the Corporation unanimously saw fit to grant some degree of dispensation'. This decision was later relaxed, in that the requirement of unanimity of votes in granting this exceptional privilege was abandoned; in 1674 the ruling was limited to those born outside the province, and in 1740 to those born outside the United Netherlands. Catholics were also excluded in various towns in Gelderland and Overijssel, such as Deventer.[2]

As well as economic and religious reasons for exclusion from the freedom of the town, sex and marital status could also count. In Amsterdam, for instance, women were only accepted if unmarried, or married to a freeman of the city.

There were four ways of becoming a freeman: by being born to a freeman, by marriage to the daughter or widow of one, by grant or by purchase. The recommended method for newcomers was generally purchase, and occasionally grant or marriage.

The Haarlemmerpoort (Haarlem gate) at Amsterdam. Print by Reinier Nooms, 1617. It was no simple matter for a foreigner to get into the town unobserved. Most towns were surrounded by a rampart or wall, pierced at intervals by gates. The town militia was responsible for opening the gates every morning and closing them in the evening. (Gemeentelijke Archiefdienst, Amsterdam)

The exclusion of the adherents of some religions applied particularly to eligibility for public office. Only male freemen who were members of the Calvinist Reformed Church could be considered, thus excluding Catholics, Remonstrants, Lutherans, Jews or Baptists.[3]

The primary distinction between residents by their religious faith, the economically based division between *poorters* and non-*poorters*, and the virtual absence of a right to vote, all disappeared with the Batavian Revolution of 1795. The constitutions adopted in subsequent years applied to *all* citizens: the opening statement of Article 1 of the 1798 Constitution reads, 'The happiness of all is the highest law'. Furthermore decision-making was based on the right to vote, and as such there was no longer any discrimination by religious belief, though there certainly was by many other criteria: for example, voting was restricted to males who paid a certain and by no means insubstantial sum in taxes.

In spite of this taxation-based franchise, the period of French occupation, from 1795 to 1815, dominated by the slogan 'Liberty, Equality, Fraternity', can yet be regarded as an interval of far-reaching democratic experimentation in comparison with the period that followed it. As we have seen, even the non-native-born were allowed, subject to certain conditions, to join the electorate.[4]

The establishment of the Kingdom of the Netherlands in 1815 resulted in a partial reaction with regard to the franchise. The Lower House of Parliament was elected indirectly by the Provincial assemblies or Estates, which in their turn were drawn from three echelons: the nobility – consisting of all the adult members of that order, the towns, and the rural areas; these last two consisted of men aged twenty-three and over who paid sufficient in land tax and wealth taxes. The special position afforded to the nobility therefore meant that the criterion of 'birth' was re-introduced, a criterion which in fact also used to apply for co-option within the ruling of 'regent' families of the Republic. The criterion of land tax put the emphasis on property, and that of wealth taxes on the pattern of expenditure and therefore indirectly on income. Land tax was based on the possession of land and property, personal tax on what can be summarized as lifestyle, such as the rental value of housing, furniture, servants and horses.

The revision of the Constitution in 1848 signified the loss of the criterion of birth for the franchise, a weakening of the property criterion, but a reinforcement of the income criterion. In the period from 1848 to 1917, men aged twenty-three and over (from 1896 to 1917 limited to twenty-five and over), who contributed at least a specified amount in direct national taxation, might vote. Included in these taxes were, as before, land and wealth taxes, but now also a 'patent' or business tax. This was payable on the independent exercise of a non-agricultural profession and thus strengthened the income element in this taxation-based franchise.

The restriction of the right to vote for parliamentary representatives to those persons who contributed at least a certain amount in taxes, which was maintained until 1917, was by no means a random one. Its foundation was the notion that only those citizens could vote responsibly who were able to carry personal responsibility. This, so ran the received opinion, could be measured by possession of sufficient vested interests, as evidenced by a tax assessment. In 1850 the total of the three taxes to be paid was set so high, that only about ten per cent of men aged over twenty-three could vote. In 1890 twenty-five per cent satisfied the requirements, and by 1900 the figure had risen (partly through the admittance of 'non-tax-paying voters') to about half of all men aged over twenty-five.[5]

Only in 1917 was universal male suffrage introduced, followed in 1919 by universal suffrage for both men *and* women. Since then, the most important restrictions have been the minimum age limit – lowered from twenty-three in 1917 first to twenty-one and then to eighteen in 1971 – and nationality.

The assumptions about who could be recognized as a full citizen, reflected in eligibility for office and the right to vote for the highest legislative body, have therefore been subject to considerable change in the last two hundred years. These assumptions and the constitutional changes in the polity did not exist in isolation. Similar ideas prevailed in other areas of society. In the churches, for example, birth, wealth and gender used to determine everyone's station. Violent disputes about the most honourable and therefore the best seats in church were not confined to nobles in the Middle Ages: well after 1500 the rich, as a symbol of their prominence, purchased their own pews for use in services and less distinguished members of the congregation hired chairs according to their status. In the nineteenth century virtually all Dutch churches had complicated systems for the sale and rent of seats. So status could be bought, even before the eyes of the Lord. Sometimes uncomfortable benches were made available to the poor at no cost; most of them, however, just had to stand.

The social divide between rich and poor, even in church, is well demonstrated by an event that occurred in the town of Grave near Nijmegen in 1855. A request was made to the Catholic churchwarden of Grave on behalf of the Catholic non-commissioned officers of the garrison stationed there that the NCOs be allocated 'respectable' seating, that is to say, 'equivalent to that of citizens of the middle class'. The argument was put forward that their equivalent ranks in the Reformed Church also occupied good seats. A telling postscript to the request asks that no places should be allocated where 'poor or mean people have their seats during the week and on Sunday mornings' since 'these seats might not be entirely clean, as you, the Churchwarden, will surely agree with us'.

The extent of this split between the different social classes in the Netherlands became clear when this system of social stratification in church actually appeared to offer a solution to the problem of caste in Ceylon (the modern Sri Lanka). In 1737 Baron G.W. van Imhoff, Governor of the East India Company there from 1736 to 1740, addressed the rulers of Matare. They had requested to be allowed to be married, as they had been previously, in the Dutch church in the fort, instead of in the church outside where the lower castes, specified as 'laundrymen and all of low birth' used to go. Van Imhoff decided that the rulers 'if they wanted to be proper Christians should put off their greatness at least in religious observances', seeing that before God 'the meanest are often the best and most worthy'. Yet he had a solution to offer for this problem of caste. He added to his admonition 'that if some distinction could be allowed in the church, this might consist of them and their families having separate seating in the same church, which was not forbidden to them, and was also the practice in our own churches'.[6]

In connection with regional and religious differences, there were also all manner of distinctions in Dutch society in cultural matters, and nowhere was this more clearly demonstrated than in the use of language. Local dialects were the language of communication for almost everyone. The use of dialect not only complicated communication between people in, say, Limburg and Overijssel, it also led to quite direct labelling of people as coming from a particular region. In urban society the use of dialect determined what class someone

Scene on the Dam in Amsterdam. Detail of a painting by Johannes Lingelbach, 1656. Paintings of market scenes and similar views often showed characters recognizable by their dress. The trio in the foreground belong to the prosperous bourgeoisie. The man and the woman on the right are much more simply dressed. (Amsterdam Historical Museum)

belonged to. Even in the seat of government, The Hague, where the ruling elite may speak in 'plummy' accents, the ordinary townsfolk have their own distinctive dialect, and always have done.

Many other examples of cultural differences in the Netherlands can be listed, such as the gradations in spiritual conviction and liturgical practice between and within the rich variety of religious communities in the Netherlands. Cultural differences are, however, not only regional or religious, but also especially class-related, as is amply demonstrated by the example of the two kinds of Hague accent.

A final difference between people in the Netherlands, not yet mentioned, is their sexual orientation. Whether it is acknowledged, denied or disregarded, a minority of the population has always shown homosexual proclivities. Society has shown varying reactions to this in the course of time. A period marked by persecution was followed in the nineteenth century by one in which homosexuality was regarded as an illness. Only recently has it been possible to speak of the emancipation of this category of people.[7]

It will be plain from this section that as well as the criterion of 'newcomer' there are many other yardsticks by which people and groups in a society can be distinguished and divided.

Living with the differences

How then have all these individual Dutch people, with all these
differences and so many conflicting interests, managed to live
together?

Everyone is a combination of several characteristics on the basis
of which he or she might be treated differently. Each individual is
either a man or a woman, has a certain age, disposes of a certain
amount of income or capital, holds a certain outlook on life or
religious beliefs, has a certain sexual orientation, is of high birth or
not and has a specific place of birth and nationality (though for the
purpose of this chapter we shall ignore the last feature). At the level
of the individual it is not always immediately obvious which characteristic is socially the most relevant. This only becomes clearer
when there are instances from which it appears that at the level of
the group one particular characteristic, at a specific time and in a
specific social context, contributes more readily to promoting the
interests of the group than does some other feature. In the formation
of the primary group of the family, gender, age and sexual orientation are inoperative as common characteristics. Within the family
these characteristics are in a manner of speaking neutralized as
potential crystallization points for the promotion of interests in
public life. The other characteristics, however, particularly the
economic and religious ones, normally coincide at the level of the
family.

In Dutch history the collective promotion of interests in these
last two areas has played a major role. One can even regard that
history primarily as the continuing conflict of interests between
religious and socio-economic groups. Only in the last few decades
have interest groups and the promotion of interests based on age,
sex and sexual orientation manifested themselves more clearly.

The conflict of religious interests was decided in the early days
of the Eighty Years War to the advantage of the adherents of the
Reformed Church. Catholics, Jews and Baptists tried to maintain
their position as best they could, but were neither prepared for nor
capable of real resistance to the prevailing order.

Elements of the class struggle, although present, for instance, at
the start of the Revolt against Spain, in strikes in the Leiden textile
industry and among seasonal migrant workers in peat cutting and
elsewhere, did not lead to any real threat to the established order.

There was occasional violent opposition to the governing class of regents, but it remained exceptional.[8]

Only the internal conflict amongst the regents themselves, and especially between the regents and those citizens who could not gain access to the higher offices, led to a shift of power at the end of the eighteenth century. A group known as the Patriots had not proved able to overthrow the rule of the regents' oligarchy and of the stadtholder in 1787, but returned in 1795 with the troops of Revolutionary France, and set up the Batavian Republic. Although this was in the first place a conflict between the old and the rising new elites, there was also an element of social protest in it. One way in which this manifested itself was when in many churches the fine boxed pews, owned by the old regent families, were destroyed, as opposed to just their coats of arms being hacked off, as had happened in the previous political crises of 1672 and 1748.[9]

We have seen that the democracy originally put into effect by the Batavian Republic under the slogan of *Liberté, Egalité, Fraternité* found expression, among other things, in the introduction of a tax-based franchise, under which twenty per cent of the male population were entitled to vote, a much larger percentage than had previously been able to exercise direct political influence. This democracy was soon reversed under the influence of international political developments. What did survive was the separation of church and state, or at least the removal of obstacles for those who were not members of the Reformed Church, and therefore the principle of emancipation for these groups.

Only in the second half of the nineteenth century did the real consequences of these reforms become apparent. On the one hand, the franchise was extended; on the other, increasing prosperity only then made it possible for the emancipation of the disadvantaged religious groups to be realized. Both developments were reflected in the most important political and social development of the last century, pillarization or '*verzuiling*', by which is meant the growth in Dutch society of vertical non-class groupings based on religious faith and later on the secular creeds of socialism and liberalism. These 'pillars', held together by all manner of political, social, and cultural organizations, came to dominate all forms of public life in the Netherlands right up to the 1950s. The widening of the franchise in the second half of the nineteenth century not only gradually gave more citizens the right to vote, but also forced those who held, or who strove for, political power, to mobilize and organize this ever-increasing mass of voters for their own ends.

From around 1870 the formation of political parties became a necessity, particularly for the religiously based emancipation groups: the Catholics and the orthodox Calvinists. This last group arose from two schismatic movements in the Dutch Reformed Church: first the Secession (*Afscheiding*) of 1834 and second, the Dissent (*Doleantie*) of 1886. Catholics and orthodox Calvinists, two groups which had been ignored, disdained and excluded from the political system by the traditional Dutch Reformed elite, struggled and fought for a position of equality in society. Their aim and their main weapon was their own confessional schools. For the sake of these they joined forces to fight the liberal, mostly Dutch Reformed, elite, who supported state schooling with a general Christian ethic.

It was not only religious groups which organized themselves: an emancipation movement based on socio-economic foundations was also launched. The socialists had been organizing themselves since the late 1860s, striving towards raising the status of the working class and a fairer distribution of worldly goods, with one of their early party journals being called, *Rights for All.*

When both the orthodox Calvinists and the Catholics saw that only by combining forces could they bring their goal closer, the principle of pillarization was born: a vertical division (in other words, not linked to class) of society based on recognition of each other's power. Catholic and orthodox Calvinist bourgeoisie and church leaders began to organize their supporters in every conceivable way. Although the ideology of class conflict inclined the socialists against the principle of a pillarized society, in the long run they were also forced to operate within pillarized frameworks. The liberals and mainstream Calvinists, too, finally had no option but to protect themselves by conforming with pillarization.

The leaders of the pillars, who frequently met each other at national level, were prepared to forge compromises – in cabinet and in parliament, and after the Second World War in the Dutch Labour Foundation, and in national co-ordinating bodies for sport, broadcasting, culture and the like. Their supporters, however, were expected to abstain as much as possible from contact with members of other pillars. A Catholic not only went faithfully to his parish church, but also voted for the Roman Catholic State Party (later the Catholic People's Party). He was also, depending on his occupation,

Comité van Werkloozen, aangesteld door verschillende Vakvereenigingen.

PROTEST-MEETING

op WOENSDAG 25 Januari a.s., des avonds half negen uur,
IN "CONSTANTIA," ROZENGRACHT.

Spreker: F. DOMELA NIEUWENHUIS.

Onderw.: Werkloosheid erger dan de Cholera.

Entrée 5 ct. tot dekking der kosten.

ARBEIDERS, komt allen op! Alleen uw gezamenlijk en krachtig optreden zal de machtigen dwingen in uw nood te voorzien.

HET COMITÉ.

Typ. BOOM & Co., Lepelstraat 76, A'dam.

a member of the Roman Catholic Workers Union (later the Catholic Labour Movement and later still the Netherlands Catholic Trade Union) or of equivalent employers' or farmers' organizations. He listened only to the Catholic broadcasting station (KRO), played in a Catholic football club, bought his clothes in a Catholic-owned department store like C&A. Even entirely non-ideological activities had to be organized on confessional lines, and so he might also be a member of one of the legendary Catholic goatbreeding associations. For their part, socialists voted for the Social-Democratic Workers' Party (later Labour Party) and were members of the Socialist Trade Union Confederation. They read *Het Volk*, the socialist daily, and listened to VARA, the socialist broadcasting channel. The orthodox Calvinists had the Anti-Revolutionary Party, the National Christian Trade Union Confederation, and the NCRV, the Dutch Christian broadcasting organization. To a much lesser extent, similarly extensive organizational structures existed for the liberals and the mainstream Calvinists. The heyday of *verzuiling* occurred between about 1920 and 1960. Only then did the system begin to lose its strength under the influence of the huge increase in prosperity, a series of events we have already discussed in Chapter 2.[10]

The socialists began to organize in the 1860s. They fought for the improvement of working conditions and for a fairer distribution of worldly goods. Domela Nieuwenhuis was one of the leaders of the movement in the Netherlands. He denounced abuses in his journal Recht voor Allen (Justice for All). (Gemeentelijke Archiefdienst, Amsterdam).

Differences among the Dutch, and social organizations based on those differences, are therefore an essential characteristic of Dutch society. The most important criteria by which people have been mobilized to fight for their interests in society seem in Dutch history to have been religious denomination and class. In the secular welfare state since 1960 these criteria have lost their significance. In the welfare state the relationship between the state and the individual has come to play an increasingly important role. New forms of promoting interests have come into being along new lines, such as age (youth culture), gender (women's movements) and sexual orientation (gay movements) and the like.

Finally some reference should be made here to the fact that social conflicts in the Netherlands have generally been solved with very little bloodshed. Political assassinations have been a rarity in Dutch history since the seventeenth century. Strikes have sometimes been resolutely suppressed, but seldom with violence.[11] After 1870, even criminals could no longer be sentenced to death. Perhaps the major exceptions to this tendency have been the persecutions of gypsies and homosexuals before the Second World War.[12]

Chapter 5

Newcomers and their descendants: the process of settlement
Approaches and concepts

After a prolonged stay, newcomers become immigrants; at that point, questions inevitably arise which go beyond the how and why of their coming, going, or staying. How do they find a place in the new society, or how is such a place assigned to them? And what happens to newcomers in the long run, and particularly to their descendants who are no longer immigrants and may not be aliens either? These are the kind of questions posed by sociologists about the process of settlement. Most contemporary research has concentrated on answering these questions at the individual level and in the short term. The process of settlement is approached from a psychological or cultural-anthropological point of view, in which the adaptation or acculturation of *individual* newcomers is measured and recorded. This kind of approach is not really appropriate for our purposes. Our attention is directed much more at the process of accommodation or fitting in of *groups* of newcomers in the long term, in other words, *over generations.*

   The difference is not simply the result of the point of view from which the subject is approached. There is also a question of basic assumptions: much research concentrating on the adaptation of individual immigrants and their children ignores the influence of the host society. This can create the impression that the way a group of newcomers and their descendants gain a place in society is determined principally by the characteristics, talents and behaviour of individual newcomers. We, on the other hand, start from the premise that not only the newcomers but also the host society determine the outcome of the settlement process, and that both must therefore be the subject of research. The importance of both factors may vary, depending on social circumstances and on the specific characteristics of the newcomers and of the host society.

The development of the social and ethno-cultural position

If we want to answer the questions posed earlier about the development of the position of newcomers in society, we must first of all look at the distinction between the social and the ethno-cultural position of the group of newcomers. Their *social position* can be provisionally defined as the place of the group as a whole in the social strata of the host society.[1] Do the newcomers gain a place in the labour market, and if so, at what level, with what income, and with what chances of improvement? What opportunities are afforded to newcomers to earn a living as self-employed persons? What is the housing situation, and the quality of housing? What about the educational opportunities for newcomers and their families? The answer to these and similar questions gives an indication of their social position.

The *ethno-cultural position* of a group of newcomers and their descendants involves their position as it is perceived by the group itself and by society at large. Relevant questions in this connection are: how 'different' or 'not our sort of people' are the newcomers felt to be? And vice versa, how alien do the newcomers find the host society? If the group of newcomers themselves stress their 'otherness', is this consciously preserved, or even cultivated? And to what extent are there tendencies in the host society which emphasize the 'otherness' of the newcomers, for example, by promoting nationalist sentiments?[2] The ethno-cultural position is harder to measure, partly because it involves matters inherent in people's perception of their environment and which are not always easy to record objectively.

If we simplify the development of the social and ethno-cultural position of a group of newcomers and their descendants, there are theoretically four possibilities:

1   Both the ethno-cultural and the social position of the group of newcomers and their descendants become in the course of time no different from that of the host society. This is called *assimilation*.[3] In this definition assimilation does not imply being completely absorbed without retaining any of their own characteristics, but that members of a group perceive themselves *primarily* as members of the host society, and are considered to be so. By far the major part of the immigrant groups reviewed in

Chapter 2, and particularly the pre-war ones, can now be called assimilated in this sense.

2 Its ethno-cultural position is defined as 'different' by the group itself and by society, but the social position proves not to be systematically different, or rather is not systematically inferior or likely to remain so. A typical early example of this is the situation of Chinese restaurateurs in the Netherlands in the 1960s. The position of the Sephardic Jews during the Republic, and that of later groups of immigrants who have successfully found a niche for themselves in the economic system, such as the Italian ice-cream makers, are also good illustrations of this category.

3 The newcomers and their descendants are not regarded as different from an ethno-cultural point of view, and do not primarily regard themselves as different, but they occupy, and retain, a systematically inferior social position. In such cases the immigrants are absorbed into another classification, that of social class. It is not easy to give clear examples of this. One can perhaps think of the thousands of German and Belgian (cross-frontier) workers who in the early decades of the twentieth century worked in the Limburg mines.

4 Being ethno-culturally different, or being considered to be so, remains linked with a systematically inferior social position. In the Netherlands it is mainly this final situation (or the threat of it) which has attracted most attention since the war in research, as well as in policy, and for which the term *minority* has been introduced.

Where possible in the chapters that follow, we shall discuss the ethno-cultural and social positions of newcomers separately. We do this because each of them forms an independent constituent of either of the possible final outcomes of the settlement process. For assimilation implies that the group of newcomers and/or their descendants are no longer distinguishable on either count.

A closer examination of the concept of 'minority'

The use of the term 'minority' as described above is slightly different from its normal usage internationally, in which what matters most is being ethno-culturally different, and being perceived as different, and in which the term 'minority' is used for both the situations outlined in 2 and 4 above. We will therefore briefly discuss the specific usage of the term in the Netherlands.

In the Netherlands it is primarily Hans van Amersfoort who has set his stamp on the use of the specific term 'minority' (*minderheid*) with his book *Immigration and the formation of minority groups: an analysis of the Dutch experience 1945-1975.*[4] This was not apparent immediately on the publication of the Dutch version of the book in 1974, but only after 1979, when the Netherlands Scientific Council for Government Policy (WRR), and the Advisory Committee for Research into Minorities adopted the theoretical framework and many of the concepts used in Van Amersfoort's book.[5]

For Van Amersfoort the central question is what social and cultural position newcomers and their descendants occupy in the new society after a few generations. The end result can at one extreme be *assimilation*, as described above. The other extreme is *minority*, described by Van Amersfoort as a group living in a situation in which its members have over generations regarded themselves primarily as belonging to a separate group and are also regarded as such by society, and moreover where the group occupies a low social position and can exercise no effective political influence. If such a group also distinguishes itself from the majority by its own culture or at least by important cultural elements, then we can speak of a cultural or ethnic minority.[6]

In this definition 'minority' is a very precise concept. In practice it will seldom occur that a group satisfies all the criteria laid down by this definition.[7] If we run through the most important post-war immigrant groups in the Netherlands, then it is plain that hardly any of the criteria apply to the East Indies Dutch. The Surinamese and Antilleans are groups of immigrants who are generally regarded as separate, but whether they perceive themselves as such is, on the authority of recent research, increasingly doubtful. Moreover, these groups do not occupy an inferior position in Dutch society across the board. Finally, few of them have been in the country for more than a short time, so that no definitive pronouncement can be made on whether the position of their descendants born in the Netherlands will be the same as that of the first generation.

The largest Mediterranean immigrant groups, the Turks and Moroccans, satisfy some of the important criteria for a minority: most of them consider themselves to be primarily members of their own group, and are perceived as such; they also occupy a low social position all-round. But again, the time elapsed since their arrival is too short for further pronouncements. Meanwhile, although it has become clear that the older children of these immigrants, who came to the Netherlands with their parents, are closer to their parents than to their Dutch contemporaries when it comes to social position and opportunities, we can still only make provisional judgements about the second generation born in the Netherlands.[8]

Of the post-war groups of immigrants, perhaps the Moluccans best fit the criteria laid down. But here, too, we should take account of the fact that although the third generation of Moluccans appears to have fewer opportunities than autochthonous groups with the same characteristics, at the same time the social position of that generation is considerably less inferior than that of their grandparents who arrived in 1951. Their ethno-cultural position also changed rapidly.[9]

When we try to apply the strict definition of minority empirically to immigrant groups in earlier periods, we encounter further problems: in several respects the concept proves to be a product of its time. For example, the criterion that a minority can exercise no effective political power presupposes a society in which there is some degree of democratic decision-making. The farther we go back into the past, however, the smaller the institutionalized social basis of political decision-making proves to be (see Chapter 4), which means that exclusion from political decision-making becomes less and less a distinguishing criterion.

A second important presupposition is that of the nation-state and the assumption that every individual identifies himself with it as a citizen to some degree. This arises from the question of whether members of an immigrant group consider themselves primarily to be members of their group or members of the host nation-state. For the period before 1800 one could take the most relevant social and administrative entity of the day, for example the province or possibly the town, as a substitute for the nation-state.

So far we have only applied the concept of 'minority' to immigrants and their descendants, but that is purely the consequence of our line of approach. The concept is not in itself linked to new arrivals. Autochthonous groups can also at certain times find themselves assigned a very special place in society, or acquire one.

A fairly recent example of a group which within a period of half a century has become a minority in the strict sense are the caravan

Caravans in Leiden, early 1970s. Because of systematic separate treatment over the years, travellers in the Netherlands have become a distinct cultural minority known as caravan dwellers. (Photo Spaarnestad)

dwellers. They fulfil all the criteria, but this is an autochthonous group which has always lived in the Netherlands and speaks Dutch. They are distinguished by a single point: they live on wheels. However, the consequences of this one difference appear to be very great. From this point of view the lifestyle of the caravan dwellers could be called a subculture.[10]

Certain expressions can start to lead a life of their own. We have described the specific content which social scientists give to the concepts of 'minority' and 'assimilation'. However, in general parlance, and also in government terminology, several of these concepts are used differently: for instance, the term 'assimilation' is usually avoided, and the term 'minority' is used in a much wider sense than that described above. If one looks closely at important policy documents relating to the so-called 'minority policy', the common denominator of all groups eligible for facilities under that policy seems to be that they might *run the risk* of becoming a minority in the sense defined above.[11] We will not follow such usage here. In considering the process of settlement of immigrant groups over a very long period, ideal-type definitions of the end scenarios are necessary. We will therefore use the terms 'minority' and 'assimilation' in the strict sense defined above.

Acquiring and being allocated a social position, distinction and discrimination

In the first paragraph of this chapter we indicated by our questions that the position of newcomers can be looked at from two different angles: to what extent has that position been gained and fought for by the newcomers themselves, and to what extent is it allocated to them or imposed on them by the established society? These questions are of great importance, for the following reasons.

The social position of most Dutch people is largely determined by factors over which the individual has little or no influence. Gender and age are not the individual's own choices, and religious or philosophical beliefs in practice are only so to a limited extent. Despite all the claims of a 'free society', most Dutch people have only a very limited choice when it comes to their position in the labour market and their income. Many of those born with a penny will never in fact make it a pound. Certainly in the past it was true for the majority of the population that the position of their parents determined the opportunities of the children. This may have changed in recent decades, but the ideal of equal opportunities for all is still far from being achieved.

We start here from the view that *position allocation* is more important than position acquisition, in the sense that the former is decisive for the potentially positive effects of individual efforts and merits. This means that we shall primarily direct our attention to society, and the way in which it prescribes more or less precisely what newcomers and their descendants may or may not do. In this context society can best be regarded as a combination of a large number of groups with varying interests. How is the distribution within this society controlled of resources which are in theory needed by everyone, and the supply of which is at the same time limited? Jobs and the incomes linked to them, and particularly the better jobs, are among the most important social resources over which battle is drawn. But somewhere to live is obviously also an essential resource, and preferably somewhere as comfortable as

*Many migrants start at the
bottom of the ladder.
Cleaner at Schiphol Airport.
(Photo Ad van Denderen)*

possible; then there is education, health care, and insurance for one's
old age, against disability, and against loss of income or of the
breadwinner.

This battle is fought at an individual level, but also especially at
the level of the group, and this is of particular interest here. In
politics, competing groups try to acquire as great a share as possible
of the social resources. Attempts to exclude rival groups play an
important role in achieving this. From the point of view of position
allocation, the crucial question is then to what extent newcomers
are in fact, or can be, excluded.

One of the easiest ways in which this can be done politically is
by provisions in legislation and regulations which create a distinction between newcomers and their descendants and other groups in
society: for example, on the grounds that they were not actually born
in the country; that they do not hold its citizenship; that they cannot
speak the language; or do not belong to the prevailing religious faith
of the host country.

None of these forms of distinction is always and necessarily linked with being a newcomer, but in practice they often go together. The one most directly linked with being a newcomer is to distinguish by length of stay; for instance, in present-day Germany the ruling applies that wives of foreign employees, who come to Germany in the context of family reunion, only acquire the right to enter the labour market after they have been in Germany for four years. A ruling of this kind serves both to put a brake on the flow into Germany, and to protect the jobs of autochthonous Germans.

But distinctions can be made in the distribution of important social resources such as jobs, housing and educational opportunities, quite outside legislation and regulations, and in fact, even directly contrary to them. Newcomers and their descendants can systematically be treated differently, even if it is in conflict with the law. In a few cases this might mean systematically better, but usually it means systematically worse. The fact that newcomers are aliens can be a readily available criterion for treating them differently. That argument also applied to the situation before 1850, when 'alien' still tended to mean 'born somewhere else'. But perhaps it is above all the combination of grounds for exclusion in a single individual which makes it easier to make a distinction: a Moroccan from the Rif is simultaneously an alien, physically and culturally identifiable, working class, and moreover, not a Christian. An alien of this type is more likely to be the victim of exclusion than a manager working for a multinational company. The multinational's powerful network will usually already have arranged entry into the Netherlands, and made sure that the stay is comfortable, so that the man or woman involved ends up far less often in situations of potential exclusion.

So far we have avoided the term 'discrimination' and only used the neutral term 'distinction'. In general parlance the meaning of the concept 'discrimination' has become rather broad; it seems to include everything from unfriendly behaviour, through making distinctions in allocating important social resources which no-one can do without, to actual bodily harm. For the position allocation the first is relatively unimportant, because it need not *per se* have social consequences. In the context of this chapter, then, we would like to restrict 'discrimination' to those cases involving *actions with direct or indirect social consequences, in which a distinction is made on grounds not relevant to the situation.*[12]

Making distinctions in the allocation or distribution of resources is therefore discrimination when that distinction is made on grounds not relevant to the situation. When an individual has the best qualities for a job, and this is denied him *because* he does not look Dutch, is an alien or a Muslim, then this is a discriminatory action if those attributes are not important for the exercise of that post or occupation.

The definition of the concept is therefore restricted to actions. The motivation of the action is therefore less important: a discriminatory action with evil intent by someone with strong prejudices about members of a particular group has in principle the same social effect as the same action carried out because of a misunderstanding. For our definition it is of little importance even whether the person discriminated against is aware of the fact or not. When housing applications for a specific group, for example the Turks, are systematically subjected to long delays – contrary to official procedures – it can happen without the people involved regarding it as discriminatory, because they simply do not know, or they regard it as not particularly unreasonable. However, this certainly amounts to discrimination in our terminology.

The main problem with this definition is the phrase: *not relevant to the situation.* When we look at it without linking it to any specific period, its material content presents great difficulties. The definition of what society officially calls 'permissible distinction', and what it calls 'non-relevant distinction', appears to be subject to change over time. In Chapter 4, in examining who was admitted to the franchise, a series of distinctions was listed which in particular periods provided grounds for excluding people from the active or passive franchise; many of these were grounds for exclusion which, with hindsight and applying present-day standards, we must regard as discriminatory.

This last comment is intended only as a warning against interpreting history too much by modern-day standards, and not to qualify or throw doubt on the present-day standards for discriminatory behaviour. When we examine the persecution of gypsies, of homosexuals, or of people with different religious or political convictions in Dutch history, we cannot escape employing our own standards, and therefore with hindsight we talk of discrimination. At the same time we must, if we wish to explain those phenomena adequately, realize that contemporaries of those events could hold other views, and that the legislation, regulations, and legal practice of that time justified those actions and distinctions. We therefore see opinions and attitudes as quite separate from discrimination, or at least we do not start by assuming that there is a direct connection between the two. However, they do have their place, and sometimes a very important one, in relations between groups.

In this connection we must explain a few concepts in more detail. The first is *stereotype*. By this we understand assumptions and expectations with regard to another group which give a markedly simplified picture of reality. The second concept is *prejudice*. Prejudice differs from stereotype in that prejudices are rigid opinions and expectations not amenable to reason; furthermore they are in essence emotionally loaded. In research practice it is assumed that prejudices are negative and represent a negative attitude on the part of their holder.[13] The actual effect of stereotyping and prejudices depends very much on circumstances and on the parties involved.

Particular concepts are employed in some specific situations. In those cases in which a dominant group, or an authoritative institution from within that dominant group, such as the government or the church, imposes a negative stamp (a 'stigma') on another group, we talk of *stigmatization*. Whenever this process occurs the next question is, who is considered to be part of the group on which the stigma is imposed. The term used for this is *labelling*.[14]

The ethno-cultural position and ethnic processes

The way in which the ethno-cultural position was defined above, and its relationship to other concepts, such as ethnicity and ethnic processes, still requires some more detailed explanation here.

The ethno-cultural position usually refers to an observed situation at a specific moment and is therefore static. If we direct our attention more specifically to the dynamic behind changes in the ethno-cultural position, then we are entering the relatively new area of the study of ethnicity and ethnic processes.[15]

Ethnicity can be briefly defined as a sense of unity and solidarity based on a common culture or history. It is a social identity connected with loyalty groups or communities. Defined in this way it is the characteristic of a group at a specific moment. In *ethnic processes* we can distinguish between the formation (ethno-genesis), maintenance, reinforcement (ethnicization) or weakening of ethnic boundaries between groups. The cohesion of a group and thinking or acting in terms of groups is of primary importance here. It assumes interaction and communication between different groups or their members. People want to distinguish themselves from others, for which cultural and other symbols or a shared past and origin are employed to mark out the boundaries between the groups; language, linguistic usage and religion can also play a role as boundary markers. Ethnic groups emphasize those cultural elements, characteristics and attributes which divide them from the rest of society, rather than those in which they do not differ. It has been shown that the formation of ethnic groups has appreciably more significance than on the cultural level alone: people can take part as an ethnic group in the struggle for their share of social resources.[16] It is quite clear, but in both Dutch and English usage still somewhat strange, that within this terminology the autochthonous Dutch should also be regarded and defined as an ethnic group.

Ethnic processes often occur among immigrant groups, particularly among those which are physically and culturally distinguishable from the majority. However, the phenomenon is neither inevitably nor exclusively linked to newcomers and their settlement process.[17] The renewed attention, for instance, paid to Frisian as an officially recognized language, one of the expressions of Frisian regionalism, can also be regarded as a component of an ethnicization process. In comparison with the surge in regional minority movements in neighbouring countries, the ethnicization tendencies of Frisian or Limburg or Brabant regionalism in the Netherlands are relatively innocent. In Flemish and (by way of reaction) Walloon regionalism, the ethnicization tendencies have for years been translated into a social conflict which has shaken and changed forever the essence of the Belgian political system and the whole of Belgian society. The Corsican, Catalan and Basque struggles for political realization of their ideals of ethnic unity and independence are also of another order of magnitude, but are based in essence on the same process.

A compelling explanation for the powerful rise of this phenomenon is offered by E. Roosens.[18] Briefly summarized his line of thought amounts to this: in the colonial period the partnership of power and ethnocentrism introduced or even imposed the Western model of culture as the best. As a consequence, for instance, the

Indians of the American continent were decimated or confined to reservations. After decolonization a discussion and a terminology developed which emphasized the guilt of the West for the destruction of earlier authentic cultures during colonization, and promoted the inalienable right to one's 'own' culture, and one's 'own' identity, as something universal and sacrosanct.

Particularly at the international level, such points of view gained recognition and were recorded in general terms in statutes and treaties as 'Human Rights'. Gradually this has developed as a norm, and anyone infringing it can be charged with being a racist or a colonial imperialist. This fact can be used as a weapon in the struggle, particularly by ethnic groups in a position of numerical minority.

In this perspective, relations between ethnic groups are usually studied as relations between interest groups. The number of other functions the ethnic group has or could have varies from case to case, and is difficult to predict. The ethnic group can vary (still according to Roosens) from a more or less temporary group linked to a certain situation and aiming at a fairly limited goal, to a coherent and permanent group of people, who in almost all situations and stations in life are regarded as a separate group, as until recently in South Africa.

Chapter 6

Newcomers and their descendants in Dutch society since the sixteenth century

What position did the many immigrants since the sixteenth century gain in Dutch society, or what place was allocated to them? What were the relations between these newcomers and their descendants and the society in which they had settled, and how did they develop? In dealing with this long period we will split it into the events up to the Second World War, and the half-century after 1945. There are various reasons for this.

In the first place there is an argument inherent in the data: for the pre-1940 immigrants the process of settlement can be traced over several generations, but the major proportion of post-war immigration is still so recent that the settlement process has not yet crystallized. What the eventual picture will look like in these cases is still unsure.

A second argument for this division is the source material available to us. For the pre-war period we are dependent upon historical sources; over recent decades studies of these have been published regularly, but are nonetheless limited, with the consequence that these data are not always easy to interpret. This makes it difficult to describe the social and ethno-cultural development of the groups of newcomers and their descendants in the past, using the concepts outlined in Chapter 5. It is less complicated for the post-war period: since 1980 there has been an abundance of social science studies of the position of those groups in particular which, since that date, have been among the target groups for the minorities policy. For this period and these groups the literature is indeed so abundant that we will restrict our references mainly to the most important surveys and bibliographies.[1]

The process of settlement of immigrants and their descendants 1550-1940

It is often difficult to disentangle from the historical source material how newcomers and their descendants gained a place in society and how they related to people, organizations and institutions in that society. Most of the historical material is concerned with contacts and relations with the government on the one hand, and with individuals and organizations on the other. The nature and the course of these relations give us an indication of the position which the newcomers and their descendants achieved.

From this material it is certainly clear that these contacts usually took a different course for newcomers compared with their descendants. We will therefore deal as far as possible with the contacts of newcomers and those of their descendants with the host society separately and in succession: first at the level of government with its legislation and regulation, and then at the level of the individual, or of individuals working together in organizations such as guilds, associations and trade unions.

The Dutch government and newcomers

During the Republic the authorities as a rule made no distinction in civil or criminal law between residents born in the Netherlands and elsewhere. The exceptions affected mainly those who were in any case regarded as undesirables: vagabonds, tramps and suchlike. An impartial policy appears to have been the rule not only in the letter of the law but also in its application. J.A. Faber was able to demonstrate that in the cosmopolitan Amsterdam of the period 1680-1811 no systematic difference was drawn between the Dutch and newcomers either in criminal prosecutions or in sentencing.[2]

In Chapter 4 it was pointed out that an important distinction was made between residents who did and those who did not possess the freedom of the town *(poorterschap)* when it came to civil rights; Chapter 3 described how there was also a distinction between native-born citizens and foreigners. In fact this distinction was primarily of practical importance for those wishing to occupy high office, for which being native-born was a requirement; however, the option of naturalization was always open to those not native-born.

Because of the advantages linked to it, the freedom of the town was important for many more residents. It meant that they could

Merchants from the East on the Dam in Amsterdam. Detail of a painting by Johannes Lingelbach, 1656. (Amsterdam Historical Museum)

acquire exemption from tolls, access to most offices, and – most importantly – the right to apply for membership of a guild. Continuous residence in the town was a strict requirement to retain its freedom, once gained. The simplest way to acquire this freedom was to be born to a freeman. Newcomers had to achieve the desired position in some other way.[3]

Relatively few newcomers will have acquired it by marriage to the daughter or widow of a freeman, or as a grant from the town authorities, although this did occur sometimes, as in 1681 when, as we have seen, the freedom of the city of Amsterdam was initially granted to all Huguenots.

The most common method of acquisition was the purchase of the freedom by interested newcomers. We have remarked that it would require at least several weeks' wages; the newcomer, after paying his fee, taking his oath, and sometimes after a specific period of residence, could become a fully fledged citizen.

There were no provisions which excluded newcomers as such, though some categories of newcomers could be affected by general restrictions laid down for gaining the status of freeman. These were mostly concerned with economic resources, and sometimes with religious denomination, gender, or marital status. It is plain that poor newcomers in particular found an almost insuperable barrier placed before them by these limitations, as is also obvious from the high fees charged for the freedom of the town.

In many towns Roman Catholic immigrants found themselves excluded from the freedom because of their religious convictions. The most severely affected were, however, Jewish newcomers. They were not excluded from the freedom, but they were from its most attractive benefit: admission to the guilds. In 1632 the Amsterdam city authorities forbade any Jew to be a member of a guild. Exceptions were only made in a few rare cases. For instance, the brokers' guild, founded in 1612, consisted of 450 Christians and fifty Jews.[4]

The requirement of the freedom for admission to a guild actually applied only to master craftsmen, in other words, self-employed practitioners of their trade. Inhabitants without the freedom, including newcomers, could be admitted as apprentices, as was indeed emphatically laid down on various occasions. Sometimes a modest condition, such as the payment of a small fee, would be imposed.

As well as being a freeman and being native-born, the authorities sometimes set other conditions for the exercise of a profession; for instance, a special permit was necessary for plying the trade of money-changer, running a pawnbrokers, or keeping a school. In addition to general conditions there were also some directed specifically at newcomers, such as those for foreign assistants to apothecaries and surgeons in Amsterdam, and for painters and art dealers temporarily resident in Utrecht.

The Batavian Republic upheld the principle of equality before the law for everyone residing in the territory of the state, and this policy was continued by the Kingdom of the Netherlands after 1813. Foreign seasonal labour migrants could, for example, successfully bring a lawsuit. This was shown when around 1850 ordinary labourers from the German principality of Lippe-Detmold carried on an action for years on end against their employer, a brickmaker in Stadskanaal, near Groningen. Not only did they sustain a lengthy action before the local magistrates' court in Zuidbroek, demanding payment of their wages which were in arrears, but they also took their appeal to the district county court in Winschoten.[5]

The new state of the Netherlands differed from its predecessor, the Republic, on two important points. It did not recognize the distinction between freemen and other residents, and in addition the guilds were finally abolished, so that restrictions on the exercise of trades by newcomers fell by the wayside. For a time a tax was still levied on work performed by foreign seasonal labour migrants, such as the one-guilder tariff in the 1805 Patents Act.[6] Sometimes one also comes across provisions in local bye-laws directed against newcomers; the refusal of local authorities in the 1930s to issue licenses to Chinese hawkers of peanut biscuits is a familiar one.[7]

During the French occupation, at first not even the condition of being native-born was still listed as a provision for exercising such civil rights as the suffrage. For several years, as we have seen, it was enough to have been resident for a specified period. So in 1798 it was laid down that aliens who satisfied all other requirements would be enfranchised after a stay of ten years, and in 1806 it was even reduced to six years.[8] In the Kingdom of the Netherlands after 1813, however, those not native-born and – after the introduction of the principle of nationality – foreigners were once again completely excluded from the franchise. Only in 1985 did parliament again grant both active and passive suffrage to aliens resident in the Netherlands, after three years of legal residence.[9]

Both in the Republic and in the Kingdom much the same restrictions on eligibility for high office remained in force with regard to newcomers and foreigners. In these cases naturalization continued to be an efficacious remedy.

The Dutch and newcomers

To what extent was the government policy outlined above, as it developed over the course of time, in tune with the attitude of the autochthonous population to the newcomers? By population we mean here both individuals and voluntary organizations of individuals, such as guilds, associations and trade unions.

Before this question can be answered, it is necessary to know whether this population could recognize the newcomers as such. For the authorities it was easy, for they always required written evidence, such as certificates of birth or baptism. For the general population it seems to have been rather more difficult in cases where the external appearance of the newcomers was not very different from their own, as with an obviously dark skin or distinctive type

A grass-mower (hanneke-
maaier). Detail of a nursery
print, late eighteenth cen-
tury. The accompanying
poem contains an allusion to
the popular etymology of the
word 'hannekemaaier',
which held that it was de-
rived from the name Hans.
(Atlas van Stolk, Rotterdam)

of hair. Nevertheless, in most cases newcomers would have been easily recognizable. Even where there were no obvious biological differences, people were usually in no doubt as to whether they were dealing with newcomers. For instance, they might dress differently. The Armenians wore caftans, but it did not need to be so elaborate: German mowers in Friesland wore blue smocks and waistcoats with white linen backs, Overijssel mowers working in Friesland wore brown smocks, while the local Frisian mowers stood out with their red woollen shirts.[10]

Most newcomers did not immediately master the Dutch language. Many popular farces satirized the comic gibberish of the immigrant Germans. In the Amsterdam theatre these shows formed for centuries the most popular repertoire with the citizenry. In his play *De Zwetser* (The Windbag) of 1712, Pieter Langendijk gave this speech, in a stage-German accent, to Slenderhinke, the simple Westphalian mower, just before he came to Amsterdam for the first time: 'Then I fell asleep, until the morning came, and I saw, ach ja, for the first time this great Jumbledam, this Amstel Holland, which gladdened my heart. Then, thought I, Hinke you will make so much money here.' ('Toen roakten ik in sloap, tot dat den morgen kam, ond zag jo, den eerstemaal dit graute Haspeldam, Dit Amstelholland; dat verbliede mik de zinnen, Toen docht ik; Hinke doe solst dikke doalders winnen.')[11] Langendijk makes his character garble not just the Dutch language, but even Dutch place-names. It is similar to the way many Dutchmen now imitate Surinamese, Chinese or Turks in an attempt to be funny.

There is also a tendency among members of the autochthonous population not to recognize things such as dress or mastery of the language as cultural differences, but subconsciously to translate them into physical characteristics. Justus van Maurik records memories of German seasonal migrants in his youth as 'those large, clumsy men who, with their turned-up noses, their wide, friendly, smiling mouths and childlike eyes, were typical of guileless innocence'.

Less flatteringly he puts the following words into the mouth of his father's old servant, Barend, about these same Germans: 'Och, you know Sir, they were really not quite human, I always took them for a kind of half-baked kaffirs. There were no greater idiots, as stupid as the back-end of a pig and, begging your pardon, Sir, they smelled little better.'[12]

Flemings and Brabanters. Marginal illustrations from Hendrick Hondius' 1631 Map of the Netherlands. He lays stress on the fashionable dress of the Southern Netherlanders, which is perceived as exaggerated. (University Library, Amsterdam)

There can be no doubt that for a long time after his arrival almost every newcomer is recognized as such. Even the repatriates of wholly European descent, who returned from the Dutch East Indies after the war, had to adapt their habits and their speech in many ways: a 'pisang' suddenly had to be called a banana.

It is impossible here to give a definitive description of the attitude of the population towards newcomers. In the first place we are now entering on a virtually untrodden path of historical research, so that for the period before the last war only a preliminary sketch can be given. Secondly, only certain groups of Dutchmen and newcomers actually came in contact with each other, whether in co-operation, or in competition.

The only approach currently open to us is one in which we try to trace two extremes through examples on the one hand of clear co-operation, and on the other – and more commonly – of clear opposition. As an example of clear co-operation on the individual plane, one can cite 'mixed marriages', that is to say marriages

between someone born in the Netherlands and someone born
abroad. For the years 1578 to 1810 it can be demonstrated for
Amsterdam that foreigners, when they married in the town, tended
to marry Dutch women and only to a limited extent women from
their region of origin. The surplus of women over men in Amsterdam will have played an important role in this. In so far as they were
able to marry Amsterdam girls, the possibility of acquiring the
freedom of the city in this way must also have played its part.[13]

As examples of clear opposition at the individual level we shall
content ourselves with a brief survey of the opinions of the Dutch
about newcomers, and – in one case – of more than just opinions.
The great objection to this approach is uncertainty about the degree
of representativeness in data of this kind.

The earliest examples in which the attitude of the population to
newcomers is manifest are derived from the arrival of the Southern
Netherlanders around 1600. Frustrations on both sides, between the
population of Holland who harboured feelings of inferiority about
their culture compared to that of the Southern Netherlands, and
Southerners who did not feel properly accepted in their new home,
are expressed in the following quotations.[14] The poet Roemer Vis-
scher addressed the Flemings as follows:

> The stolid Dutchman pulls the flounder from the brine,
> He milks fat butter from the robust kine:
> Then why do you, more stolid still, who call the Dutchman
> names,
> Give him for fish and butter coin and grain?
>
> (De botte Hollander haelt de Bot uyt de zee,
> De vette botter melckt hy van het grove vee:
> Dan ghy alderbotst, die voor bot den Hollander schelt,
> Waerom gheft ghy hem voor bot en botter cooren en ghelt?)

In 1614 Jacobus Trigland preached in the Old Church in Amsterdam:

> And that is to be lamented most, that those from Brabant and
> Flanders who have fled here to Holland because of the perse-
> cutions, to seek a refuge here, have brought their arrogant
> manners here with them. About which you often hear the
> Hollanders complaining and saying: the Brabanters have imposed

these new manners upon us here. Formerly there was nothing to be seen here but humility and simplicity, but since the Brabanters have been here, so have their arrogant ways begun to gain the upper hand here, too. But neither side is to be excused. You Brabanters should think: we who come here into a plain, simple and humble country, we do not want to introduce arrogance here, and we do not want to set a bad example, but we will imitate their humility and simplicity. You Hollanders, though having a more arrogant manner than yours may look good on a Brabanter, should not imitate this arrogance, but should keep to your modesty and humility...

If these fragments express the Dutch frustration about the immigrants, the latter in their turn will for the most part have echoed the Southern Netherlander Willem Usselincx:

It is true, that some of the refugees have done well here, and they have also assumed that it was their homeland, although practice proves otherwise, because they are not treated differently from strangers and are not consulted any more than the French, English, German or any other nations.

Remarkably enough we know of no similar emotions expressed at the time of the arrival of the Huguenots. This was not the case with the continuing arrival of new armies of seasonal labour migrants. It is not so much the fact that we can collect a number of negative reactions to seasonal migrants which makes what follows so important, but more that these pronouncements were not general. The specific circumstances in which they did actually occur should give us an indication of the conditions under which xenophobia could thrive.

Concerning the seasonal migrants in the Netherlands, most of whom came from Germany, there was anything but a positive impression.[15] The farces satirizing the *Moffen* (*Krauts* or *Boches*) depicted them as simple clodhoppers and in Justus van Maurik's work we find the last echo of this. Indeed, Germans in general were not seen in a favourable light for a long time. In 1760 an anonymous writer went much further than stressing their boorishness when he said: 'This brood of Boches should be allotted a special district in the town, just like the Jews, labelled "Bochery".'

It was not only men of letters, dramatists and writers of farce who spread this negative image of the Germans; it appears to have been

'Holland bound'. German grass-mowers, probably in Friesland. Drawing by C.W. Allers, 1896. (Open Air Museum, Arnhem)

experienced more generally. A traveller on the Purmerend to Alkmaar steamer, with its deck packed with grass-mowers from Hanover, tells how they were continually abused by women and children from the banks, and by deckhands on passing ships, shouting '*mof, mof* ' at them, and that the Dutch sang derogatory songs about them. According to this traveller, a German himself, the Hanoverians only occasionally answered back in kind.

Only the great economic, cultural and scientific boom in Germany after 1870 brought about a change. This meant an end to the seasonal trek to the Netherlands, with Dutchmen going to work in Germany in large numbers instead; at the same time respect for German achievements rose in the Netherlands. This fresh evaluation can be well illustrated by the values recorded by a 1913 editor of the leading dictionary of the Dutch language, *Woordenboek der Nederlandse Taal*. In his discussion of the word *mof* he gave the negative meanings of this concept, which probably dates from the sixteenth century. He concluded that it was a term of abuse for 'Germans in general, who were held in contempt by prosperous Dutchmen' but, he concluded, 'These days the Germans are usually judged differently, and the term *mof*, however common, is often free of contempt'. This was to change again around 1940. In recording the picture as a negative one, one must therefore be careful of anachronisms.[16]

A second comment concerns the actions which could accompany these negative images and the consequent verbal abuse. In searching for examples of violent collective action against newcomers, we have come across very few. Nor are any groups known to us before the twentieth century which flew the banner of xenophobia. In his study of riots in Holland in the seventeenth and eighteenth centuries, Rudolph Dekker certainly records the participation of aliens in rebellious actions, but mentions not a single riot directed against them.[17]

The first example known to us of organized actions against aliens on a large scale during the Republic took place in the 1730s, years marked by other actions against minorities as well.[18] In the summer of 1734 Belgian seasonal migrant workers were chased off the islands of the provinces of Zeeland and South Holland, and in the Westland the German workers had trouble, as they did in Harlingen in Friesland.[19] The common characteristic of these victims was not only, and not even in the first place, the fact that they were newcomers, but that they were Catholics. In the years 1733 to 1734 a widespread flood of rumours arose to the effect that the Catholics wanted to break up the existing Protestant hegemony. Some Catholic seasonal workers were even said to have had visions about imminent events. For instance, it was said in Franeker in the summer of 1734 that 'there was a Kraut in Harlingen, who told how the Calvinists would go to bed on St John's eve in the year 1734 as Protestants, and would wake up the next morning as Papists'.[20] The same was true of the events in Flushing of 1778.[21] There, and also elsewhere, there were outbursts against merchants fleeing from Dunkirk, again not primarily because of their French nationality, but because of their Catholic religion.

In the nineteenth century a new criterion, other than religion, appears to become dominant; the first signs of it can be observed in Belgium in the 1830s. The young country, which had risen in revolt against the Northern Netherlands in 1830, expressed its hostile feelings against its former fellow-countrymen in the labour market as well. Dutch navvies working on excavation projects near Antwerp were turned away and chased off. In their turn, over the next few decades Belgian navvies were discriminated against in the Netherlands. Particularly in the construction of the railway from Flushing to the German border, and the accompanying canal through the island of Walcheren, Belgian workers had a hard time of it; sometimes even their lives were at risk.[22]

Here then is an example of xenophobia apparently no longer nourished primarily on religious considerations, but rather on nationalistic ones. This Dutch nationalism, which received an important stimulus from the Belgian Revolt, gained in strength in the 1840s, as was demonstrated earlier in the discussion of the first Aliens Act, passed in 1849.

More individual actions against newcomers, solely or mainly on the basis of the fact that they were newcomers, are also known from the nineteenth century. One extreme case is worth closer examination. In the Greidhoek of Friesland, German seasonal migrant labourers habitually took on the mowing of the grass for hay-making, in June. They knew the farmers and the farmers knew them personally, and relations were in general satisfactory. Yet it was here that the following incident happened in the 1860s. Two German mowers were on their way home after finishing their work at the end of the season, and were travelling by barge from Harlingen to Leeuwarden. They lay relaxed on the deck, singing cheerfully, as was their wont. Near the hamlet of Deinum they passed another boat, a cargoboat with a crewman and the ship's boy on the deck who, as they were passing, first began to tease the German 'Krauts' for fun, and then to splash them, until the game turned to bitter earnest and they began to prod and poke at the Germans with their long boat-hooks. Suddenly the crewman pulled one of the Germans off the deck of the barge with his boat-hook. He fell backwards into the water and drowned.[23]

The contrast between the reasonable and often friendly relations on the farm and this deadly assault near Deinum can perhaps be explained by the anonymous situation in which it occurred. The anonymity of the two ships passing each other echoes that of the insults shouted at the Purmerend-Alkmaar steamer at about the same time, mentioned earlier.

There may be a similar explanation in the case of the navvies. It was the custom to put them to work in gangs of about ten to twelve.

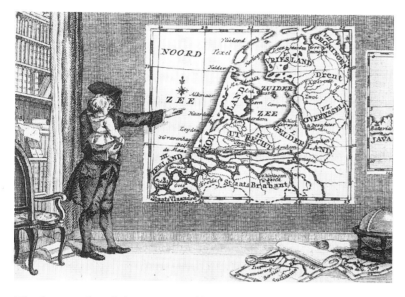

The letter N from 'My national ABC book for Dutch children' by J.H. van Swilden, 1781. The caption accompanying the letter N (for Netherlands) tries to foster patriotism in schoolchildren. (Atlas van Stolk, Rotterdam)

The bosses played these gangs off against each other to speed up the rate of work. Animosity and especially anonymity between the gangs was therefore a fact of life. In a situation like this nationalistic arguments and sentiments could, as we have seen, lead to a dangerous escalation.[24]

The conclusion we can provisionally draw from this impressionistic survey is that newcomers were rarely exposed to risk of violence solely for being newcomers. It is true that they were at risk – but only in a limited number of cases – because of other characteristics which at particular times drew attention to them: religion in the seventeenth and eighteenth centuries, and factors concerned with the labour market especially in the nineteenth century. Furthermore there are indications that the national state increasingly encouraged nationalist feelings, and that this made newcomers stand out all the more. Finally the degree of anonymity in a situation also appears to play a role.

We can close this review of the relationship between the Dutch and newcomers with the observation that animosity and 'finding each other strange' are phenomena of all periods. In certain circumstances this animosity can deteriorate into xenophobia, the most obvious case being the growth of nationalism, which seems to provide a more ready justification for such actions. Other possible legitimating circumstances are those situations in which newcomers share other essential characteristics, which at that moment, in the eyes of their attackers, are negative. Until the late eighteenth century, religion seems to have been an important criterion. Factors such as an anonymous situation, or one where a crowd is involved, are generally seen as potentially dangerous; this also applies, though not exclusively, to social relations between the Dutch and newcomers.

Dutch government and the descendants of newcomers

In this section the position of newcomers' descendants will be examined, and particularly the influence of government on this group. Under what conditions did they become assimilated? Did they remain socially or culturally 'different', or both, and did this lead to minority-formation, possibly followed by discrimination, collective violence and extermination? And how much time, how many generations, did these processes take?

One group is excluded from this set of questions, because almost by definition it always consisted of newcomers: the seasonal labour migrants. As a rule they did not settle, and so neither were there any descendants in our sense. The same applies more or less to most transients. We are therefore left with the descendants of political or religious refugees, and of predominantly economic immigrants, up to about the Second World War.

In the attitude of the authorities to these descendants, we find a remarkable phenomenon. As long as these authorities continued to draw a distinction of principle based on the difference between native-born and other inhabitants, the descendants of newcomers, who were native-born, became invisible to any special official policy. They could, of course, suffer inequality as a result of being poor, working class, or female, but their descent from an immigrant no longer had any influence.

A first exception to this rule is provided by elements of the official policy with respect to Jews under the Republic. Faber has established that in Amsterdam between 1680 and 1810, for Jews just as for newcomers, no difference seems to have been made from other inhabitants either in criminal prosecutions or in sentencing.[25] One might imagine that this conclusion would also apply to other legislation and regulation, especially in view of the fact that in 1657 the States General declared that Jews 'truly are subjects of the state and should consequently have the same allowances and guarantees, rights and privileges ... agreed and obtained for the inhabitants of this state'.[26] Nevertheless, we have already listed several examples which do not seem to tally with this statement, either in the policy on entry or in that affecting Jewish newcomers.

As conversions to Judaism were rare, one can assume that anti-Jewish measures were by definition also directed against their descendants. Certainly the Amsterdam regulation mentioned earlier, excluding Jews from almost all guilds, also applied to them. And other anti-Jewish measures could be cited. The Court of Holland imposed as one of the requirements for the admission of advocates that they should be practising Christians; in 1685 it therefore refused to accept Mozes Israel d'Acosta, a Jew who had qualified at Harderwijk. In Amsterdam in 1737, all Jews were forbidden to engage in the fish trade.[27]

With the emancipation of the Jews in 1796 all these official anti-Jewish measures disappeared. Only with the German occupation in 1940 did they return, with a severity which led to the extermination of almost all Dutch Jews.

A second exception was the official policy concerning gypsies under the Republic. Here again it was the case that since it was difficult for outsiders to become gypsies, measures against gypsies affected not only newcomers, but particularly their descendants as well. As we have so far only referred incidentally to this group, their immigration and the position they were allotted by the authorities will now be examined more extensively.[28]

On linguistic grounds, most authors have accepted up to now that gypsies originally came from northern India, and from there travelled to Western Europe via western Asia and the Balkans. Their presence was certainly documented in 1417 for the first time in North-Western Europe, and in 1420 in the Low Countries. In March of that year a group of a hundred people was welcomed by the town authorities of Deventer. This was done in accordance with letters they carried from the German Emperor, from which it transpired that they were believers, refugees for their Christian faith, and worthy of alms. As the Netherlands were then part of the Empire, this request was complied with.

From that time onwards groups of gypsies regularly visited the various regions and towns of the Netherlands, and for almost a century they acquired new letters of introduction from towns and provinces, testifying that they had behaved properly and as good Christians. The last of these letters were provided by the town of Nijmegen around 1500 and by the Duke of Guelders in 1506 and 1518.

At about the same time proclamations began to appear, directed against them. The earliest is from Gouda in 1512, directed against beggars, including gypsies; then followed a proclamation in Holland in 1524, and so it went on. What is the explanation for this reversal of attitude? Some claim that it lay in the misbehaviour of the gypsies, but if one analyses the more than a hundred references to gypsies from 1420 to about 1530, there were only four cases concerning theft. The cause of the reversal of attitude seems rather to have been an external one, and in our view is a good example of a higher government authority forcing local authorities, and then the people, to discriminate.

In 1497 in the Imperial Diet at Lindau there occurred the first complaints about the parasitic behaviour of gypsies. A year later, in the Diet at Freiburg, they were banned from the whole of the Holy Roman Empire, and so also from the Low Countries. The local effect was delayed for a while, but the unification of all the Low Countries under Charles 5 in the first half of the sixteenth century brought about a central authority which, in 1537, entirely in line with the Diet's decision, ordered all gypsies to leave the Netherlands, 'and this on pain and forfeit of their lives and goods'.

Evidence can be found right up to the eighteenth century of a favourable or at least a neutral attitude to gypsies: there is even a record of a gypsy child being baptized in Ermelo in 1694. Nevertheless, a process had now started in which a section of the gypsies, together with other nomadic groups, started to indulge in criminal behaviour, the authorities imposed more severe punishments, the outcast and hunted behaved ever more anti-socially, and so on.

It is our impression that in this process the gypsies rapidly mingled with others who had turned their backs on society, and were then confused with them. The authorities had increasing difficulty in identifying gypsies. There is very little positive evidence of actual gypsies in the seventeenth and eighteenth centuries. Nevertheless, the authorities increasingly hunted down what they identified as bands of gypsies. In Gelderland, for example, the process was as follows: from 1536 expulsion, from 1631 expulsion with force of arms, from 1637 flogging followed by expulsion, and in the same year the first 'gypsy hunt' in the heath area of the Veluwe. In the late seventeenth and early eighteenth century these hunts were regular events, particularly in Overijssel and Gelderland. Sometimes they were also targeted at the so-called 'Smouses', German and Polish Jews who were suspected of crimes against property. Whereas the provinces usually guarded their independence jealously, in this case they were ready to organize interprovincial or even international hunts. At this time these ended in executions and for the women floggings, which pregnant women and children had to watch. In a proclamation of 1725 in Holland it was laid down that a gypsy who committed any nuisance or violence should immediately be hanged without any form of trial; in the following year the Overijssel gypsies were declared outlaw, and a reward of fifty guilders was promised for any gypsy, dead or alive, handed over to the authorities. There was no longer any point in these measures; the gypsies in the Netherlands had been forced into anonymity or driven out. It was to be a century and a half before the first gypsies were recorded again in the Netherlands.

So the general rule that until the end of the nineteenth century the descendants of immigrants were invisible to official policy is tempered by the exception of the anti-Jewish and, in particular, the anti-gypsy measures during the Republic. Moreover, this rule was turned on its head, as it were, when in 1892 citizenship became 'hereditary'.

The consequence of the application of the hereditary principle to nationality is that if the descendants of immigrants are to keep their foreign nationality, then they too have fewer rights than the country's own citizens. That the number of provisions which drew this distinction increased sharply, is clear from an inventory drawn up in the Netherlands in 1983.[29] H. Beune and A. Hessels found about 1,300 discriminatory provisions in the legislation and regulations, a high proportion of which were concerned with distinction by nationality. But Dutch regulation was also shown to contain restrictive conditions for newcomers and their descendants on grounds of being born outside the Netherlands, of speaking a particular language or following a particular religion.

Not all the discriminatory provisions are equally important: quite a large number are found in ancient, sometimes obscure legislation, with little or no social effect. But some of them are important, and some very important. If a foreigner needs a work permit to work in the Netherlands, that places him in a different situation from his

Dutch workmates. But even when an alien possesses one of these permits, a number of occupations, like certain types of official post, are not accessible to him. Exclusion from active and passive suffrage is another important difference. In the sphere of social security there is the fundamental difference that under the terms of the Act and under certain conditions, a benefit is a right for the Dutch citizen, while for an alien under the same conditions it is a favour. In other words, it can be refused, which can then lead to expulsion on grounds of a lack of any means of subsistence.[30]

In only one case does there seem to have been no interruption in official policy with regard to the descendants of newcomers: the policy towards gypsies in the Kingdom of the Netherlands after 1813 displays similarities with that during the Republic.[31] The policy of extirpation in the early eighteenth century has already been described. From that time onwards there were for a long time no gypsies in the Netherlands, or hardly any; at least the authorities no longer listed anyone as such, and did not feel themselves obliged to take any action against them. That was the case until 1868, when a

A group of gypsies near Vaals, 1928. (Photo Spaar-nestad)

first group of colourfully dressed people, made up of various families from Hungary, entered the Netherlands at Almelo in Overijssel.

At first most authorities did not know what to make of these newcomers. They consulted the Aliens Act, and when they discovered that the gypsies possessed the proper travel documents and could keep themselves financially – mainly as tinkers or by making a bear do tricks – no obstructions were put in their way. The apparatus of the Ministry of Justice, in part alarmed by foreign reports, soon, however, had second thoughts, and the first expulsions date from 1869. After this expulsions were rather the rule than the exception, and endless problems started at the frontiers with groups of gypsies.

In 1904 a campaign by the Burgomaster of Vianen near Utrecht, who managed to mobilize his colleagues in the vicinity, resulted in the Ministry of Justice resorting to a secret regulation lacking any legal basis. The Ministry instructed all Queen's Commissioners, who were the chief officers of government in each province, no longer to apply exclusively the Aliens Act to the admission of gypsies. In accordance with this instruction the Commissioners instructed their Burgomasters 'under no circumstances to admit gypsies. I request you emphatically to ensure that no publicity of any sort be given to the content of this Cabinet instruction'.

This 1904 regulation was the first of many. During the Nazi occupation, the Dutch government worked hand in hand with the occupying Germans on the solution to the 'gypsy problem'. As late as May 1944 raids throughout the country collected as many gypsies together as possible. The infamous concentration camp at Westerbork held 279 'anti-socials' (by which was meant Dutch caravan dwellers who were not gypsies) and 299 gypsies. Of the latter 245 were transported to the German extermination camp of Auschwitz-Birkenau on Friday 19 May 1944. Most of them, including all 147 children, died in the last mass gassing of gypsies on 31 July 1944. According to the Red Cross only thirty returned after the war.[32]

The continuity of official measures against this group displays an essentially different picture from official policy towards the Jews.

The Dutch and the descendants of immigrants: between assimilation and minority-formation

The official attitude to the descendants of newcomers up to the end of the nineteenth century, as described here, makes it plausible

– assuming that the attitude of the population did not deviate too much from it – for assimilation to have been the rule rather than the exception. With hindsight we can indeed confirm that the majority of the descendants of refugees and immigrants in the Netherlands before the twentieth century have been assimilated, with the occasional retention of a few cultural characteristics.

The Southern Netherlanders had already disappeared from the scene as a group by around 1630.[33] Literary works mocking them, preachers addressing them reprovingly, authorities publishing provisions to their benefit or detriment: nothing more was heard of it.

It is difficult to make any general statements about the time it took to assimilate a group of immigrants. J. Briels believes that the Southern Netherlanders as a group had already gradually been absorbed in the Dutch population with the passing of some twenty or thirty years.[34] Others are of the opinion that a process of this kind takes longer to work. C. Berkvens-Stevelinck points out that the assimilation process was not only a difficult one for the Huguenots, but reached its final stage relatively late. For instance, only in the early nineteenth century did the fifth to the ninth generations of French refugees start to use Dutch versions of their French surnames.[35]

In individual cases more details of the process of assimilation are sometimes known, as seen both by the descendants of the immigrants and by the host society. In 1613 Pieter de la Court senior, at the age of twenty, moved from his home near Ypres and settled in Leiden, where three years later he married a girl from the region he came from. Thirty-five years later, when there was a scandal about the family, Pieter Senior was described in a defamatory pamphlet as a 'garlic eater', a 'son of a *Hoere Waert* [pimp] near Ypres', who had run away from home with 'always more Walloon lice than dollars or ducats; with rag on rag and scabs and scum, and begging on the streets'. The second generation, well-known businessmen in the Leiden textile industry, whose relatives included town councillors and university professors, were still forced to hear themselves called immigrants for a long time. In 1668, fifty-five years after the family settled there, a scurrilous pamphlet was published about the well known Pieter de la Court Junior, who had been born in Leiden, claiming that the Leiden weavers shouted after him in the street: 'Strike the Walloon dead, strike him dead, devil take him.' According to the same pamphlet the Leiden 'Walloons' – apparently still seen as a single entity – had taken up the cudgels for him and intrigued with high-up politicians, which was probably a thinly veiled reference to the De Witt brothers.[36]

However this may be, some of them certainly retained their cultural identity for longer. At the time of immigration in many places the Southern Netherlanders had set up 'Chambers of Rhetoric', a kind of amateur dramatic society. These societies, founded in the 1580s and 1590s, sometimes lasted a few years, but often for several decades. There are two examples of Chambers which survived the first half of the seventeenth century: the Flemish Chamber in Leiden, called 'The Little Orange Lily' (*De Oranje Lelijkens*), later renamed 'Growing in Love' (*In Liefde Groeyende*), which existed until 1652, and the Flemish Chamber in Haarlem, 'The White Gillyflowers' (*De Witte Angieren*), with the motto 'Steadfast in Love' (*In Liefde getrouw*), which was not disbanded until 1739. The Walloon church congregations, established by French-speaking Southern Netherlanders, in general lasted even longer. They dif-

The Walloon Church on the Oudezijds Achterburgwal in Amsterdam. Print by C. Pronk, c. 1736. The church was founded in 1578, when large groups of refugees from the Southern Netherlands settled in the area. A century later the Walloon churches also played an important role in the reception of the Huguenots. (Gemeentelijke Archiefdienst, Amsterdam)

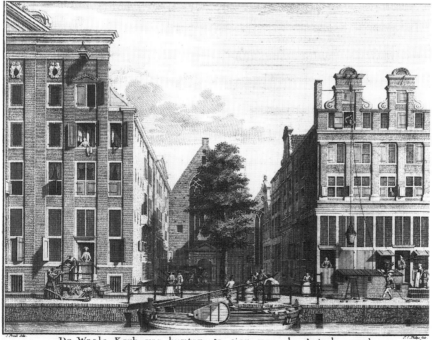

De Waale Kerk van buyten, te sien van de Agterburgwal.

fered from the Dutch Reformed Church primarily in language, and so were able to fill a useful function in the reception of the Huguenots in the late seventeenth century.[37]

The assimilation of these Huguenots also took about two generations. In 1743 the Amsterdam town authorities decided that the children of poor Huguenots should henceforth attend not French but Dutch schools, and in the early nineteenth century many descendants of Huguenots started to use Dutch versions of their surnames. Sometimes they chose a straight translation, so that Le Jeune became De Jonge, Le Noir became De Zwart, and Dumoulin Van der Molen; sometimes there were also some corruptions, so that Malfait might become Malefeyt, and Laict de Beurre Ledeboer. Only an elite continued to retain their own identity longer in the still existing 'églises Wallonnes', where Calvinist services are conducted in French.

The pattern among immigrants who came not as refugees but for economic reasons also seems to point to a tendency towards rapid assimilation within a few generations, with their cultural identity sometimes being retained for longer through the existence of a separate church congregation. In the Lutheran churches in the Netherlands, for instance, the difference from the dominant religion lay primarily in the language used and was not doctrinal. The true German Evangelical-Lutheran congregations in the Netherlands only date from the mid-nineteenth century.[38]

A final example of the assimilation process undergone by most immigrants in the course of a few generations is that of the Polish, Slovenian and Italian miners in South Limburg, who were recruited from the beginning of the twentieth century.[39] P. Brassé and W. van Schelven conclude that there was full assimilation after a few generations, but also the retention of some cultural traditions. There are still Polish and Slovenian cultural clubs in South Limburg, where they keep up the dances, folklore, sports and games of the original countries from which they came. Brassé and Van Schelven quote an apt summation of the function of such clubs by a second generation Slovenian: 'As a child I was jealous of the Dutch. However, now I am not only their equal in all respects, but I have also something extra: I am a Yugoslav. That gives me a *hobby*.'

If assimilation was the rule in the long run, at least as far as we can now take stock, two qualifications are necessary. These concern the speed of assimilation of Jews in the Netherlands,[40] and the failure to assimilate the gypsies.

We have observed that the Dutch authorities published a number of measures against Jews during the Republic, mainly involving severe restrictions on the professional opportunities of poor Jews, most of them German. The majority of them were dependent on hawking and peddling, and even there they sometimes encountered difficulties. When we go on to discuss the attitude of the Dutch population to the descendants of Jewish newcomers, a problem arises for the period from about 1650 to 1796, because the group was continually being supplemented by new waves of refugees from Eastern Europe. There were pogroms in Poland in 1648 and in Lithuania from 1654 to 1656. In the second half of the eighteenth century the Jewish population of Amsterdam grew by more than half, which indicates substantial immigration once more. Hence it is difficult to distinguish the attitude to Jewish newcomers from that towards Jewish descendants. However, it will be discussed primarily in the context of whether or not they were assimilated into Dutch society.

The failure to assimilate is demonstrated by the use of their own language, Yiddish, and by their living together near the synagogues – though the poorer German Jews were excluded from them – so that a kind of voluntary ghetto came into existence, with their own organization.[41] In Amsterdam, where most Dutch Jews then lived, the town had in fact given great political power to the spiritual leaders of the Jews, the *parnassim*, which went beyond their religious leadership. For instance, they even administered justice in civil cases between members of their own community. Indeed, the Jewish population demonstrated another characteristic which categorized them as a minority. They were mostly poor, or as a pamphlet described them in 1795: 'They have been allowed to sing Psalms in public ... and to starve to death.'[42]

Towards the end of the eighteenth century the *Haskalah*, the Jewish Enlightenment, objected to this exceptional position, particularly that of the German Jews.[43] In 1789 a pamphlet was published in the Netherlands entitled: *A demonstration of the need to teach the young the Holy Law in a language they understand, and hence here in Holland in Dutch (Bewijzen der noodzakelijkheid om de Heilige Wet in een verstaanbare taal aan de jeugd te onderwijzen en dus hier in Holland in het Nederlandsch)*. In the revolutionary atmosphere in which the leaders of the Batavian Republic came to power, the Jews subsequently gained equal rights. This gave the

'T GESIGT VAN DE PORTUGEESE EN HOOGDUYSE IODEN KERKEN TOT AMSTERDAM

Vüe en perspective des Eglises des Juifs Portugais et Allemands a Amsterdam   A Prospect of the Portugese and High German Jews Churches at Amsterdam

View of the Portuguese and German synagogues in Amsterdam. Print by P. van Gunst, early eighteenth century. (Gemeentelijke Archiefdienst, Amsterdam)

supporters of the Enlightenment the opportunity, often against the will of the religious leaders, to carry on the fight for full emancipation, and in this process the use of Yiddish disappeared almost entirely from the Netherlands. The voluntary formation of ghettoes became relatively less operative in the second half of the nineteenth century because Jews began to spread to other districts of Amsterdam and to other parts of the country, including the rural areas. Job differentiation also increased, and in the second half of the nineteenth century an extensive industrial proletariat came into existence, particularly in the diamond and clothing industries. The labour leaders in these branches of industry, particularly those of the diamond workers, played an important role in building up socialism and the socialist trade-union movement in the Netherlands.

Anti-Jewish pronouncements had regularly been heard in the Netherlands before their emancipation, and did not cease after it. Many organizations continued to keep their doors closed to Jews, for example, the Society for Public Welfare which had actually developed out of the Enlightenment. From the Protestant side there had traditionally been an interest in Judaism, particularly because of the increased interest in the Old Testament since the Reformation; at the same time anti-Jewish sentiments were expressed, for instance by the orthodox Calvinist leader Abraham Kuyper. Between these two extremes there was quite an active movement for the conversion of the Jews, which registered successes with the well known adherents of the *Réveil* movement, Isaac Da Costa and Abraham Capadose. Among the Catholics a fairly strong anti-Jewish attitude appears to have been prevalent. A survey of the Rotterdam press reveals this in the Catholic *Maasbode* in the late nineteenth and early twentieth centuries.[44] In 1924 the Dutch bishops still forbade Catholic girls to work for Jews as domestic servants.[45]

In spite of all this the emancipation continued, in the twentieth century also taking the form of an increase in mixed marriages and secularization. This development was abruptly cut short by the German occupation and the subsequent extermination of Dutch Jews and of the foreign Jewish refugees who had sought refuge in the Netherlands.

Although after the First World War there were actually Dutch organizations propagating anti-Semitism, in our opinion the extermination of the Jews should primarily be seen as having been caused by external developments rather than by an internal Dutch reaction to a presumed Jewish failure to assimilate.[46] The organized Dutch anti-Semites – very small in number – included many members of right-wing splinter groups, such as the National Socialist Dutch Workers Party, part of which merged in 1933 with *De Bezem* (The Broom), a fascist union founded by Alfred Haighton, a true anti-Semite. The Black Front, after 1940 called the National Front, with adherents particularly in the south, was also anti-Semitic. At first the NSB (National Socialist Movement, the main Dutch fascist party of the 1930s and World War II), was not, and had Jewish members, but under foreign influence, and after their leader, Antoon Mussert, had become familiar with the Dutch East Indies, it also became anti-Semitic. However, this was when their greatest electoral successes were already in the past.

Another question which must be asked about the rise of organized anti-Semitism is whether it was primarily directed against descendants or against newcomers. It is, for instance, quite possible that it was also influenced by the flow of refugees starting to come from Germany and Austria. Moreover, many of these refugees had pronounced left-wing political opinions, which did not make it any easier for their opponents on the right to welcome them with open arms.

The gypsies' isolation in society was, as explained earlier, strongly supported by Dutch government policy, which in practice closely matched the policy of the occupying Germans, unlike the case of the persecution of the Jews.

Two aspects deserve further examination in the case of the gypsies: was the attitude of the population in fact at variance with that of the government and is this therefore a case of *terrorization of the discriminant* ? And secondly, what is the relationship between the attitude on the one hand to gypsies, and on the other to a group of Dutch who, by a process of ethnicization, had become caravan dwellers?

There is some evidence that the attitude to gypsies and also to caravan dwellers was mainly imposed upon the population from above. It is not our intention naively to defend the proposition that the population always and everywhere rather welcomed gypsies with open arms, but there are at least reasons for doubting whether there was a general feeling of hatred for gypsies. We will limit ourselves to the period after the second arrival of the gypsies, after 1868.

The commander of the military police in Breda wrote in 1868 in a report on the gypsies, who were itinerant tinkers, 'that the exercise of their trade adequately equipped them to provide for their travelling and subsistence costs, since they were able to obtain good prices for the work they carried out ... [on the basis of the fact that he had seen] the work produced by gypsies, no coppersmith in the Kingdom was capable of carrying out such repairs in such a way, so that they could in fact be called works of art'.[47]

In spite of and partly on the basis of this report, the procurator-general in 's-Hertogenbosch nonetheless thought fit to write to the Minister of Justice: 'Though the said report makes it plausible that these travellers have committed no illegal acts in Breda for their subsistence, yet in view of their major expenses, which are not covered by the income from their craft, it is plain that they are persons whose wandering about the Kingdom should be prevented as far as possible.'[48]

This mechanism, in which senior people held a negative opinion not shared by the more junior officials who had personally been in contact with the gypsies, was not uncommon in the late nineteenth century. Apart from this negative opinion promoted by the government, a negative image of gypsies was created in another respect. J. Kommers has pointed out how negative the image of gypsies was in

Dutch children's books: their depiction as kidnappers in particular is a constantly recurring theme.[49]

Around 1900 the gypsies changed over from travelling with tents and horses to caravans. From that time on, the Netherlands has also experienced a growing population of autochthonous caravan dwellers, a development which still continues today. The government took increasingly forceful action against these caravan dwellers as well. There has been much criticism of the government's policy of confining these 'travellers', by force if necessary, to large camp sites, and the policy was accompanied by restrictions on their freedom to travel, which in practice comes down to a ban on a nomadic life. Many caravan dwellers considered this to be the death knell for their occupation and income.

To a significant extent, the rise of a caravan dwellers' sub-culture can certainly be interpreted as a reaction to their exclusion by government and society.[50]

The settlement process of immigrants and their descendants after 1945

In the first half of this chapter we have tried to distinguish between the treatment of newcomers and of their descendants by government and society. For the period after 1945 this systematic distinction would raise problems for a number of immigrant groups, because their immigration is more recent and the position and treatment of a genuine – Dutch-born – second generation is in many cases not yet quite clear. This applies particularly to groups who have arrived in the Netherlands since 1970. There is, however, now a second, and in some cases a third generation of those who came earlier, like the East Indies repatriates, the Moluccans, the Polish, Hungarian and Czech refugees, and the early guest workers from southern European countries.

To extend our historical perspective as much as possible, in this section we shall devote separate attention to those earlier post-war groups of immigrants, and after that discuss the more recent post-1970 newcomers. For this period, however, we will not employ the distinction between newcomers and their descendants as a classification criterion, though where possible – and naturally this is easier for the earlier post-war newcomers – we will devote separate attention to the descendants of immigrants. The dichotomy of 'government and newcomers' and 'society and newcomers' will be maintained, as in the first section.

Pre-1970 immigrants and their descendants

Government policy 1945-1970

As we saw in Chapters 2 and 3, the Netherlands emphatically did not consider itself to be an immigration country after the Second World War, and the general opinion was that it should not become one either.[51] The paradox was, however, that this same Netherlands was indeed a host country: for repatriates from the former Dutch East Indies and for Moluccan ex-servicemen in the 1950s, for guest workers in the 1960s, and after that for countless other groups.

This paradox could arise because Dutch policy and government had interpreted and defined what was actually immigration in a very particular way. The use of the term 'immigrant' was avoided.[52] The Netherlands was only concerned with 'short-stay migrants'. This applied specifically to the 'guest workers', but just as much to the Moluccans (then still called Ambonese) and the 'citizens from the overseas part of the Kingdom' (as the Surinamese and Dutch Antilleans were known).

At first even the position of the repatriates from the former Dutch East Indies was assumed to be temporary, and diligent efforts were made to find a final destination for them 'elsewhere', at least for some of them. The Dutch orientation of the larger part of this group, their legal position as Dutch citizens, and their bonds with groups in the Netherlands turned out to be strong enough to exercise political pressure at an early stage in favour of an active policy of integration. After some initial hesitation the Dutch government accordingly opted for an intensive policy aimed at the 'resocializing and integration' of this group. They accepted the direct costs of the material provisions for the policy, including accommodation in contracted boarding houses, and definitive re-housing by means of reserving five per cent of subsidized public or social housing for allocation to repatriates. Social counselling and spiritual guidance were farmed out to private organizations, for the most part attached to the churches. The provision of resources by the government could certainly be called generous in comparison with that for previous groups of immigrants.[53]

However, for all other groups it was assumed that they would only be in the Netherlands on a temporary basis, which led to a dual policy: for as long as these migrants were to stay in the Netherlands some degree of adaptation and operation in society was thought necessary. Fitting in 'while retaining their own identity', as it was called for a long time, was not, however, seen in terms of a prolonged or even permanent stay, but was based on the assumption that they would return home. The policy therefore did not require the intensive provision of resources needed for repatriates; it was mainly limited to reception and guidance in the welfare area, and to special measures to cope with any problems that might arise.

In as much as there was a policy to implement, each of the groups was dealt with separately. The official point of view was that there could be no common denominator for all these migratory movements, or for the problems experienced in the Netherlands by those who were members of them. Responsibility for policy and co-ordination for each of these groups lay with the Ministry deemed to be most involved with that group: 'guest workers' came under the Ministry of Social Affairs, Moluccans (and later the first groups of Surinamese and Antilleans) under the Ministry for Culture, Recreation and Social Work, and refugees under Foreign Affairs. For other groups there was no policy at all.

The idea of a temporary stay took a very particular form in the policy for the Moluccans. In Chapter 2 we saw that this group came to the Netherlands in rather special circumstances. Both the Moluccans and the government started out with the idea of a temporary stay. The Moluccans looked forward to returning to an independent Republic of the South Moluccas, but this never happened; moreover, the Dutch government did not support that political ambition.

A special office, the CAZ (Commission for Ambonese Affairs), was set up to carry out this policy. After arrival in the Netherlands the Moluccan soldiers were demobilized. The ex-service men and their families were put into camps and residential quarters mainly in the east and south of the Netherlands, where they led an existence cut off from the rest of society. At first the state offered a welfare service, carried out by the CAZ, which covered all their basic needs: housing, food, clothing and pocket money. At first, and up to 1954, they were not allowed to take paid employment. The children's education was often at schools in the camps.

From the early 1960s, on the recommendation of a special committee, named after its chair Verwey-Jonker, special housing estates
were built in some sixty communities 'as temporary accommodation, until they start to live by themselves'.[54] The Committee
thought that on the one hand this would not affect their own life
as a group and their expectations for the future too much, and on
the other would help to integrate them in a number of ways. Only
in the late 1960s was the CAZ, which the Moluccans had felt to be
very patronizing, abolished and what remained of the policy was
administered by a Moluccans Department in the Ministry of Culture, Recreation and Social Work.

Newcomers and Dutch society up to 1970

We earlier stated the rule that for every group of newcomers one at
first encounters stereotyped images, together with hard or soft
prejudices. This also applies to the early post-war immigrants. For
example, the following summary of images of Dutch Eurasians has
been assembled from contemporary sources: 'Eurasians are Indonesians adopted by the Dutch; they are Muslims converted to Christianity; they live in bamboo huts; they have hardly outgrown being
illiterate. These are some of the opinions from a motley collection
of recorded views. Alongside them, and probably occurring much
more frequently, there is a total lack of any conception of their
situation, or an awareness of not being able to conceive of it, so that
when judgements have to be made, people have no basis for judgement other than the principle of "being different". This can result
in being excluded or expelled from the links by which one identifies
oneself or the group to which one belongs [...].'[55]

There grew up a whole collection of anecdotes, circulating among
the repatriates themselves, about their being frequently confused
with Indonesians; the stories were constantly recounted, and even
quoted as personal experience, without that necessarily having
occurred. For instance, many versions of the following story have
been recorded: a Dutchman, surprised that a repatriate speaks such
good Dutch, asks where he learned it. The repatriate, appalled at
such ignorance about Dutch life in the Indies, answers ironically:
'On my way from Indonesia to the Netherlands', an answer which
the Dutchman finds quite plausible.[56]

Comparable stereotyped images and prejudices can be found in
contemporary sources for each of the early post-war groups of

immigrants.[57] Another phenomenon which occurs regularly in the period soon after immigration is the animosity between groups of young men from immigrant groups and groups of autochthonous youths. The background and manifestation of these confrontations can vary: competition for girls or for public spaces and facilities often plays a role. Among the Moluccans the phenomenon of youth groups starting confrontations with the indigenous groups lasted well into the 1970s.[58]

How then has the process of integration fared for these early post-war immigrants? Studies of that period are limited, but still give some clear indications. In answering this question it should be remembered that until about 1974 the period in which these groups were settling was one of economic development and boom.

This was a time when employment was growing almost continuously – albeit with a few brief interruptions – and when government policy was aimed at full employment. By the mid-1950s there was already a shortage of labour in some industries, and this led to the first recruitment of newcomers by large businesses such as the State Mines and Hoogovens Steelworks. From the early 1960s onwards, unemployment had fallen so far that it amounted to a structural shortage of labour, which caused the systematic organization of recruitment of foreign workers.

In this kind of period of economic expansion and heavy demand for labour it was possible for the first post-war groups of immigrants – the post-war refugees, the repatriates, at first the Moluccans too, and the 'guest workers' – to find jobs on the labour market, even if in the early stages they were restricted to those in which the indigenous population had little interest.[59] At any rate this gave them a modest starting point for their integration into society.

In 1971 Verwey-Jonker drew up the following balance-sheet for the post-war *refugees* : 'materially the integration of the group of recognized refugees into Dutch society has on the whole been quite successful.'[60] The immaterial aspects are given less prominence in the research. In this sphere reports did indicate certain problems, such as the loneliness of the unmarried and the old, but they also listed a great many factors pointing to integration: there had been a large number of marriages with Dutch women, and (partly as a result) there was good mastery of the Dutch language. Job satisfaction increased with the length of stay. Each of the refugee groups set up its own clubs and associations with the aim of maintaining

awareness of their own culture by contacts among themselves, but
it did not seem to play an important role in public or political life.
The picture painted by Verwey-Jonker is one of rapid and almost
complete assimilation. After 1971 these groups vanished from the
scene both in research and as targets for policy.

The course of the integration process of the *repatriates* from the
Dutch East Indies is remarkably thinly documented. We have
already seen that this first post-war large-scale migration provoked
many reactions in Dutch society,[61] but there was little academic
interest in them.[62] It is striking that as early as the early seventies, a
number of general studies had already come to the conclusion that
the adaptation or integration of these newcomers had gone relatively
successfully.[63] Even before 1970, it was no longer thought necessary
to have an explicit government policy for them.

Not until the 1980s were questions asked, partly by academics[64]
and partly by associations of Eurasians and their descendants and
welfare organizations, about what some called the 'myth of success'.
At the same time, within the group of immigrants from the Dutch
East Indies and particularly the Eurasians, and at least some of their
descendants, there was increased interest in their history, which in
their quest for an identity is partly being rewritten.[65] An increasing
interest in the past and in their identity can also be found in novels.
In addition to the earlier organizations, new ones are being set up,
such as NINES (Descendants of the East-Indies Dutch and their
sympathizers). What is striking is that the second and third generation are interested not so much in the specific history of the Dutch
East Indies, but more in modern Indonesia. As far as the older
generation is concerned, the migratory past is coming to be seen in
a different light: partly because some people find that their traumatic
war-time experiences are resurfacing in their minds in their old
age,[66] and partly because in the care and nursing of the elderly who
have become dependent, their East-Indian connections and their
East-Indian past has revealed itself more clearly.[67]

These phenomena are important for the course of a process of
integration, but they appear to do little to weaken the general
conclusion that from a social point of view the group of repatriates
and their descendants have won themselves a place and are not
regarded as a separate group within Dutch society.

The *Southern Europeans* – Italians, Spaniards, Portuguese,
Greeks and Yugoslavs, and their descendants – have ended up in

Dutch society for the same reasons and in the same position as the later groups of Turks and Moroccans, but they have undergone a different development.[68] Their social position has substantially improved over the years. Their early arrival in the Netherlands, the better opportunities they had there, a different pattern of migration with a substantial and selective returning migration, and a relatively large number of mixed marriages, seem to have been significant factors. They, too, are now scarcely regarded by society as separate groups, and outside the area of cultural expression they do not behave as such.

The settlement process of the *Moluccans* has in contrast to these former groups been much more problematic. Their unforeseen transfer to the Netherlands, the traumatic experience of being demobilized, and the isolation in which they lived, meant that for them the process of integration was beset with problems from the start. Their camps and quarters were set up with a view to maintaining Moluccan culture, and specifically one based on cantonment life. There was little privacy in the camps: there was strict social control, and cultural traditions were rigidly adhered to. The political ideology of the Republic of the South Moluccas (RMS) was able to thrive in such an environment: the first, and the overwhelming majority of the 'in between' and second generations of Moluccans were strongly influenced by it. But in the end all this, even after fifteen or twenty years' stay in the Netherlands, did not lead to any result, whether on the political level, or in improving the group's position. In 1974 Van Amersfoort judged that the Moluccans were the only post-war group of immigrants in the Netherlands who had developed into a minority in the strict sense.[69]

Between 1966 and 1977 certain Moluccan youth organizations perpetrated a number of violent occupations and train hijackings in the Netherlands calling attention to their social situation and their political demands for a Republic of the South Moluccas. D. Bartels interprets these actions as resulting from the lack of progress or prospects in the political struggle for the RMS, and as an appeal for compensation for the injustice of demobilization from the Royal Netherlands Indian Army, which had been forced upon their parents by the Dutch government. He points out that all the train hijackers had been raised in the Schattenberg camp in Drenthe: 'Although most Moluccans condemned the violence, they collectively accepted the responsibility for it.' At first instance and in the short term, the actions negatively affected the attitude of Dutch society,[70] but at the same time they brought home to the Moluccans with considerable force that their political ideal was unattainable, and the idea of a collective return a pipe-dream. After that it was possible to talk more realistically about the situation in the Netherlands. Since then their social and ethno-cultural position in Dutch society has become a principal subject of debate among Moluccans. A new organization, the Moluccan Welfare Forum (Inspraakorgaan Welzijn Molukkers), was set up under the new policy and led the way.

In Bartels' view it is not these events which set all this in motion: he maintains that for some time there had been changes taking place below the surface in the Moluccan community, like secularization, the increasing importance of the individual, and a younger generation which was partly returning to its 'roots' and partly chose other symbols to mould its identity. These developments below the surface have accelerated since 1977, and have led to 'a strong upsurge of Moluccan identity, including a re-evaluation and reinterpretation of traditional values and customs', and at the same time to 'a greater readiness to accept a permanent stay in the Netherlands, resulting in better adaptation to life in Dutch society'.[71] These developments did not apply to the whole group, but were valid for the mainstream.

The social position of the Moluccans, measured by their position in the labour market, deteriorated seriously after 1974.[72] Only since the early 1990s has their very high level of unemployment declined, due principally to the results of a 'thousand-jobs plan' for Moluccans. In education, the second and subsequent generations have certainly made progress compared to their parents, but the few studies we have which draw comparisons with autochthonous pupils suggest there is still some ground to be made up.

Concerning the ethno-cultural position of the group, and especially its relations with the Dutch authorities, developments were positive after the dramatic crisis of the train hijackings in the mid-1970s. The situation and orientation of the group was significantly redefined, and redirected towards a future in the Netherlands, both on the part of the majority of the Moluccans themselves, and by the Dutch government (and in their wake, probably a substantial part of society). The change on the government side was formally marked by a policy document of 1978,[73] in which the idea of a temporary stay was definitively abandoned and a policy outlined for integration. The Moluccans as a group have concentrated since then, more than they did before, on improving their position in society. Their orientation towards their own group now occurs primarily in private life, for example in a revival of Moluccan language and culture, which can be combined with efforts to improve their social position in the Netherlands. This change of tack is manifested most clearly in the agreements of April 1986 between the Badan Persatuan (the most important Moluccan political organization in the Netherlands) and the Dutch government, which in addition to restoring the honour of the Moluccans, contained a number of agreements on the group's employment and housing. Now it seems there is more of a development towards emancipation within Dutch society than towards the minority position which Van Amersfoort observed in 1974.

Recent immigrants since 1970

Government policy since 1970

The ambivalence we have observed in policy on immigration and immigrants living in the Netherlands continued into the 1970s. The conviction that the Netherlands should not be an immigration country survived until the end of the seventies. On the other hand the Netherlands appeared much less ready than most of its neighbours to take strong and consistent measures against immigration in practice. No regulation of Surinamese migration was forthcoming, though it was proposed and discussed several times from the late 1960s onwards. Family reunion for 'guest workers', though officially unwelcome, was not the subject of serious restriction in the period 1976 to 1981, as it was in other countries.[74] At municipal level, ways were even found for by-passing the formal procedures for family reunion in favour of the families in question.[75]

A solution to the increasing 'tension between standards and fact',[76] was found in the 1970s in the emphasis on the opportunities for returning home. In politics and government circles there were discussions about the desirability of introducing a 'rotation principle' for guest workers, and a proposal was later submitted for the introduction of a bounty for returning home. The facilities for what the Ministry of Culture, Recreation and Social Work called 'migrating groups' consisted of welfare provisions designed to make the life of these migrants livable, for as long as they were in the Netherlands.

Education for guest workers' children was based on the prospect of their returning home, and education in their own language and culture was an essential component of it.[77] The policy also fitted in with certain trends among the Surinamese elite who supported a 'return ideology', in spite of the fact that research into return migration, and the capacity of the labour market in Surinam to absorb it, pointed in the opposite direction.[78] There was clearly a 'fiction of impermanence' about the stay of all these immigrants, which was deeply rooted in the practice of legislation and regulation and of admission policy, but also in policy on reception.[79] The Netherlands was not only an immigration country in spite of itself;[80] it was also an unwilling one.[81] The effect of defining the situation in such terms was that it had repeatedly to be emphasized that the groups involved occupied a separate and temporary position in Dutch society, but that their future lay elsewhere.

Only towards the end of the 1970s was there any sign of a change in political and government circles, so that in 1978 for the first time the impermanence of the Moluccans' stay was recognized for the fiction it was, and policy became centred on the future position of the group in Dutch society.[82] A report in 1979 entitled *Ethnic Minorities* by the Netherlands Scientific Council for Government Policy gave an important stimulus to declaring this approach applicable to other groups of immigrants as well. In 1980 a general policy on minorities was announced, in 1981 a draft policy document was published, and in 1983 the reversal in policy received the political imprimatur in a definitive policy statement on minorities.[83]

In this new policy, certain groups were explicitly named as target groups: foreign workers from the eight 'recruitment countries',[84] Moluccans, Surinamese, Antilleans, refugees, gypsies, and caravan dwellers.[85] There were two sides to this policy. On the one hand it aimed at a tolerant, multicultural or multi-ethnic society, in which cultural and ethnic 'distinctiveness' should be accepted and valued. (In this respect the new policy differed, at least officially, from the policy formerly applied to such groups as the East-Indian Dutch and refugees, which had been aimed at assimilating the newcomers.) On the other hand there was the objective of combating and eliminating social disadvantage and institutional discrimination. All this is redolent of the ideology of equal opportunity and equivalent participation, which gained greatly in strength with the emergence of the welfare state.

The first objective demanded group-specific categorical provisions, and so accentuated the special position of these groups. It starts from the assumption that organizations within the group itself should play an important role in the 'maintenance and development of their own culture and identity', concepts which were left vague and general in policy documents. There was a desire to avoid a prescriptive role in these matters. The task of the authorities was primarily to remove obstacles and to fight intolerance on the part of society or of groups within it.

To achieve the second objective a consistent policy of combating disadvantage and creating equal opportunities had to be set up, preferably within the general policy pursued by the government on employment, education and housing. Access to organizations and facilities, equal opportunities, and the fight against discrimination, became key phrases. For government agencies and services the concept of 'proportional distribution' was even introduced as the yardstick for an effective treatment of migrants.[86]

It cannot be denied that the government displayed a certain amount of drive in the early stages of the new policy. In 1980 extra financial resources were released which were allotted structurally to the newly agreed budget for the minorities policy. The budget then rose from 595 million guilders in 1981 to more than 800 million by the late 1980s.[87] Furthermore, a powerful organizational structure was set up, at first mainly at national level, both within each of the ministries involved and interdepartmentally. Co-ordination of the minorities policy was delegated to the Minister of Home Affairs. But to put the policy into effect, a tight network of organizations, most of them subsidized, also arose alongside government itself.[88] From the mid-1980s there was a growing inclination to replace the policy from on high with a more decentralized one, in which local authorities (municipalities) acquired a more important role.

How was this new policy to acquire concrete form? To understand this and then to be able to judge its effect, the most important measures will be briefly outlined. In doing so a distinction is made between policy on social disadvantage, policy on the legal position of newcomers, and cultural policy.

The *policy on social disadvantage* had to be put into effect in the areas of employment, education and housing. Although the policy statement on minorities[89] indicated that in the early 1980s the position of employed immigrants in firms was low and that unem-

ployment among minorities was disproportionately high, the government proposed no radical measures to change the situation. The
high unemployment was seen mainly as an inevitable effect of the
restructuring and modernization of the industrial sector, in which
immigrants had previously been able to find work. The policy
measures proposed were primarily directed at improving the starting
position of migrants by training, and on better services to assist in
seeking employment. Employment offices had to improve the service they gave migrants; new educational and training programmes
were set up for them; members of minorities were to participate
proportionately in job creation schemes, and they were to be given
more opportunities to set up their own businesses. In this policy the
employers did not come into the picture at all, except when the
employer was the government itself. Within its own workforce the
government stipulated the need for proportional representation of
minorities even in the early stages of the policy.[90]

However, the diagnosis appeared to be faulty and the measures
too limited. Participation by minorities in training and job creation
schemes had increased to some extent by the late 1980s, and the
proportion of minorities in government employment had grown,
but there was certainly no question of proportional representation.
Meanwhile unemployment had risen to between 25 and 50 per cent
of the labour force in the various groups, many times higher than
among the autochthonous population.[91]

In the meantime research had shown increasingly clearly that to
a large extent the disproportionately high level of unemployment
among immigrants was to be explained by discrimination against
them – sometimes direct, but more often indirect – by employers
in recruitment and selection, and by the over-representation of
migrants when jobs were lost, particularly in mass redundancies. In
1986 the Advisory Committee on Research into Minorities (ACOM)
therefore advised that immigrants should be given a 'fair chance' by
taking positive measures, like those already in force in the United
States and the United Kingdom.[92]

However, ACOM's recommendations fell on stony ground. The
powerful statutory Social and Economic Council proposed in its
1987 recommendations a series of measures in the areas of immigrant
training and joint action by employers and trade unions to improve
the position of minorities, but categorically rejected any form of
compulsory positive or affirmative action. In 1989 the Netherlands

Scientific Council for Government Policy (WRR) published recommendations on *Immigrant policy (Allochtonenbeleid)*, which inched towards positive or affirmative action by proposing a law for improving job opportunities on the Canadian model, in which employers would be obliged to publish details of the ethnic composition of their workforce every year. However, no sanctions were proposed. The effect would have to come from pressure of public opinion and from the ethnic minorities.

The WRR's recommendations, and debate about possible obligatory requirements for business, resulted in the employers and trade unions coming to an agreement in the Labour Foundation (STAR) in November 1990 to combat the high level of unemployment among minorities. They set themselves the target of bringing unemployment in these groups down to the level of that of the autochthonous population within five years. To achieve that aim, stated the agreement, 60,000 extra jobs for minorities would have to be created. Shortly after the STAR agreement was made public, the Minister of Social Affairs and Employment announced that a law promoting job opportunities for immigrants, like that demanded by the WRR, had now become superfluous.

In the early part of 1992 and of 1993, two research reports were published evaluating the joint efforts of employers and trade unions in the context of the STAR agreement.[93] It was clear from these reports that hardly any employers were familiar with the terms of the agreement, let alone implementing it. The effect of these publications was twofold: on the one hand the social partners renewed the promises they had made in the STAR agreement; on the other, both the Minister of Social Affairs and Employment and a coalition of politicians led by Paul Rosenmöller, a Member of Parliament for the Green Party, put forward a bill promoting equal job opportunities for immigrants. The Dutch Lower House of Parliament approved Rosenmöller's draft bill in July 1993 and passed an Act requiring public reports by employers on the ethnic composition of the workforce in their businesses. There was great opposition to this new Act by the social partners, partly based on the argument that the voluntary initiative of the STAR agreement would be undermined by it, and that registration by ethnicity would be difficult, undesirable and too expensive. Over two years after the Act (known as the WBEAA) came into force, it has become clear that the great majority of employers do not comply with it, and have never done so: they have not submitted the required data on the composition of their workforce.[94]

Where *social security* is concerned, the development of policy took quite a different course. On the whole those immigrants who have been in the country for an extended period had officially acquired over time a position which was virtually the same as that of the autochthonous population. Both general social insurance and insurance linked to employment are equally accessible to immigrants, though this does not necessarily mean that in practice they are always treated equally. Formally it is only social security benefits which still apply to aliens as a favour, but in practice agreements with most of their countries of origin lay down that subjects of the parties involved are in fact entitled to these benefits.

Government policy in the area of *education* for minority groups developed differently from that concerning the labour market. In 1980 the Ministry of Education published a plan for education for 'cultural minorities'. The two main objectives were equal opportunities and equal status in the curriculum for minority cultures. The first objective was to be achieved by laying more emphasis on education in Dutch as a second language and by more intensive contacts between parents and schools. Extra facilities were made available for instruction in the Dutch language in the first two years after migrants' children arrived, particularly for those without any kind of Dutch-language background.

To achieve the second objective, equal status for cultures, two provisions were available: the OETC (Education in own language and culture) and Intercultural Education. OETC education had actually been set up in the early 1970s, at that time with the aim of making the reintegration of the pupils in their country of origin easier after their presumed return. In the 1980 policy plan the aim was stated quite differently: it was now a matter of promoting welfare and ethnic identity, and protecting children against alienation from their parents and family. It was also intended, indirectly, to contribute to improved performance at school.[95] Whether it actually works that way in practice is a question which still arouses violent controversy in educational circles today.[96]

Intercultural Education was based on a different concept. The idea behind it was that both indigenous and immigrant pupils should be prepared for a harmonious co-existence in a multicultural or multi-ethnic society. In practice, however, it has proved difficult to incorporate that aim in a specific educational programme. Some suggested that the programme should concentrate primarily on combating prejudice and discrimination. In the event, multicultural education seems to consist mainly of information about immigrants, and the history and folklore of immigrants and their countries of origin. It is confined to some of the schools which have a mixed pupil population.[97]

From 1985 onwards all provisions for the children of immigrants were incorporated into the general framework of the educational priorities policy. This was based on the belief that the educational problems of immigrant pupils were to a large extent comparable to those of indigenous pupils from the lower socio-economic classes, and that they could therefore be combated in the same policy framework. Schools in what were designated educational priority areas would therefore receive extra financial support based on the number of their pupils from minority groups, but also, though to a lesser extent, on the autochthonous pupils from lower socio-economic environments. Recent research and policy recommendations have attacked the points system used as inefficient; it is suggested that a general policy for the disadvantaged directed at all lower socio-economic groups would be more effective.[98]

In addition to mainstream education, in the 1980s and 1990s specific educational provisions for immigrants have also been developed in adult education, particularly for language courses. Public debate about the integration of immigrants and their reception since 1989 has contributed to a greater availability of such courses for migrants, though the supply is still insufficient to meet the demand in full.

With regard to *housing*, two lines of policy can be distinguished. First, in a number of cases the government has reserved some of the subsidized newly-constructed rented housing for allocation to newcomers; this was originally done for the repatriates from Indonesia and for the building of housing estates for the Moluccans in the 1960s, later for the immigrants from Surinam and the Netherlands Antilles between 1975 and 1980, and up to the present day for invited and recognized refugees. Guest workers and their families have never been able to take advantage of such measures.

In addition, from the early 1980s attempts were made to make the market for rented housing accessible to immigrants on the same terms as it was for the indigenous population. Differentiation between immigrants and autochthons in registration, rules for prioritization, and allocation, was forbidden. This kind of 'neutral' application of the rules has made that section of the rental market in the hands of local authorities and housing associations particularly accessible for immigrants. In the private sector minorities are still at a considerable disadvantage.[99]

Recent debates on the housing situation of minorities concentrate on the specific effects of two general developments in housing policy in the Netherlands in the 1990s. The first is the gradual retreat of government from the housing sector: an increasing proportion of new housing has to be built and financed by the private sector, while rents for public or social housing have increased and rent subsidies have been curtailed. The second is that a new system for the distribution of public or social housing is gradually being introduced, based on the public advertisement of social housing to be let, and on bids or applications by potential tenants for that accommodation. The housing is then let to applicants according to a set of criteria based on need, urgency, and the like. Little is known as yet about the particular effects of these new measures on minority groups, but it is assumed by some specialists that they may have a negative influence on these groups. It is thought that they may lead to stronger forms of concentration of minorities in certain areas or quarters, and that they may ultimately, under certain conditions, increase social segregation.[100]

A second cluster of policies after 1980 affected *the legal position of foreign immigrants and the combating of discrimination*, and there follows a brief summary of the most important developments in this area.

First there is the policy with respect to security of domicile for immigrants not possessing Dutch nationality. From the early 1980s this has been consistent. Aliens who have entered the Netherlands legally can acquire a permanent residence permit after five years. Those who have come for purposes of family reunion qualify for this permanent permit after three years. Withdrawal of a permanent permit and expulsion are only possible in exceptional cases; unemployment and lack of income are not sufficient grounds. As a result the majority of legally entered aliens have now acquired a reasonably secure right to remain.

A second aspect concerns the equal treatment of legally resident aliens and indigenous Dutch citizens. To obtain a clear picture of inequality of this type an inventory was drawn up of articles and clauses in legislation and regulations in which a distinction was made on the grounds of nationality, country of birth, religion, culture or language.[101] Subsequently a large number of such rulings were repealed. Although policy on this point has been fairly successful, voices were still raised in favour of banning all forms of distinction at a stroke with a Bill on Equal Treatment for Immigrants,[102] demands which were partially met by a General Bill on Equal Treatment introduced in 1994. It forbade unequal treatment on the grounds of nationality and ethnic descent, and also of religion, sex, age, and other grounds.

A third way of improving the legal position of aliens, and particularly of their children, was provided by the new law on Dutch citizenship introduced in 1985, with its procedures for the acquisition of Dutch nationality. The most important changes were:

a. that children of the third generation, born to parents who were themselves born in the Netherlands, automatically acquire Dutch nationality;

b. that children born of aliens in the Netherlands, who have then lived continually in the Netherlands, acquire the opportunity between the age of eighteen and twenty-five of opting for Dutch nationality on application by a simple declaration;

c. that as well as children of a Dutch father, henceforth also children of a Dutch mother (with a foreign father) can acquire Dutch nationality without difficulties;

d. that the spouses of Dutch nationals acquire special rights for the acquisition of Dutch nationality.

Another change was that henceforth naturalization would be authorized by Royal Decree or Orders in Council, rather than by statute.

Also of great practical importance is a recent change of policy: it is no longer a requirement in all cases that the original nationality be dropped on naturalization. This possibility of holding dual nationality, and the changes listed above, have led to a sharp increase in the number of naturalizations since 1985.[103] A law regularizing this policy on dual nationality is still awaiting approval from the Upper House of Parliament.

A fourth important change has been that aliens also have partial access to politics. Those who have resided legally in the Netherlands for more than three years have since 1985 acquired the right both to vote and to stand as candidates in municipal elections.

In addition to improvement of the legal position on residence and official equality before the law, the final element in government policy has been the fight against discrimination. Both in criminal and civil law a number of changes have been put into effect with the aim of confirming the principle of non-discrimination and giving more legal opportunities for the prosecution of individuals and organizations. In the new Constitution of 1983 the principle of non-discrimination was emphatically restated.

In implementing the policy, measures have been taken to make complaints procedures easier. The police and public prosecutors have been instructed how to deal effectively with cases of discrimination. The government has subsidized the National Bureau against Racism,[104] which co-operates with a large number of local organizations in reporting and fighting racism. A final element in the anti-discrimination policy is the indirect route: fighting prejudice by information campaigns, by training government employees, and by subsidizing private organizations promoting a similar message.

Of course all these measures have not been able to prevent the continued existence of discrimination, or even the recent sharp increase in racist incidents since 1992,[105] although it is true that the norm of equal treatment and non-discrimination is quite well rooted in public life, certainly in comparison with neighbouring countries. It will become apparent that this does not necessarily mean that these norms are equally solidly rooted in the attitude of individual Dutchmen.

A third key aspect of the minorities policy is concerned with *culture, religion, language and ethnic organizations.* The policy statement on minorities of 1983[106] outlined a multicultural society as the ideal, in which immigrants would and should have the same rights and opportunities to develop their cultural and religious identity as other groups in society. It was up to the government to create scope for this. The *right* articulated to the preservation and development of one's own culture, religion and language, and the right to organize has never been a matter of dispute in the Netherlands. 'Pillarized' Dutch society had already recognized these fundamental rights much earlier, and there was in principle nothing against extending them to immigrants, as long as the 'fundamental norms of our pluralistic society' were not put at risk. The existing facilities were therefore also accessible to newcomers on the same terms as they were to indigenous groups.

However, the government initially reasoned that in practice newcomers would be less able to take up these *opportunities*, because they were few in number, and moreover they were disadvantaged. Some effort to support minorities was therefore allowable, and several measures were taken to strengthen their position, such as government support for organizations set up by minority groups.[107] These would also be expected to contribute actively to the formation of policy, and separate organizations were set up for participation and comment. The national and local authorities committed themselves to consult with these organizations about the proposed policy.

Similar measures were taken in the field of education and the dissemination of information. The provision of 'Education in own language and culture' (OETC) has already been mentioned. Special programmes for minorities were introduced into the national broadcasting networks. From the mid-1980s a number of experimental local radio stations for minorities were also set up.[108]

In the field of religion the government took a series of measures over the course of time which were designed to enable followers of religions such as Islam, Hinduism and Buddhism to practice their faith in the Netherlands. Until 1984 a number of regulations were in force which made the partial subsidy of places of worship possible.[109] Slaughter according to the Islamic rites was made legal. In 1988 the public call to prayer from the minaret of a mosque was made equivalent to ringing the bells of Christian churches. But an important contribution to the new religious institutions was also achieved by appealing to the 'pillarized' legislation and regulation of Dutch society. For instance, in 1985 the authorities recognized an official Islamic Broadcasting Foundation as part of the public broadcasting system, followed in 1994 by a Hindu Broadcasting Foundation. From 1988 onwards, Muslim and Hindu parents founded primary schools based on Muslim and Hindu religious principles, entirely within the rules of Dutch 'pillarized' legislation. By 1995 there were more than thirty state-funded Islamic schools and three Hindu ones across the country.[110]

In evaluating the measures and their effects in the course of some fifteen years of minorities policies, in terms of the aims formulated in the early 1980s, one reaches mixed conclusions. Firstly, the results of these policies in their various domains turn out to be so divergent that a general judgement of their effectiveness is premature and therefore probably unjust. In certain areas significant progress has been made, concerning for example the housing sector, the legal position of alien immigrants, the participation of immigrant organizations in policy formulation and implementation, and the institutionalization of religions like Islam and Hinduism. It is precisely in these areas that the situation of immigrants in the Netherlands seems to be more favourable than in neighbouring countries. In other matters, however, progress has been much less unequivocal and the original aims remain in the distance, in education and anti-discrimination policies, for example. And lastly, there is one domain, and a crucial one, in which the situation of minorities has deteriorated: the labour market. Here the diagnosis of the problem appears to have been too one-sided; the application of resources was limited and the support for further measures, like affirmative action, was inadequate.

The differential success in the various policy areas leads us to a second conclusion: in those areas where there is found a combination of an institutional framework in the form of existing legal provisions and enforcement agencies, with the political will and consensus to take action, progress can be achieved in a relatively short period. The housing sector is a good example: the fact that much of the distribution of public or social housing can be politically controlled on the basis of existing law, and the fact that in the early 1980s a consensus emerged in favour of the equal treatment of immigrants in the distribution of housing, led to a rapid improvement of the housing situation, especially for workers from the Mediterranean countries, and their families. An important contributory factor is that a large share of the housing in the major cities in the Netherlands is controlled by local government and the housing associations. The private sector (in which much less progress has been made) is relatively small. The same two conditions are apparently applicable, *mutatis mutandis*, to other policy areas which have enjoyed success, like the legal position of immigrants and the institutionalization of their religions.

Finally a comment is appropriate on the unintended potential effects of the minorities policy. That policy is inherently contradictory; it tries to remove disadvantage and to make distinction between groups redundant, but for the policy to be implemented it must itself initially make distinctions. Which groups qualify for facilities and which do not? And for how long? By explicitly labelling target groups as disadvantaged, the policy itself can have a stigmatizing effect, which will be all the greater if these groups are presented not only as disadvantaged, but also consistently as deviating from main-stream Dutch culture. Opinions differ on how great a negative effect this might have had. It is, however, by no means fanciful.[111]

If we step back further, and put the relatively recent development of the post-1980 minorities policy described above in its long-term historical context, some interesting conclusions can be drawn.

In the first place there seems to have been a sharp increase in the political involvement of the authorities with newcomers. This is particularly reflected in the large number of policy statements, and the data partly commissioned and collected by the government, about the groups targeted in the minorities policy.[112] But if we look too at the financial resources and the multiplicity of activities, the policy – certainly when compared to other countries – is very comprehensive.

In the second place we must, in the light of historical experience of the settlement process of immigrants, state that expectations of the results in the short term are too high. This is also shown by the Scientific Council for Government Policy (WRR) report on *Immigrant policy* of 1989: only six years after the 1983 policy statement on minorities, it expressed disappointment with the results of implementing the policy.[113]

If we analyse the content of the policy, there are several interesting departures from past practice. In its ambitiously formulated objectives it is possible to recognize the basic principles of the welfare state: a guarantee of minimum standards for all legal inhabitants (regardless of nationality), equality of rights and opportunities, proportional participation and equal treatment. The minorities policy can therefore be regarded as a specific form of the policy of such a welfare state.

The ideology of the nation-state and its exclusion of aliens appears to have lost much of its strength in that policy, at least for those aliens residing legally in the country. In fact the legal position of aliens who have stayed for an extended period has in most respects become equivalent to that of nationals. Even institutions which were previously the exclusive privilege of nationals, such as the right to vote in local elections, have become accessible to legal aliens. Moreover, formal access to Dutch nationality has been made appreciably easier since 1985.

Within the minorities policy and the public debate on it the battle is now mainly between the ideology of equality, equal treatment and equal opportunity for individuals in the welfare state on the one hand, and the ideology of 'pillarized' society on the other. The traditional pillars may have lost a large part of their support in recent decades as a result of secularization, but the structure of pillarization established in legislation and regulation has largely remained intact. The significance of this development for newcomers is equivocal. On the one hand the surviving pillarized structure represents the principle of respect for one's own culture, religion and language, and this structure also offers real opportunities to immigrants, for instance of setting up their own broadcasting network and schools based on religion. On the other hand a section of the secularized and individualized population of the Dutch welfare state opposes the organization of religion and culture in new pillars. They regard the integration and emancipation of immigrants by means of pillarization as 'an outdated and counterproductive strategy'.[114]

Newcomers and Dutch society since 1970

We have now seen in broad outline how the authorities have reacted to newcomers living in the Netherlands, and to their descendants, since 1970. But how did society as a whole react? To answer this question we will look first at the development of the social and ethno-cultural position of the post-war groups of immigrants, and then try to answer the question of what role society and the immigrant groups themselves played in this. We will look mainly at the largest target groups of the minorities policy – the Turks, Moroccans, Surinamese, and Antilleans. By far the largest amount of information is available for these groups.

a. The development of the social position

What is the position of immigrants in the labour market, in education, and in the field of housing in the Netherlands?

If we measure the place of immigrants in the *labour market* by whether they can obtain paid employment or manage in some other way to earn their living, then it is very quickly clear that the answer is largely determined by the general development of the economy and particularly of employment.[115] Roughly speaking there have been two distinct periods since the Second World War. The first is that of the economic reconstruction and the boom which succeeded it until about 1974. We have seen that the early post-war immigrants found it relatively easy in this period to gain a reasonable position for integration into the labour market.

After the first oil crisis in 1973 this changed drastically. The process of restructuring and automation of production in industry gained strength, and this led to a substantial reduction of employment opportunities, particularly for the unskilled and semi-skilled. The concrete expression of this restructuring process were reorganizations, usually accompanied by mass redundancies, and the displacement of labour-intensive industries to countries with lower wages. This rendered a large proportion of the foreign workforce unemployed, and also of the first generation of Moluccans who worked in just these types of industry. Unemployment rose and became structural in nature after 1974: it remained high even at times of economic prosperity. There is no longer any question of a policy aiming at full employment: those who can no longer earn their own living are accommodated within one of the provisions of the expanding welfare state (disability insurance, unemployment and other benefits). Competition in the labour market is on the increase, and the better educated supplant the less skilled. With a plentiful supply of labour employers can increase their requirements, and avoid employing groups representing potential risks.

The effects on migrant unemployment are observable from 1975 onwards: from that date the unemployment of foreign workers (which before 1975 had always been lower than that of the indigenous population) rose appreciably. By 1983 it was already on average more than three times as high as for the autochthonous Dutch, and it continued to rise after 1983, when it began to fall among indigenous workers. Similarly, the average duration of unemployment among the minorities is also longer than for others. In the period 1989-1991 – when the labour market developed relatively favourably – unemployment of both indigenous and immigrants decreased, but the ratio between them was very unequal, and worse for Moroccan and Turkish immigrants in particular; the unemployed sections of the working population of these groups were 42 and 35 per cent respectively, as against 7 per cent for the indigenous workforce. For Antilleans and Surinamese the percentage was 29 per cent, still four times that of the autochthonous Dutch. This proportional distribution of unemployment did not change essentially in the period 1991-1994.[116]

Two provisional conclusions can be drawn from this. First, that after 1975 it was appreciably harder for newcomers to find a place in the labour market. Secondly, that the policy objective – propor-

tional participation by immigrants in the labour market – is now
further off than when the policy was formulated in the early 1980s.
The policy was obviously not sufficient to reverse the negative
developments in this respect.

If we look at the position of immigrants who are in work, they
seem to be filling positions which are for all groups – except the
Antilleans – substantially lower than those of the indigenous population. The level is lowest among the Moroccans and Turks: more
than two-thirds of them are either unskilled or semi-skilled workers.
The younger Turks and Moroccans are proportionately less often
found working at the lowest levels, but the differences from their
parents' generation is very small, and that from their Dutch contemporaries is great.

The second yardstick of social position is the *level of education*.
For adult members of minorities, particularly the Moroccans and
Turks, this is low. The school-leaving standard of the other Mediterranean migrants, and of the Moluccans and Surinamese, is
higher, but is still well behind the average for the Netherlands. Only
the Antilleans approach that level.

Children of minority groups who follow normal full-time education also display clear disadvantage compared with indigenous
children: their learning performance in primary education is lower,
and they therefore tend to be channelled more often into lower
forms of secondary education, such as lower technical schools for
boys, and domestic science training for girls. The greatest disadvantage is usually found among Moroccan and Turkish schoolchildren:
more than half of them go straight from basic primary school into
lower technical and vocational education, compared to a fifth of all
schoolchildren in the Netherlands. Although some improvement
can be detected in recent years, they are still well behind the Dutch
average. The position of the Antillean, Surinamese and Moluccan
schoolchildren is also disadvantaged, though not quite so much.

If we examine the school performance of migrants' descendants
more closely, then most of their disadvantages can be blamed on the
fact that they have only been in the Netherlands for a short time,
and have not been in Dutch education from the start: the longer a
child lives in the Netherlands, and the younger he is when he starts
in a Dutch school, the less his disadvantage appears to be. Re-
searchers have compared the school performance of children born
in the Netherlands to earlier groups of immigrants, such as the

Italians, Spaniards, Chinese and Surinamese, with indigenous Dutch children: among these children the educational arrears appear to have almost disappeared.[117] The choice of type of secondary education by these locally born children of migrants differed from group to group, but on balance the average level was the same. It is too early to say whether this positive development will also apply to more recent immigrants such as the Turks, Moroccans and Pakistanis, as the number of children in these groups born in the Netherlands and who have completed their education is still too small. Although there is a tendency for improvement here, too, the process of making up the arrears of these last groups seems to be coming up against further problems.

The third yardstick for social position is *housing*. That of the first generation of Turks and Moroccans is still the worst: they live in relatively cramped conditions and often in old cheap premises of inferior quality. In comparison with some twenty years ago, however, their housing situation is much improved. Many of them then still lived in boarding houses and special billets, and had great difficulty in getting accommodation for their families. The market for cheaper rented housing has become more accessible to them since 1980.

Surinamese, Antillean and Southern Europeans occupy a halfway position between the Turks and Moroccans and the indigenous Dutch. In the period 1975-1980 some of the Surinamese and Antilleans were housed by the government, scattered throughout the Netherlands: five per cent of all new council or public housing was reserved for them.

After their arrival in 1951 the Moluccans were 'temporarily' put into camps, mainly in the east and south of the Netherlands. When their stay went on being extended, special housing estates were built for them in the 1960s in some sixty towns and villages. This gave them a relatively good standard of housing. Over the years, however, this has deteriorated everywhere in both absolute and relative terms, and therefore in recent years renovation work has commenced on several of these estates.

b. The development of the ethno-cultural position

To what extent are immigrants regarded by society as a separate, different group, and to what extent do immigrant groups consider themselves as being culturally, religiously or ethnically different, and what emphasis do they put on it?

For society we can answer the first part of the question by analysing how politicians and policies regard and treat these groups. Political mobilization against minorities is another yardstick, as is the media reporting on minorities. At the level of the individual we can look at changes in the attitude and 'discrimination tendency' of the Dutch. For the immigrant groups we must obviously look at the nature and orientation of immigrant organizations and of individual immigrants: to what extent are they concerned with the Netherlands and their present or future position in Dutch society? All these elements will be briefly reviewed.

In the 1970s there were several unfavourable developments in society. In the first place there was at that time, as has been explained, a policy that put strong emphasis on the distinct and temporary position of immigrants and gave expression to this in regulations: these included a housing policy which put 'guest workers' into boarding houses and encampment huts, and which made family accommodation difficult, and proposals which aimed at confirming the temporary nature of their stay and encouraged their return, such as the two-year rule[118] and return premiums, and also special 'education for return' for the children of labour migrants.

At the same time an anti-immigrant political movement was started, originally by the Dutch People's Union (*Nederlandse Volksunie*) and later by the Centre Party (*Centrum Partij*).[119] Reports on immigrants in the press and other media were often negative, which helped to create a negative image among the Dutch audience. Public opinion with regard to foreigners and minorities became much more hostile in this period, as can be demonstrated by the opinion polls taken regularly from 1966 onwards. In some areas tensions also arose between newcomers and sections of the resident population, and on several occasions these even led to riots and clashes, as in the Afrikaanderbuurt in Rotterdam in 1972 and Schiedam in 1976.[120]

For the minority groups themselves there is little evidence in the 1970s of their deliberately profiling themselves as distinctive groups, except for the Moluccans. Within their own migrant communities the first generation of labour migrants tried to reconstruct the environment of the familiar way of life they had left behind. They set up – as migrants in a foreign country almost always do – their own places of worship, formed their own organizations, established teashops and coffee houses, shops, and other social and cultural amenities. Activities of this kind were primarily intended for their own people and not really aimed at outsiders; they wanted to create a haven within their own community where they could feel socially and psychologically at home. But this, of course, also contributed to society seeing and identifying immigrants in the first instance as a separate group.

From the early 1980s onwards there seems to have been some degree of reversal in the negative developments we have described. Politicians and policies abandoned the idea of the immigrants' stay being temporary, and in the new minorities policy an equal place in society had to be reserved for minorities as a matter of principle. A wide-ranging policy, outlined previously, was put in hand for this, for which there appeared to be, at least in the first half of the 1980s, broad political support.

Particularly after 1983 – when the Centre Party won nine per cent of the votes in mid-term municipal elections in the town of Almere[121] – there also arose considerable counter-forces against anti-immigrant political movements and against discrimination in general. The political parties felt obliged to take a stand against such movements more clearly than ever before. Action groups and working parties which had already been formed to support minorities and to fight discrimination and racism were given a new lease of life and grew in number – in churches, schools, and in residential areas. The norm that racial discrimination cannot and must not be permitted became firmly rooted not only in law, but also in society's consciousness.

In the same period the public climate, as measured by questions about the acceptance of minorities, appears to have stabilized. There was certainly a section of society that continued to oppose the arrival and presence of certain groups of immigrants and there were also regular racist incidents, but on the other hand some degree of habituation seems to have developed in the relationship between newcomers and residents, and in residential areas there was an attempt to find a way of co-existing, or at least of living peacefully next to each other. The frequently forecast outbreaks of collective violence, such as took place in English cities, did not occur in the Netherlands of the 1980s. This does not, of course, mean that there were no problems in the relations between residents and minorities, but they were not seen as insuperable.

From the end of the 1980s there was evidence of yet another change occurring. The Scientific Council's (WRR) report on *Immi-*

grant policy set the tone in the first instance: according to the report the integration of immigrants had been disappointing and the policy approach needed to make more demands on the members of minority groups. The consensus among the political parties on minority policy began to break up. A number of international developments, including the Salman Rushdie affair and the Gulf War, led to a polarization in the discussion about Islam and about the position and integration of Muslims in the Netherlands. In comparison with other countries the consequences in the Netherlands could be limited by the efforts of the government,[122] and of Muslim and indigenous organizations (religious or otherwise), but nonetheless it is plain that negative imagery has attracted new levels of support.[123]

This change coincided with a major increase in immigration, of which the family-forming migration of Turks and Moroccans, and the great stream of asylum seekers has attracted most attention. Asylum seekers in particular regularly feature as an 'insoluble problem' in the public view. Moreover, the politicians and the media have loudly proclaimed the threat of further flows of migration, like the East Germans after the fall of the Wall in 1989, ex-Soviet citizens after the collapse of the Soviet Union in 1990, and projected internal migrations within the European Union after the abolition of internal frontiers on 1 January 1993.[124] None of these migrants have actually arrived, but the publicity about them did nothing to create a positive climate surrounding immigration and immigrants.

Finally, in this same period the unification of Europe has also played an indirect but important role in this field. The hardening of political attitudes towards immigrants and asylum seekers in countries such as France, Germany and Belgium in the 1980s also had its repercussions in the Netherlands – though for the time being somewhat toned down. The 'taboos' surrounding minorities and their integration (or lack of it) in the Netherlands needed to be removed, in some people's opinion. In the Netherlands these European developments played into the hands of the racist parties. The elections to the Dutch Lower House in the spring of 1994 brought the extreme right-wing parties two of the 150 seats available, in comparison with the single one occupied by the Centre Democrats in 1990. Even greater success was registered by the extreme right in the local elections which were also held in 1994: they gained more than a hundred council seats across the country.

The attitude of individual Dutchmen, again measured by subsequent comparable annual polls, showed no change until 1991,[125] but has hardened slightly since 1992. It is expected, given the evidence of recent elections, that this will deteriorate further.

The crucial question for the next few years is whether Dutch society is capable of mobilizing effective counter-forces against these tendencies, and of keeping under control or neutralizing the opposition to immigrants.

Among the immigrant groups themselves one occasionally sees small groups taking the public stage, as happened in the debate about Salman Rushdie's *Satanic Verses* with a group of orthodox Muslims. Reactions of this kind seem to have been more moderate in the Netherlands than, for example, in Britain. In general there are few indications that immigrants are consciously distancing themselves from society, organizing themselves, and setting themselves up as separate groups. Nonetheless it is clear that most first-generation immigrants are still strongly oriented towards their country of origin, or at least ambivalent. Many of them still cherish the intention, or at any rate the wish, to go back to their country of origin one day, but actually carrying out this intention in practice always becomes delayed and postponed. This ambivalence on the part of many first-generation immigrants can, of course, have a negative effect on their future in the Netherlands. If, for example, they think that knowledge of the Dutch language or Dutch education for themselves and their children is only of secondary importance, because they are planning to go back, then decisions of this kind can severely limit their opportunities in the Netherlands when they eventually decide to stay.

The second generation (that is to say, immigrants' children, born in the Netherlands) has in general become much better acquainted with Dutch society, partly because of education. But on the other hand they know much less of the language, culture and life of their parents' country of origin. Their frame of reference generally tends to be much more Dutch society, or sections of it, such as the youth culture.[126] Precisely because they are more familiar with the norms of Dutch society, they adopt in general a much more conscious attitude, certainly when there is any hint of discrimination. At the same time, at least in certain circumstances, they also stress the fact that they are different, and have different origins. They often appeal, albeit selectively, to symbols and elements originating in their

parents' country or culture. A good example is the succession of
subcultures amongst Surinamese-Creole youths in Amsterdam,
such as the disco-freaks and rappers, as described by L. Sansone for
instance.[127] This ethnicization process leads to a great diversity of
group-formation among the second generation, manifesting itself
mainly in the field of recreation and leisure occupations, and also
in the sphere of religion and ideology.

Between these first and second generations there is a group of
young people who came to the Netherlands as children or youngsters. They have often had little chance of integrating into the
educational system, so that their prospects in Dutch society are very
limited. Is is mainly this group which determines the current image
of problem youngsters from minority groups. A number of them
have developed 'alternative lifestyles': running away from home,
dropping out, drug abuse, and so on. These lifestyles are often very
similar to those of marginalized indigenous young people.[128]

However much the image of these groups of young people may
dominate the media, the general picture is that group-formation
and ethnicization mainly occurs in the area of recreation and in a
private environment, and that its function is mainly expressive. In
public life they do not generally set themselves up as a separate
group, but try to protect their interests in existing, general organizations. In municipal elections, for instance, immigrants rarely put
forward a party of their own, and in the instances where they have
done so, they have received no support from their own groups. The
migrants who were elected as councillors in 1986, 1990, and 1994
stood as members of established political parties, such as the Labour
Party or the Christian Democrats, and recently also for the Liberal
and Green parties.[129] The same applies to trade union activities.

Conclusion

What conclusions can be drawn from this highly summarized
description of the way in which the position of post-war immigrant
groups has developed? Is there any question of the formation of
minorities, as they were defined in Chapter 5?

In the first place we can confirm that a number of the early groups
of immigrants, entering the country soon after 1945, have been
assimilated. Their social position is not low across the board, they

have gone through a process of upward social mobility, are not considered primarily as a separate group by society, nor do they consider themselves to be one, although they have retained their individuality in a number of aspects. This profile applies to the early post-war refugees, the repatriates, the Southern Europeans, and the descendants of these groups.

The settlement process of the Moluccans has gone much less smoothly. Until late in the 1970s they seemed to be moving strongly in the direction of minority-formation. Changes both in policy and in the orientation of the majority of the group itself have since then put the process of settlement of this group onto a new course, directed at integration.

When it comes to the largest target groups of the minorities policy, the Moroccans, Turks, Surinamese and Antilleans, the picture is still somewhat unclear, partly because these groups are more recent immigrants. Their social position on arrival was in general low, and their opportunities on the labour market have deteriorated appreciably over the last twenty years. As yet the employment situation of the younger generation seems not much better than that of their parents.

In the area of education, first-generation adults have a poor starting position. Migrants' children in general fare just as badly in comparison with every indigenous group, as measured by the levels of secondary education they attain and their final examination results. Improvements among these groups as a whole have been modest, both in absolute and relative terms. This is associated with the fact that most immigrant pupils were already quite old when they arrived. There are, however, clear indications that the examination results of immigrants' children born in the Netherlands differ much less, if at all, from those of their indigenous contemporaries with similar characteristics.

The housing situation of minorities has improved for most groups during the last twenty years. The market for rented housing, particularly for public or council and housing association accommodation, has become more accessible. In relative terms it is mainly the position of the Turks and Moroccans which displays great disadvantage. In this area, too, there is little difference between the position of the first generation and their current younger successors.

However, the negative developments in the field of employment weigh heaviest. Because of their low incomes the greater part of the minorities are tied to cheap rented accommodation, and the educational opportunities of their children are to some degree also determined in this way. It is above all developments on the labour market which maintain the arrears.

Relations between minorities and established society worsened in the 1970s, but changed for the better in the early 1980s. The norm in Dutch society that there should be no discrimination has taken firm root. In the period up to the late 1980s, forces developed opposing racism and supporting minorities in order to counter those which had turned against immigrants. For a variety of reasons the 1990s have heralded a further period in which anti-immigrant sentiment has been on the upswing. The result has been a polarization of opinion about immigration and immigrants in Dutch society, though still a moderate one in comparison with neighbouring countries.

The third condition for the formation of minorities can be dealt with very briefly: the minority groups discussed here involve relatively small numbers. The largest group, the Surinamese, makes up only 1.5 per cent of the population of the Netherlands, and all the target groups of the minorities policy combined amount to only 5.7 per cent. Although these groups have formally been given opportunities for political participation, at least at municipal level, this does not mean that they can exercise any direct and effective political influence, even in situations where strong local concentrations exist. Their indirect influence through participation in the mainstream political parties has supposedly increased.

Finally there is the fourth criterion, that a minority only exists in the strictest sense if the three previous conditions have been satisfied for several generations of the same group. This criterion obliges us to exercise great caution in pronouncements about the current situation. The position is that the great majority by far of the groups discussed here are made up of people who are immigrants themselves, and that the number of descendants born in the Netherlands and now adult is still small. Where they do exist, there is often no systematic information available about them.

The developments outlined here are not equally significant for every group. All research data indicate that the Turks and particularly the Moroccans have fared worst on almost all fronts. The outlook for sections of the Surinamese, Antillean and Moluccan groups may be no more rosy, but subgroups can increasingly be found among them, who no longer belong to the lowest socio-economic strata.

Chapter 7

Reflections on the settlement process of newcomers and their descendants

Processes which ultimately lead to assimilation or to the emergence of a minority take time. Only after several generations of descendants can any final pronouncement be made. These processes do not therefore in the first place apply to newcomers themselves. From the descriptions in Chapter 6 the conclusion seems to emerge that the behaviour of the various groups of immigrants show fairly strong similarities in their reaction to the new society. They organize themselves in the first instance in their own associations, not only to share within them the atmosphere of their common origin, but also to use those organizations and institutions as a base from which to strengthen their position in their new surroundings. Usually immigrants are encouraged in this by the attitude of the host society, which regards them at the least as newcomers, but often also as 'not one of us', different in culture and religion. In short, precisely because immigrants bring much of their cultural and social frame of reference with them from their country of origin, and continue to hold on to it, their place in the new society offers few indicators for what their descendants, born and bred in the new country, will do.

In order to analyse the differences between immigrants and their descendants in the way a position is allocated or acquired, the processes will be discussed separately for each of these two categories.

Immigrants and their specific situation

Immigrants have a number of things in common. They share the experience of having left for good the place where they were born or lived previously. In most cases this did not happen voluntarily, or not completely so, and meant leaving behind family and friends. This is followed by the equally common experience of having to fit into different surroundings, often in a completely different society. A great deal is new, unexpected, and does not (or not entirely), come up to expectations. Some of the skills useful in the earlier situation appear to produce little or no result in the new. They have to learn a new language and get used to the customs and usages of the host country. Not only is the social environment not what they are accustomed to, but even the climate can be quite different, which can cause physical discomfort.

These and similar experiences are common to immigrants, and they differ in these respects from the established members of the new society and also from their own descendants. Even without encountering any difficulties which might result from a hostile attitude in the host society, the definitive transition from one society to another may require a great deal of effort. The stories of those concerned bear witness to the problems of transition even in situations where the reception of the immigrants is ideal. Without too much exaggeration it can be stated that the permanent change from the one situation to the other is always a traumatic experience.

The degree to which the migration and the subsequent new situation is experienced as difficult, even under ideal conditions of reception, can vary enormously. For the political refugee, who may arrive in the Netherlands after a calvary of torture, matters are, of course, very different in comparison with an immigrant who settles in the Netherlands after marrying a Dutch wife.

The conclusion can be drawn from all this that there is no such thing as a group immigration free of problems. However, it is important to distinguish between those problems inherent in migration which immigrants always or almost always encounter, and problems which are caused by specific requirements and conditions set by the host society. Some of the important factors inherent in migration itself or in the starting position of the migrant will now be reviewed.

From the immigrant's point of view, it can be accepted first of all that he or she is poorly equipped for competition and performance in the new society. This applies particularly to those who cannot speak, read, or write the target language, which in the case of the Netherlands means the majority of newcomers. Adults, and particularly those not accustomed to learning foreign languages and who have had no preparatory training, in practice rarely seem to attain a good active and passive mastery of the new language. Through their contact with their Dutch contemporaries and the education process in general, immigrants' children born in the Netherlands learn to speak and understand Dutch well, although their mastery of and feeling for the finer points of the language may be less than that of their Dutch contemporaries. This applies particularly to those children who normally speak no Dutch at home or in their immediate environment. The Dutch-language skills of most second-generation Moluccans is a clear illustration of this.[1]

Unfamiliarity with the new society is a second important factor which applies to all immigrants, if to a varying degree. Even groups of immigrants who seemed well equipped in the matter of language and theoretical knowledge of Dutch society, such as the repatriates, the Surinamese and the Antilleans, seem to have encountered a society, which was different, and which functioned differently, compared with their expectations. Even for these groups there was much to learn in the period immediately after arrival, not only about regulations, institutions and organizations, but also about the rules of behaviour and conventions in the new society. Naturally this applied to a much greater extent to groups who had no command of the language and who were in many cases simultaneously making the transition from a rural agricultural area in a developing country to an urban industrial centre in the Netherlands; this was the case for most of the families from Morocco and Turkey.

But yet more factors may be mentioned which play a restrictive role for newcomers, and which therefore contribute to the allocation of their position: an important one is the collection of rules, customs and procedures which, often unintentionally, have an *indirect* restrictive effect on newcomers. For instance, in the Netherlands the principle of 'last in, first out' usually applies in large firms when there are mass redundancies. In times of economic recession such a general rule leads by definition to the more frequent dismissal of newcomers. There is a similar mechanism at work at the recruiting end; research has shown that in times of high unemployment employers recruit relatively more frequently through unofficial channels, that existing employees have a strong voice in deciding who will be taken on (by co-option), and that the unemployed

A tightly organized common religion can fulfil the function of a network. Moroccans in Amsterdam. (Photo Ad van Denderen)

increasingly need some kind of strings to pull. Newcomers are thus more likely to lose out.[2]

In general the importance of *networks* should not be underestimated. Although Dutch society has sometimes been described as over-organized and over-regulated, this does not mean that the use of personal networks is no longer of any significance. They certainly exist and gain strength in times of scarcity. This need not only take the form of direct advancement, the old-boy network, or nepotism; networks can also be decisive for lesser services such as the provision of information. By definition newcomers have smaller networks, but in particular they cover a much narrower spectrum of society and in general include fewer people in positions of influence. For this reason alone therefore, newcomers as a group are almost always at a disadvantage.

All this does not mean that immigrants, if they have the opportunity, do not make use of networks. On the contrary, they have more need of them than anyone else. In a great many cases it appears that arrangements for their arrival have been made in advance through a network of relatives and acquaintances. They provide the first reception, and negotiate and help in finding accommodation and work. In short, the familiar picture of chain migration. And in many respects these networks continue to be of great importance after settlement. But as long as they are restricted entirely or mainly to members of the immigrant group, all of whom are newcomers, and who have not, or not yet, achieved important positions socially, these networks prove to have little power in situations of strong competition. They do not yet include individuals in positions where important decisions are taken, or important resources allocated.

Of course, there are also rules or procedures which have unintended effects, quite apart from the economic situation: the fact that the tests most used in the Netherlands are designed for people who have been brought up and raised in a Dutch system of education almost automatically means that many newcomers cannot surmount such barriers. The fact that there is no straightforward recognition for educational qualifications and diplomas gained abroad results in newcomers being more likely to be unsuccessful.

This summary may perhaps give the impression that nothing can ever go right for immigrants. That would be incorrect, as the history of newcomers in the Netherlands over a somewhat longer term shows us. It is important, however, to realize that these limitations exist, and it prevents us from harbouring inflated expectations or making exaggerated demands for the improvement of the position of immigrant groups and their descendants. In Chapter 4 it has already been emphasized that inflated requirements for adaptation should not be set for immigrants who come to the Netherlands as adults after completing their education, particularly where it involves adaptation that goes beyond the instrumental: to norms and values. To this we can add that in general no great leaps up the social ladder should be expected from these same immigrants. There may be a few exceptions, but for the immigrant group as a whole, partly for the reasons given above, it would not be realistic. For this reason the concept of 'minority' in our definition implies that a group occupies a low social position over several generations. The crucial question is what opportunities are open to their descendants, and whether advantage is taken of those opportunities.

Allocating a position to immigrants

The spiritual and material baggage, the qualities and characteristics of newcomers, to a large extent determine the starting position of the group. This spiritual and material baggage, but above all the value accorded to it by the host society, appears to vary greatly between the groups under review. The first groups of prosperous and well-educated Southern Netherlanders, Sephardic Jews and Huguenots started in a favoured position, high up the social ladder. The unskilled Mediterranean labourers who were recruited in the 1960s and early 1970s started with little more than a job for which no Dutchman could be found. They started at the bottom of the social ladder, like many other groups of immigrants: a substantial proportion of the later waves of Southern Netherlanders and Huguenots, almost all the Ashkenazic Jews, most of the immigrants from Germany, Poland and Slovenia, and the Moluccan ex-servicemen.

The starting position obviously affects the likelihood of minority-formation. Immigrant groups whose members have little or no education, who bring no material prosperity with them and who, moreover, are regarded as being culturally different, start from a point which already has all the characteristics of a minority but one: their position only needs to be made permanent by their descendants.

The social position of newcomers can be seen as being determined to an important degree by the host society, in principle in either a positive or negative sense. A positive sense would mean that

Cleaner in a swimming bath. (Photo Ad van Denderen)

newcomers receive preferential treatment in some respects. Allowances are made for them which are not granted to the rest of the population, or a proportion of important social resources are reserved for them from the general distribution. There are relatively few historical examples of such preferential treatment, but they do exist. The list of measures taken originally by a number of towns in the Republic to entice Southern Netherlanders and later Huguenots to their gates is a clear, if incidental, example. Other instances can be produced in modern times, though less extensive and less spectacular than those of the Southern Netherlanders and Huguenots. For instance, in the post-war period the 'five per cent rule' was applied for the permanent housing both of the repatriates from Indonesia in the 1950s and the Surinamese and Antilleans in the mid-1970s. This meant that five per cent of all newly built public or social housing subsidized by the state was reserved and could be used for allocation to these groups. This share of public housing was therefore kept outside the normal distribution. This rule is still being applied for the housing of invited refugees.[3]

The provisions of what is known as the government's minorities policy, which apply only to the listed target groups of that policy, can in fact be classified as positive allocations. In policy documents, however, it receives a minimum of emphasis, and such provisions are defended in terms of the philosophy of social disadvantage and compensation.

Position allocation in a negative sense, by excluding newcomers from the distribution of certain social resources, is seen much more frequently. The most obvious distinctions in legislation and regulation for the period before 1850 seem to be the legal ones between freemen and the rest in the towns of the Republic, and between residents who were born locally and those who were born elsewhere. In 1850 the legal distinction between aliens and nationals came into force. During the last hundred years in particular, this legal criterion has created a firm basis for distinction between residents. The way in which the legal position can operate in a restrictive manner for the alien is quite profound: in theory the continuation of his stay is subject to explicit permission, particularly in the first years after arrival. An important criterion affecting whether or not an extension is granted is, as it was under earlier rules, that the alien should not be a burden on the community, either financially or from the point of view of public order.

Whether they obtain permission for an extended stay or are expelled is not, however, the only aspect associated with alien status; indeed, it becomes less important after a rather longer stay, because the security of domicile increases and the likelihood of expulsion becomes steadily less. What becomes more important are the laws, rules and provisions in society which make a distinction by nationality, and in general allow fewer rights to non-citizens or impose more obligations upon them.

Up to this point we have almost exclusively discussed the distinctions in laws and regulation between immigrants and others, and the way the authorities treat them as a consequence of such legislation. In doing so we have oversimplified at least two things. Firstly, within any society a systematic distinction can be drawn, quite separate from legislation and regulation and perhaps even running counter to them, between immigrants and the indigenous population; and secondly, it is not only the authorities who are involved. Society does not react to the arrival of newcomers as a homogeneous unit, and potential measures against newcomers and the ways in which coalitions of different groups in society conspire against them can be very varied.

An obvious example, and one frequently encountered, is when an interest group in society, fearing for their own earnings or income or thinking they have reason to fear for them, opposes the arrival of immigrants, and if that fails, tries to protect its particular source of income or jobs. This occurs particularly when a group of immigrants, or part of it, show themselves to be a strong and homogeneous occupational unit, so that newcomers coincide with an occupational group. The Italian ice cream vendors in the Netherlands were hardly received with open arms by their Dutch colleagues. On the contrary, for a long time they laid difficulties in their path, and not always by particularly delicate means. Long after the Dutch public were used to Italian ice cream on their menu as a favourite and regular treat, the Dutch ice cream vendors continued to bar their Italian colleagues from the official training courses for the trade. A similar case is that of the Amsterdam diamond cutters, who in a petition of 1748 to the Amsterdam city fathers asked among other things that new Jewish colleagues should be barred. Their request was not granted: the Amsterdam authorities also had other interests to consider.[4]

But even when the situation is less clear, and a group of immigrants does not form a homogeneous occupational group, argu-

Jewish pedlar. Anonymous print, late eighteenth century. Because they were excluded from the guilds, Jews had to turn their hand to those sectors of the economy which were not subject to guild regulations. German Jews engaged mainly in small-scale trades, rag-and-bone and second-hand clothing, street selling and public markets. (Biblioteca Rosenthaliana, Amsterdam)

ments are often advanced about jobs and incomes, and the possible competition or costs associated with them. The trade unions, for example, have often shown alarm about the possible negative effects or the undesirability of particular immigration flows. They did so, for instance, in the case of the stranded Chinese seamen in the early 1930s, but also about repatriation from Indonesia after the Second World War.[5]

Direct opposition and attempts at expulsion by existing fellow workers are not always effective by themselves, though they can be when established institutions, such as the guilds in the time of the Republic, hold a monopoly position. The exemption from membership of guilds originally granted to the Huguenots in Amsterdam met great resistance in this way from the guilds themselves. However, in many cases there is no question of a direct monopoly position, and then the effectiveness of opposition depends on the number of members in the coalition, and the power they can wield. It is possible, for instance, to approach the authorities with a request for action, as has indeed often occurred; influence can be exerted through the political system or, alternatively, public opinion and popular images can be utilized. Then the means are legion: you can cast doubt on colleagues' integrity by calling their professional methods into question or by throwing suspicion on the quality of their product. There are plenty of instances in the literature of the standard accusation that Chinese peanut biscuits, Italian ice cream, and the food in Chinese restaurants, shoarma shops and pizzerias are all prepared under dubious hygienic conditions from inferior ingredients.

The question arises of whether it is possible, on the basis of the limited evidence, to give any indication of the conditions under which society tends towards a positive or negative attitude; it is particularly important to examine the power factors which play a role in this matter.

A first factor involved is the *size* and *visibility* of the group of newcomers. Relatively large numbers of newcomers arriving within a short period of time seem to generate considerable resentment, even in situations where there is a strong demand for their labour, and strong ideological support for their arrival. As J.H. Kraak puts it, 'This general feeling of being threatened in some way by the arrival of the repatriates was clearly manifest in the press reports of the arrival of ships from Indonesia, carrying large numbers of them: the news was usually limited to giving the totals of repatriates expected, with mention of the percentages who were homeless, had no income, and who had never been in the Netherlands before'.[6]

A similar mechanism came into operation when the number of persecuted co-religionists emigrating from France to the Netherlands after 1690 became too large: 'All this applied mainly to the first wave of refugees reaching the Republic. After 1690 an increasingly restrictive policy was applied in Amsterdam and elsewhere. The measure introduced in 1681 (which granted Huguenots the freedom of the city, three years exemption from taxes, and the right to ply a trade outside the guilds) was withdrawn, partly to curtail too large a flow of poor refugees. Thus it would appear that the reception of refugees, and so their fate in general, is highly dependent on a precarious balance of special circumstances, political attitudes, economic interests and humanitarian motives.'[7]

Although small groups of newcomers have relatively more opportunity to make themselves more or less socially invisible, and therefore do not arouse mass resistance, this does not mean that there is no opposition to them. Van Heek reports, for instance, that in the 1930s, under pressure from the Dutch vendors, several towns refused licences to Chinese peanut vendors: the Chinese were too successful, not so much at selling, as Van Heek adds, but in exciting sympathy and therefore making money.[8] In some cases, as with the gypsies, small groups have even encountered general and large-scale hostility and repression. One should therefore not make too much of the argument that the threat results from large numbers, for smaller groups can stir resentment as well.

A second factor is *economic functionality*: the better the newcomers supply the economic needs of the host society, the more favourable their treatment. The services offered by newcomers can take a variety of forms; highly trained skills, but also more modest skills which are in short supply, a new product, or even in some circumstances ordinary unskilled labour. The other side of the coin is that where newcomers can only offer what there is already a surplus of, and so by definition only increase the competition, the attitude of the host society tends to be negative. This argument has reappeared regularly in recent discussions about limiting the numbers of family reunions and asylum seekers.

This brings us to the third important point: the *significance of the economic situation*. If the state of economic development, and in particular the labour market, takes a sudden turn for the worse, an originally positive or at least a neutral attitude can easily turn into a negative one. The sensitivity to the economic situation which is shown in the attitude of the host society is most clearly illustrated by the history of the foreign mineworkers in South Limburg in the late 1920s, and the sharp change in attitude to foreign workers in Western Europe after the oil crisis in late 1973. Both cases involved groups who had originally been recruited to carry out specific kinds of work, and who were therefore welcomed. After the crises of 1929 and 1973, the demand for their potential return took a central place in the discussion.⁹

Position acquisition and the characteristics of immigrants

Though scope for choice and freedom to acquire a reasonable or improved social position is often restricted for newcomers and sometimes for their descendants, it is rarely entirely lacking. To some extent the characteristics of the newcomers themselves determine the development of their social position.

One of the most important ways in which this is achieved is by founding and building up institutions and organizations for immigrants and their descendants. In their organizations immigrants often combine social and cultural activities with the promotion of their interests, which is what matters here. Their own institutions and organizations and (in less concrete form) the informal networks of immigrants can perform an important function in the position acquisition of newcomers. This applies particularly where the immigration of a particular group takes place over an extended period, and a system for the reception of newcomers by those already established can be set up. The theory is that through these networks and organizations newcomers can profit directly from the knowledge and perhaps even the influence of their predecessors. The interests of the newcomers are promoted by 'caretakers'; compatriots who have arrived earlier and meanwhile found means of entry into the established society, or sometimes established members of that society as well, who are asked to represent the interests of the groups either voluntarily or for payment. The role played by the Walloon churches, established by the Southern Netherlanders, in welcoming the Huguenots who arrived later, and the role of Jewish organizations, are good examples.

What channels of advancement are open to immigrants and their descendants depends very much on the opportunities offered by society. One pattern, however, seems prominent across the centuries. Over a period an immigrant group or a section of it often specializes in a profession or industry in which the established interests are absent or ineffective, because it involves new activities, products or trades. Immigrants discover or create the proverbial gap

Immigrant groups often specialize in a particular occupation or industry. (Photos Bert Nienhuis)

in the market. German bakers and butchers, Italian chimney sweeps, granite masons, image sellers and ice cream vendors, German cloth merchants and pedlars, Chinese peanut biscuit sellers (who later introduced Chinese-Indonesian restaurants to the Netherlands on a grand scale), pizzerias run by Italian immigrants (but also for example by Turks), Turkish off-the-peg tailors in Amsterdam, and so on. These are all activities which are aimed at all members of society as potential customers.

The small independent enterprise, particularly in industries in which it is possible to set oneself up with a minimum of regulation and for which relatively little capital is needed, forms an important channel for advancement in society. Why should immigrants choose this kind of channel relatively more often than indigenous people from the lower classes? It is a possibility that the migrant, searching for opportunities, who has to relocate in a new situation, has a relative advantage over his autochthonous opposite number, whose view of social opportunities is perhaps more blinkered. In many cases the migrant is also under more pressure to choose these routes because others appear closed. Thus the boom in ethnic enterprises run by Turks in recent years can in part be explained by the increasing unemployment among this group.[10] Often, too, migrants bring with them from their background more attributes and qualities which fit them particularly well for independent enterprise. A very high proportion of immigrants seem to come from farming communities, where an independent small business is the highest goal to aim for. The lifestyle and qualities which lead to that goal are well known: hard work, long hours, thrift, and so gradually trying to expand.

To keep things in proportion, however, we need to note a number of qualifying comments on the subject of independent small business being an important conduit for the upwardly mobile. First of all many attempts to follow this route end in failures, which only become visible at the moment of bankruptcy, and are soon forgotten. The success of German newcomers like Clemens and August (C & A) Brenninkmeyer, founders of the C & A empire, is well known, but set against it are the thousands of others in the 'rag trade' who have disappeared without trace.[11] Today there is an enormous turnover in the Chinese-Indonesian restaurant industry, in which the density of establishments is now so great that they do not provide sufficient income to all restaurateurs. It is true that this industry has

H. Hollenkamp's illustrated catalogue, 1898. Hollenkamp was a German newcomer who started in the textile trade in the nineteenth century, and succeeded in expanding his business into a chain with a large number of outlets. (Gemeentelijke Archiefdienst, Amsterdam)

encountered fierce competition from other specialities introduced by immigrants: shoarma, pizzas, döner kebabs, and all manner of Greek, Turkish or North-African delicacies.

What stands out among immigrant enterprises are the resounding successes. Those who tried, but who lost what they started with and had to fall back on waged labour, or even returned to their country of origin, are much more difficult to track down.

Immigrants and the role of government

In the examples given above the government appears in various roles. In the case of the Huguenots and the Southern Netherlanders we see the authorities actively attracting them, particularly in the first phase of these migrations, taking a series of measures to make things easy for the newcomers and to give them scope for development, even to the point of defying resentment and suppressing opposition to such preferential treatment. After 1980 the government adopted a policy aimed at the integration of legal immigrants, particularly of those groups starting from a weak position, which was also sometimes achieved by giving the immigrants preferential treatment. On the other hand the government played a completely different role when, as in the early 1930s, they ordered the state-owned mines in Limburg to sack foreigners wherever possible, the same foreigners who had been recruited abroad not so many years previously with government connivance. What is more, in almost all cases the sack meant expulsion.[12]

It is essential to examine the role of government, because it controls important sources of power and because its intervention can be very influential. In the first place there is the government's influence on legislation and regulation, and the degree to which this lays down distinctions and exclusions for certain groups of immigrants and their descendants. In the second place the government is very influential in its executive role of implementing and supervising the legislation. If the rules give little or no opportunity for distinction or exclusion, it is of great importance whether the government supervises their application and so prevents discrimination. A government which only lays down the norm of non-discrimination, but does not supervise its observance, or which applies no resources to it, can see the norm in effect undermined in the course of time. And whenever legislation makes substantial distinctions, and creates grounds for exclusion, the attitude of the government also plays an important role: it can exercise strict supervision so that the distinction is in fact made, and so create a leadership role for itself. This was the case in the example quoted of the foreign mineworkers, and concerning gypsy policies.

In any case the government faces a difficult task in this context, because they not only have to apply a policy for resident newcomers, but also for the preceding stage: their admission and the legitimation of their stay. Particularly after 1975 this has been an area of increasing tension. The growing availability and diminishing costs of travel have in theory made it attractive for very many foreigners to try to settle in a welfare state such as the Netherlands, with its high standard of living. The pressure on the frontiers of the Netherlands and the EU has become heavy. A large and constant inflow, particularly one which is greater than the economy of the welfare state needs or can support, puts that same high standard of living potentially at risk. And this leads to an ever stricter admission policy, as described in Chapter 3. Thus a sterner side of the government is shown and the distinguishing label of 'alien' is rigidly applied. However, in the ideology of the welfare state its role with respect to legally admitted aliens should be a different one: once legally admitted they should be treated as much as possible as residents. For the welfare state takes care of the welfare of all its residents.

This solution to the dilemma, steadfastly against newly arriving aliens, and helpful and offering services to newcomers once they have been admitted, results in groups of the newcomers themselves often seeing the government's role as ambivalent. This, of course, applies particularly where the dividing line between those who are and those who are not admitted runs across family or kin.

The Dutch government's policy towards newcomers must also be looked at in this perspective, particularly since the government has accepted that most immigrants' stay is likely to be of some duration or permanent. That policy embraces a large number of provisions which, particularly for immigrant groups starting from a low social position in the Netherlands, should make it easier to make up these arrears, so averting the risk of their becoming a minority.[13]

Descendants of newcomers, position allocation and ethnicization

A great many of the factors which we have discussed in the allocation of position to immigrants do not apply, or do so to a lesser extent, to the generations of their descendants born in the Netherlands. For example, the specific circumstances directly associated with the actual migration are completely absent. Language is no longer a problem, or at least far less. In terms of law and regulations, before 1850 we have seen that the restrictions which were applied to their immigrant forebears no longer affected the descendants, for they were Dutch by birth, and not simply residents. Later on, and particularly after 1892, being born in the Netherlands was no longer the decisive criterion, and therefore descendants born in the Netherlands could still be aliens and be excluded from some rights on that score. In spite of this their legal residential status, because of their birth in the Netherlands and long residence, was a fairly sound one. Moreover, naturalization was relatively easy for them; precisely because of their long residence they almost always satisfied the most important requirements: speaking the language and being reasonably established in the country. The new 1985 legislation made it even simpler for descendants: aliens born in the Netherlands can on reaching their majority (at eighteen years old) opt for Dutch nationality by means of a simple procedure. The grandchildren of aliens, who have always lived in the Netherlands, acquire Dutch citizenship automatically.

Young Turks learn how to play traditional Turkish instruments. (Photo Hannes Wallrafen)

Meanwhile these descendants have built up networks and organizations, or have joined existing organizations in the community to promote their interests. Usually they have made a conscious choice between the two alternatives: organizations for immigrants and their descendants, or those common to the whole community. Sometimes descendants systematically choose their own organizations and their own group in all situations and for all purposes: from membership of a religious group up to and including their own schools and sports clubs, in so far as they are available. Sometimes such a choice is forced upon them because other possibilities are closed off.

More often the choice is partly for general organizations in the wider community, and partly for their own, which are chosen because they offer something related specifically to the common origin of immigrants and their descendants. Also common, and the more so as the number of generations increases, is the choice of descendants to opt only for networks and organizations which do not hark back to an alleged common origin as descendants of immigrants. Whichever choice is made by the descendants, their frame of reference is always Dutch society. The choice is made because it is considered to be best one in a Dutch context. In this descendants differ from immigrants.[14]

The main reason why the situation is different for descendants is that the society is no longer unfamiliar to them. Descendants born in the Netherlands usually have a pretty accurate idea of what is expected of them in various situations, both by members of immigrant groups and by members of the Dutch community as a whole. Not only can they act as interpreters between the immigrant group and the host society in both a linguistic and a cultural sense, they can also play various roles themselves: roles which respond to the expectations of their immigrant parents and their generation and also their partners in adversity, and roles responding to the expectations of the established host community.

By the same token, by the time an adult second generation of immigrants' children arrives on the scene, born and bred in the Netherlands, society at large has also lost some of its unfamiliarity with the newcomers and their descendants. Attitudes, opinions and behaviour have by that time generally taken shape, in one of two directions. It may be that the host society finds workable compromises which are acceptable to the immigrants and their descendants on a number of points that originally appeared to cause friction. Alternatively, it may be that the parties involved only clarify their points of difference but do not resolve them, resulting in fixed attitudes, accompanied by mutually negative images.

Can we learn anything from the descriptive material in previous chapters about which conditions are likely to lead to the descendants of immigrants being assimilated, and which may lead to their ending up in a minority position?

The discussion of this question which follows must necessarily be tentative and cautious in nature. We are basing our conclusions on limited material from a small geographical area in a prescribed period: up to about 1970, so including the early post-war immigrants. We can generally say very little about the immigrant groups arriving later, because the adult second generation born in the Netherlands is still too small.

If we review the descriptive material, we are drawn to the conclusion that for almost all the immigrant groups who have entered the Netherlands since 1550, an irreversible development towards assimilation started in the second and later generations. That is to say that in more and more instances these second and later generations saw themselves primarily as members of society as a whole, or of a relevant, generalized sub-group of it, rather than as members of a former immigrant group. In certain cases some identifying features may still remain visible for several generations, sometimes for still longer, or even permanently. Examples are particular church congregations or associations oriented towards the culture or folklore of the country of origin. But these cases usually involve making selective use of such institutions: the descendants who join them form a select group and they also have a specific object in joining. Provisionally it would appear that there are two exceptions in Dutch history to this general rule. The first is that of the gypsies. The second is that of the Jews in the Netherlands up to 1796 and during the German occupation of 1940-1945.[15]

What then is the essential difference in the development of the position of immigrants' descendants who were assimilated and these last two groups? This difference can be described very concisely: in both cases there is evidence of systematic discrimination and therefore of position allocation in the negative sense on grounds of membership or alleged membership of a particular group, accompanied by a strong and enduring prejudice on the part of society against the group; at the same time, and often as a reaction to the hostile attitude of society, a powerful group-formation takes place or is continued, accompanied by a strong group-consciousness.

In contrast to the phenomena generally seen in other groups of immigrants, particularly in the first phase immediately after their arrival, in these cases there is 'systematic discrimination'. In the first place this involves a specific distinction, based neither on being a newcomer, nor on the legal status of being an alien, but on some specific criterion for exclusion aimed at that group. In the case of the Jews they were barred until 1796 from certain professions because they were Jews; in other words, members of a Jewish community. Secondly, that specific distinction is inescapable for members of the group. In other words, the specific target group of the artificial distinction is rendered permanently visible in society, for example by giving them segregated housing, or seeking out systematic cultural, religious and even physical characteristics. This visibility can even be physically imposed, as with the obligation during the German occupation to wear a Star of David.

The element of strong and enduring prejudice can be considered primarily as a consequence of systematic discrimination. After all, almost all immigrant groups have suffered from stereotyped images and often rigid prejudices as well, but it did not inevitably lead, apparently, to systematic discrimination. If there is such a thing as a direct link between prejudice and discrimination, it should rather be sought in the other direction. In other words, where the conditions are present for the development or maintenance of systematic discrimination, an appropriate legitimizing prejudice is always available or can be thought up. That is certainly so in the case of newcomers who were previously relatively unknown, and so about whom there is no formulated prejudice available in the cultural heritage of society. It is not impossible, however, that a more independent or stimulating role needs to be given to groups about which there is a long tradition in the community of stereotyping and prejudice, but these can never be sufficient condition for the beginning of systematic discrimination.

That element of group formation, group consciousness and ethnicization can also be illustrated by comparison with the same phenomena among immigrant groups which later appear to have merged into society. As we have demonstrated the basis for group formation is almost always laid in the first phase of an immigrant group's stay, when, as immigrants, they try to strengthen their position in the new society through their own networks and organizations. For their descendants, with their theoretically wider freedom of choice between their own organizations and more general ones to achieve their social objectives, the determining factor is whether they have access to these general organizations and are not systematically barred from them or kept at a disadvantage. If that is not the case, these general organizations and institutions will almost always be more effective. This usually means in the long run that their own organizations are pushed into the background except in those areas where there is no alternative, for instance with cultural or religious activities specifically oriented towards the immigrant group and its descendants.

At the same time this qualifies the concept of 'assimilation'. Assimilation need not be absolute. Rather, it describes a tendency in which descendants have the opportunity – if they so desire – to make use of general provisions. However, if the general organizations, agencies and institutions of the host society appear systematically barred or in many aspects inaccessible to a particular group and its descendants, then this discrimination forces the members of the group to seek solutions within their own ranks and to utilize their own institutions and organizations for the purpose. Society's hostility to the group concerned, which accompanies this discrimination, strengthens the process of group formation, group consciousness, and the closing of ranks. It seems to be a self-perpetuating process.

If it is now clear in essence what happens in a situation of minority-formation, then the next question is as follows: why, for the Jews at certain periods, and to a much greater extent for the gypsies almost without interruption since the sixteenth century, was the settlement process fundamentally different from that of other groups?

No definitive answer can be given to this question. As we have pointed out, the limited material allows no generalizations. Nevertheless, we would like to put forward some thoughts which provide a possible explanation.

We have already stated several times that in Dutch society distinctions have been and are still being made on many and various grounds, and that a single distinctive characteristic, such as being a newcomer or an alien, of itself has rarely been sufficient to survive for long as an identifying mark for a group. More usually a combination of a number of characteristics is involved on the basis of which distinctions can be drawn between individuals and groups. In general therefore the likelihood of a development leading to minority formation probably increases with the number of distinctive characteristics which systematically coincide in a majority of members of a particular group. An example would be a case in which a group simultaneously has a separate religion unfamiliar to the host society, is seen as culturally different, has an anomalous legal status as aliens, can be identified by physical characteristics, and above all occupies a very low social position.

The sum of characteristics in this example may seem remarkable, and suggest that something of this kind inevitably leads to minority formation. That is, however, not the case; if, for example, one considers the pre-war Chinese peanut-sellers, then in Van Heek's description they entirely match the summary just given. If this description is compared with a later study of those self-same Chinese by Vellinga and Wolters in 1966, then they are shown to have become prosperous restaurateurs, most of whom had married

Dutch wives in the mean time, and had acquired a sound position for themselves in Dutch society through their own organizations and through their wives' Dutch networks.[16]

The sum of the distinctive characteristics is not therefore the determining factor. We must supplement this supposition with some consideration of which phenomena in Dutch society in the period under investigation have been and are considered to amount to important differences between groups.

Differences in religious conviction played an important, even a dominant role in the first part of the period covered. They applied not only to differences between various denominations of Protestants, and between Protestants and Catholics, but particularly also between Christians and non-Christians, in this case Jews.[17] Although the Netherlands certainly has to be judged tolerant on this point in comparison with other countries in the same period, the long anti-Jewish tradition of Christianity also played a role amongst the Dutch.[18] This is clear from the position allocation of the Portuguese *conversos* in early seventeenth-century Holland. The first of them to acquire the freedom of the city of Amsterdam did so on the condition that he remained Christian, and at first no synagogues were allowed to be built.

Since the emancipation of the various religious groups this has changed officially. In reality, religion remains a very important criterion for distinction; for while at the top of pillarized Dutch society, freedom of religion has been agreed and is protected, society itself is divided into segments which to an important degree are closed to members of other religions. Only with the growth of secularization after 1960 has the importance of religion declined in the actual distribution of social resources.

Differences in culture, which can conveniently be summarized as the totality of the behaviour, lifestyle, norms and values of a group, have in the course of history demonstrably led to a great many pronouncements of an ethnocentric nature, in which the culture of immigrants and their descendants has been portrayed as inferior, immoral, ignorant, or at best as completely different from that of 'our kind of people'. Often established residents, convinced of their own righteousness, wage war against the evil and dangerous aspects of that foreign imported culture. The Southern Netherlanders from Antwerp had to be cured of their frivolous and immoral culture, just as immigrants currently living in the Netherlands and their descendants, would – according to certain groups of people – do better to relinquish some of their customs, and adapt themselves.

The concept of 'culture' in a wide sense therefore probably takes us no further, because it is too all-embracing and differentiates too little. In many areas a society appears unconcerned about the 'otherness' and different ways of thinking and conduct of certain groups within it; other points apparently touch the core of society, or at least are thought to do so by the established society, and on these points society is hardly ever indifferent. The persecution and extirpation of gypsies, the continual persecution of vagrants and vagabonds, the minority-formation in the space of less than half a century since 1900 among caravan dwellers, all these events could point to a single *cultural paradigm*, consisting of a sedentary life, combined with respect for others' property, and being held responsible for one's actions.

To all appearances the opinions, lifestyle and practices of non-sedentary groups, as perceived by established society (which need not in all cases match the true facts), are seen as a fundamental threat to that society, which reasons that the basic values of the established society are not shared by these groups, and that they do not observe rules which are felt to be essential. A nomadic life is in itself suspect, because an ever-shifting home makes it difficult to maintain certain bourgeois obligations and conventions of social intercourse, and above all to sanction them. If nomadism is further combined with not apparently being useful to society, not having any proper occupation or regular source of income, then the stigma can take on serious proportions.

If the assumption is correct that fundamental differences, or at least what are seen as such by society, offer an inherent explanation for the fact that certain groups are systematically discriminated against, and therefore end up as minorities, then it is also possible to explain why the government almost of necessity plays an important role in such cases. Where differences are concerned which are seen as fundamental, the protection and priority of vested interests is established in law, and where it is not, then new laws will be devised to effect that protection. We have seen the authorities taking such measures against both the Jews and the gypsies. In the case of the Jews, town authorities legalized discrimination by, for instance, officially establishing large numbers of exclusions from occupations in law, and by supervising their implementation. In the seventeenth and eighteenth centuries other government measures with respect to the Jews placed them effectively in a separate position in society, leading to virtual social isolation. In the case of the gypsies the role of the authorities went substantially further; at one time they not only legalized every form of violence against this community, but they actively promoted that violence and the prosecution of gypsies or of anyone who was or could be taken for one.

If the problem outlined here is viewed from a dynamic perspective, then it seems that in the case of the Jews and gypsies there are fundamental prejudices against specific groups, which are therefore hardly the subject of conscious formulation, and which play an independent role in the process of discrimination and minority-formation. If society wishes to resist this, then it must *at least* be aware of these prejudices, as the Dutch government at the time of the Batavian Republic in 1796 was with respect to the Jews, and as some people are now with respect to gypsies and caravan dwellers.

We deliberately write 'at least'. An awareness of prejudice and its consequences, particularly among politicians, and legal emancipation and particularly the will to achieve it, are essential but not in themselves sufficient conditions for reversing the processes of discrimination and the minority-formation. For the Jews a process of reversal from a minority position to a movement for emancipation started in 1796. Although the time when this reversal was achieved can in no way be characterized as one of harsh discrimination when seen in a European context, and although the emancipation was followed up in law and had the enthusiastic participation of most of the group itself, it must nonetheless be admitted that anti-Jewish feelings had not yet died away nearly a century later. Foreign influences, notably the German occupation, made many people realize how Dutch the Jews were, as was demonstrated by the widespread strike in February 1941 against Nazi round-ups in the Jewish quarter of Amsterdam; on the other hand they led others to take part in organized anti-Jewish campaigns. In spite of all this one cannot deny the success of the developments since 1796, and the reversal of discrimination and minority-formation is demonstrably possible, if not easy.

Another example of how long a prejudice can survive is the Dutch attitude to gypsies. Although in 1868 there had been no reports of persons identified as gypsies in the Netherlands for about a century and a half, and although consequently no one by then had any sure idea what kind of people they were dealing with, yet centuries-old prejudices were very quickly revived, especially among the authorities. In spite of the fact that the legal protection of the citizen had been greatly increased in the interim, and criminal law and the administration of punishment had been humanized, in the nineteenth century a negative official policy towards the gypsies was revived and at the same time the victims made every effort to maintain their identity. Our brief comparison with the autochthonous minority group of caravan dwellers is more than sufficient demonstration that these problems are not confined to newcomers and their descendants. The excruciatingly slow pace of liberation from deep-rooted prejudices applies to all groups who are discriminated against, whether indigenous or foreign.

Epilogue

An important reason for writing this book, revising it, and now translating it, is our conviction that by a systematic study of the history of the Netherlands as a host country for immigration, we can shed more light on the current phenomenon of immigration, its associated problems, and the developments to be expected in the future. Not that our empirical knowledge or body of theory have yet reached the stage from which we can predict future events. We are equally incapable of listing the precise conditions which will cause the process of settlement to proceed quickly and smoothly, or will lead to minority-formation. Anyone with such high expectations and who looked to this book for ready-made solutions to the problems of today will be disappointed. However, for anyone who is prepared to stand back a little in looking at both historical and present-day newcomers and their descendants, there are certainly a number of 'lessons' to be drawn. Let us try and take stock of some of the more important conclusions.

One of the most significant is that the vast majority of newcomers entering the Netherlands in the course of the last four hundred years seem to have been absorbed into society after several generations, with or without the retention of some specific identifying features. Not that it was ever a smooth passage: at the arrival of almost every group of any size, opposition developed from within the host society, stereotyped images and prejudices about these immigrants and their descendants had to be overcome, and the group of newcomers was discriminated against, sometimes in law and sometimes not, or at the very least was treated differently by the resident population. The process of absorption of newcomers and their descendants usually took more than one generation born in the Netherlands to be completed. Collective action on a large scale, and certainly action of a violent nature against these people, does not, however, appear to be a feature of Dutch history.

Of course we can make no forecast on the basis of this conclusion about future developments with respect to present-day immigrants and their descendants. However, we should perhaps query some of the expectations and prophecies which are regularly heard these days. Are not the expectations and demands often imposed on present-day immigrants concerning the tempo of their adaptation and assimilation often pitched far too high? And are the problems of adaptation and assimilation therefore not dismissed too quickly as insoluble? If in the past it has appeared to be the rule that from the first generation, meaning the immigrants themselves, we could generally only expect adaptation on a number of practical aspects, then we should have good grounds before assuming that adaptation and assimilation of present-day immigrants will happen any faster now.

The same obviously applies to their descendants. After all, in the past the process of assimilation seems to have taken two or more generations rather than just one. And it is our view, arguing again from the historical perspective, that the prophets of doom who regularly arise to warn society of 'social time-bombs' being set under society by the presence of immigrants, should first demonstrate why the situation and problems now should be so utterly different from those in the past, and why the outcome should be different or, for that matter, more violent. Of course, a regularity observed in the past has no prophetic value. It does, however, place the onus of proof on those who prophesy a completely different development in comparison with the past, to show on what grounds they expect this different outcome.

A second important conclusion is that in at least two cases in Dutch history an immigrant group has had to take a different course. For Jews in the Netherlands up to 1796 this meant occupying a minority position in the strict sense in which we have defined it, followed by a slow and laborious emancipation throughout the nineteenth and the early part of the twentieth century. For the gypsies it meant extirpation and expulsion in the seventeenth and eighteenth centuries, and a minority position imposed in the course of the last hundred years, incidentally together with an indigenous group of caravan dwellers, who share with them a life on wheels.

Two important lessons can be drawn from this second conclusion. The first is that the attitude and behaviour of the authorities, where the position of immigrants and their descendants are concerned, can be of great importance. In the examples quoted of the Jews up to 1796, and of the gypsies, this role was actively discriminatory, and therefore legitimized discrimination by others. The public advertisement of rewards for bringing in gypsies, dead or alive, by local authorities at the time of the gypsy persecution legitimized every form of violence against this category or against those who were taken for them. Fortunately at the present moment this kind of role is not encountered on the part of any European government in its overt form, but it certainly exists more covertly. One should not underestimate the legitimizing effect this has throughout society at large. For instance, the British government, in the interests of the selective admission of *Commonwealth citizens*, has created various categories of Commonwealth immigrants, among which are *patrials*. This category consists of those who in physical appearance are white descendants of colonists, who were born in the colonies. These 'patrials' are now allowed entry into Great Britain, while non-white people who carry similar passports and were born in the same country are not admitted. 'Race' has therefore been introduced here as a distinguishing criterion in legislation and policy, which clearly contributes to legitimizing discriminatory tendencies in society as a whole.

Where opposition to and resentment of the arrival of immigrant groups is regularly seen to come from parts of the host society, the government needs to act as an impartial umpire. It must lay down the norms and make sure that no distinction be made on irrelevant grounds between people living legally in the country. In a democratic welfare state, in which the ideal of equal opportunities is highly valued, special temporary policies may be introduced to eradicate the arrears of those immigrants in clearly disadvantaged situations.

The second lesson we can draw from the two exceptional cases of the Jews and the gypsies is that prejudice against certain groups is apparently very deep-rooted. Whatever the causal relationships between prejudice, discrimination, and segregation of the Jews in the period before 1796, it is clear that from that date the last two were abolished by the government in law, but that this did not mean that all prejudice and discrimination against Jews had vanished from society. Prejudices against gypsies seem to be equally enduring.[1] Even a fairly long period when there were no gypsies, after the attempts to extirpate them and drive them out in the eighteenth century, did not prevent the resurrection of prejudice against them in the late nineteenth century. Quite soon after they started coming back there followed a long period of special rules and measures which were imposed upon them as a 'nomadic' population. We have explained the systematic persecution and extermination of both Jews and gypsies during the Second World War as events which were in the main externally determined, and therefore not the direct consequence of developments occurring in the Netherlands. It must, however, give cause for thought that at such a short distance from the Dutch frontier the two prejudices which were so familiar to the Dutch from their own past could have been revived in such a monstrous form. And in these cases the role of government was not just to legitimize, but also to initiate.

Finally we would like to dwell for a moment on the following. The objection may be raised that although in the past there has been no tradition in the Netherlands of systematic and collective action against newcomers and their descendants, we are now faced with an essentially different situation. Post-war immigration, and particularly that immigration currently perceived in the Netherlands as presenting a problem, involves the entry of people who are directly physically identifiable. This means that, compared with the past, there may now be a 'race problem', which might put a completely different complexion on the settlement process. The supporters of this theory add that there is also in the Netherlands a long tradition of colonialism, of slave trading, and of negative representation of other peoples, particularly of non-Europeans. From this some even draw the conclusion that we should start by assuming an almost innate racist attitude among the white Dutch.

Several arguments can be brought against such an almost deterministic assumption about the significance of 'physical identifiability'. It is our view that the colonial situation should be seen primarily not in terms of race relations, but of power relations. By this reasoning racial attitudes in colonial circumstances are a consequence of power relationships. Moreover, racial attitudes in colonial territories often seem to have had little significance in the mother country itself. Certainly this applies whenever, as in the Dutch situation, those who occupied an inferior position in the colonies hardly ever visited the mother country.

It can easily be demonstrated that stereotyped images existed – and still exist – in the mother country as well. This was also apparent when the Eurasians from Indonesia arrived in the Netherlands. But these stereotyped images were not linked to real people whom one might meet every day; nor were they held in the context of fixed rules, like guidelines on how one should behave towards non-whites. The stereotyped images which existed in the Netherlands were premature judgements rather than prejudices. Outside its colonies the Netherlands has no history of an ideology and practices maintained for generations in which there was an established division of labour between black and white, or within which definite rules existed about the desired social position of each group, as was the case (and to some extent still is) in the southern states of the USA, for example.[2] The physically identifiable groups who came to the Netherlands after the Second World War came as free and equal citizens with the same rights, and into a society which, in contrast to that in the colonies, was not stratified by race. We believe therefore that we must regard this as an 'open' situation.

The most overriding argument against this deterministic reasoning is perhaps the empirical one: the rapid assimilation of the Eurasians into Dutch society. Let there be no misunderstanding of the significance of this statement: many of them had to fight hard to find a place in society; they often had to combat or listen to highly bizarre stereotyping and prejudices; the course of their stay has often been far from easy over the course of some fifty years. Perhaps for those very reasons they are now accepted in Dutch society. That they are physically identifiable is beyond dispute and has perhaps contributed to the fact that they have had to receive and challenge more stereotyping and prejudices than would otherwise have been the case. But it is our considered opinion that physical identifiability has not become an independent factor which works systematically to their disadvantage and to that of their descendants. One could argue that this factor perhaps played less of a role in the case of the Eurasians because they were not only of East Indies extraction but also Dutch or European. In that case this factor would only apply to physically identifiable newcomers who are not of mixed ancestry. But this seems improbable: society as a whole is remarkably bad at making such fine distinctions: a foreigner is easily taken for a Turk, for example, though in fact he may be a Moroccan.

We do not, of course, wish to rule out that physical identifiability might be an important factor, or might become one. This was the case to a limited extent in the past, as it is now; there always seem to be individuals and groups who believe in the existence of inferior and superior kinds of people, and who operate on the basis of this kind of racial delusion. For us, however, the important question is whether the factor of physical identifiability is generally used, or is even starting to be generally accepted throughout society. It does not seem to us to be something which will necessarily happen. Based on an analysis of the past – and that, too, is another lesson from history – we might accept that the probability of this occurring increases if there is a systematic connection between separate characteristics on the grounds of which a distinction has always been made in Dutch society. In other words: if 'colour' systematically coincides – and continues to do so – with a low social position, with a different culture, language and religion, with being an alien, and possibly with yet more characteristics on the basis of which distinctions can be made, then 'colour' might become the co-ordinating symbol of all these characteristics.[3]

The starting position of the first generation of some recent groups of immigrants into the Netherlands, such as Moroccans and Turks for example, is a highly unfavourable one from this point of view. That starting position satisfies all the criteria we have set for a minority situation, except the requirement that this situation be continued from generation to generation. In the coming years the decisive question will be what equal opportunities mean for immigrants' children born in the Netherlands: will their opportunities be equal to those of their parents, or equal to those of any other inhabitant of the Netherlands?

Notes

Notes to the Introduction

1. For a recent overview of decisions and recommendations of the European Union in relation to immigration and the position of immigrants, see Guild/ Niessen 1996.
2. Potts 1990.
3. See Moch 1992; Lucassen/Lucassen 1997.
4. Tilly 1978:68.
5. Lequin 1988; Noiriel 1988; Green 1986.
6. Bade 1987; Herbert 1990; Hoerder 1985.
7. Holmes 1988; Lunn 1985; for an earlier survey, see Cunningham 1897.
8. Morelli 1992; Deslé *et al.* 1993; Caestecker 1993.
9. Only on the Italian immigrants in Luxembourg: Gallo 1987.
10. Lucassen/Penninx 1985 and 1994.
11. For conditions of historical comparison, see Green 1997; for Dutch migration history placed in a European context see Lucassen 1987a, 1994b and 1995b.
12. The most important is Moch 1992; see also Lucassen 1987a; Canny 1994; Cavacciocchi 1994; Engman 1992; Soly/Thijs 1995; and Noiriel 1991.

Notes to Chapter 1

1. This relatively new term was introduced in the report by the Scientific Council for Government Policy, *Allochtonenbeleid,* in 1989. Literally it means 'from a different soil' or 'from another country'.

The term had been used once before, in Verwey-Jonker 1971.
2. For a more exhaustive list of terms used, see the bibliography of ACOM, the Dutch Advisory Committee on Research into Minorities (their review of research into minorities: *Overzicht onderzoek minderheden* 1985). In this book the term 'minority' is used in a specific sense: see Chapter 5.
3. The transitions in terminology and a description of the actual changes can be found in Lucassen *et al.* 1974; Penninx/Van Velzen 1977; Penninx 1979; Van Amersfoort/Penninx 1993.
4. Surveys: Jackson 1968; Böhning 1984; Koot/Van der Wiel 1982; Penninx/Selier 1992; Vermeulen/Böcker 1992.
5. It should incidentally be mentioned that the use of the terms in statistics, e.g. by the CBS (Central Bureau of Statistics) is different and narrower. They only indicate whether people are entering the country or leaving it. In international specialist literature the number of variations on 'migrant' is even greater than it is in the Netherlands; see Bovenkerk 1974.
6. In 1990, for example, 5,731 children were born in the Netherlands with Turkish nationality (Roelandt *et al.* 1993:22). Of the group of 'Turks in the Netherlands', defined as all individuals with Turkish nationality (203,000 on 1 January 1994), 64,000 were born in the Netherlands, or 32 per cent.
7. Calculation from MS table 18 in the *Jaarwerk van de Buitenlandse Migratie* 1984.
8. Elich/Blauw 1981:14; Elich 1987.
9. See e.g. Swart 1978; Leenders 1993; Heijs 1995.

10. This last figure is the average annual total for the period 1989 to 1994: a total of nearly 200,000 naturalizations. For a detailed account of the post-war migrations and the composition of immigrant populations, see Penninx *et al.* 1993.
11. For a more comprehensive discussion, see Penninx 1984:8ff.
12. Penninx 1979:127ff.; Groenendijk 1989 and 1992a and b.
13. Baker 1983.
14. Cf. Zolberg 1981, 1989; Zolberg *et al.* 1989; Freeman 1986.
15. Detailed data on foreign migration are published annually by the Dutch Central Bureau of Statistics (CBS) in *Statistiek van de Buitenlandse Migratie*. Each year until 1987 the CBS also published *Niet-Nederlanders in Nederland 1 januari 19 ...* From 1987 the CBS with the ISEO has published *Minderheden in Nederland, statistisch vademecum* annually. The data in this paragraph are derived from *Maandstatistiek van de Bevolking* (CBS) (1994), no. 3; and Muus 1996.

Notes to Chapter 2

1. For recent literature on the Golden Age see Van Zanden 1993; Davids/Noordegraaf 1993; Israel 1994/5; Davids/Lucassen 1995.
2. See the literature in note 1, also especially Noordegraaf 1985; for the regional split and the consequences of this for migration and migrant labour, see also Lucassen 1984:159ff.
3. Noordegraaf 1985:145ff; Van Zanden 1985:378-383; see especially Noordegraaf/Van Zanden 1995.
4. Griffiths/Van Zanden 1989.
5. Lucassen 1991a and 1994b. In this respect the Netherlands differed from most of the countries which experienced strong economic growth before the nineteenth century: see Lucassen 1995.
6. For Locke, see Kossmann 1984; for another view of Descartes' stay in the Netherlands, see Galard 1985.
7. Paine 1791: 78; cf. Kossmann 1984:8 (a first Dutch translation had already appeared in 1791 in Rotterdam). For the historiography of toleration see also Mijnhardt 1983:165-168 and Gijswijt-Hofstra 1989, especially 13-24.

8. Kossmann 1978:277ff; Rogier 1956, especially 75-76 on the wording of the papal bull. See also Van de Sande 1989:103-105.
9. Lijphart 1968; for the historiography of pillarization see Ten Have 1983, and various articles in Luykx/Bootsma 1987.
10. This was planned for the Community of the Twelve for 1 January 1993, but put into effect somewhat later; within the Benelux the frontiers had in practice already been abolished much earlier.
11. McNeill 1985. This racist thinking was still to be found in Chorus 1964; for the lack of scientific validity for the concept of 'race', see Van Arkel 1984:438-439. In Dutch history of the Middle Ages and the sixteenth century no general survey exists of the history of migration. For the incidental examples listed here see for Dravants: Van Kappen 1965:212-221; for Balts: *ibid.*, 110-116; for Jews before the seventeenth century: Gans 1971:8-15; for gypsies: L. Lucassen 1990:21-27.
12. Briels 1976, 1978, 1985 and 1987; Daelemans 1975: 165-168; Tanja 1987; Koopmans 1991.
13. Bots *et al.* 1985; Berkvens-Stevelinck 1985; Bakker 1985; Bots *et al.* 1986; Buning *et al.* 1987; Cruson 1987 and 1990.
14. This in fact far more complex story is set out briefly and clearly by Salomon 1975; see also Gans 1971:15-28; Kistemaker/Levie 1987; Fuks-Mansfeld 1989; Israel 1989; and Huussen 1989.
15. In this difficult material we expressly follow Salomon's interpretation (1975), who points out, for example, that relatives of this group and others with a similar background who ended up in Antwerp, stayed Catholic. In this way a Jewish 'Portuguese Nation' in Amsterdam and a Catholic one in Antwerp existed a short distance from each other, in many cases descended from the same ancestry.
16. According to Jansen 1979 economic considerations and eschatological expectations also played a part.
17. Schöffer 1981; Gans 1971.
18. Zilverberg 1980.
19. Fafié 1981.
20. For the Belgians: Von der Dunk 1979:46-48; Van den Heuvel-Strasser 1986; Van Hees 1987; Bossenbroek/Kruishoop 1988; Leenders 1993. For Jewish refugees in the late nineteenth and early twentieth centuries see Hofmeester 1990:15-18;

Lucassen 1994a. For the Hungarians and the Russians: Verwey-Jonker/Brackel 1957:2.

21. De Jong 1969:492ff; Verwey-Jonker/Brackel 1957:2-3; Weijdeveld 1986; Berghuis 1990; Lucassen 1994a.

22. For artists, see especially Dittrich/Würzner 1982; also see previous note.

23. Van der Wal 1979. The most important sources on the repatriation and reception of newcomers from Indonesia are: Kraak *et al.* 1957; Surie 1971; Cottaar/Willems 1984 and 1985. See also Willems 1990, 1991 and 1992; Poeze *et al.* 1986; Ellemers/Vaillant 1987; Willems/Lucassen 1994.

24. Ringeling 1978.

25. Kraak *et al.* 1957. There are no known accurate data on this. Surie 1971:97 mentions that 17,840 of the repatriates are thought to have migrated on to the United States. Equally, for a long time little was known about numbers of immigrants from Indonesia and their descendants. From 1 January 1990, based on data in the Dutch population registers, it has been possible to count the number of people of 'Indonesian origin', in other words, persons with Indonesian nationality and/or born in Indonesia, plus persons with at least one parent meeting either of these criteria. On 1 January 1990 they apparently totalled 473,000. About 40% of them were born in Indonesia; this includes the Moluccans: see Beets/ Koesoebjono 1991.

26. Ambonezen 1959; Van Amersfoort 1971; Penninx 1979; Manuhutu 1987; Bartels 1990; Manuhutu/ Smeets 1991; Smeets 1992; Steijlen 1996.

27. Chauvel 1990:39-48 and 396-397; Bossenbroek 1992:252-253.

28. The Dutch policy, which aimed at controlling migration from Surinam by means of granting independence rapidly, appears to have had the opposite effect; see Van Amersfoort/Penninx 1993 and 1994; Oostindië/Maduro 1986.

29. According to a wide definition: all persons with Surinamese nationality and/or born in Surinam, plus persons with at least one parent born in Surinam; Tas 1994; Van der Heijdt 1995: 19.

30. Until 1986 it was simply the Netherlands Antilles. In that year Aruba, one of the six Antillean islands, gained an autonomous status within the Antilles; hence 'The Netherlands Antilles *and* Aruba' since 1986.

31. The definition employed here is: persons born in the Netherlands Antilles or with a mother born there; see Tas 1994:8. The total population of the Netherlands Antilles islands at that time was estimated at 290,000; see Penninx *et al.* 1993:15.

32. Verwey-Jonker/Brackel 1957:2ff.

33. Hungarians: Kijlstra 1960:231 gives a total of 2,849 individuals who arrived in the Netherlands in November/December 1956. Elsewhere (p. 235) he speaks of 'over 3,000 Hungarian refugees'. See also Ten Doesschate 1985 and Kuyer 1963. Ten Doesschate 1993:42 mentions the figure 3,300. See also Kövi 1987. Czechs: based on various sources Ten Doesschate 1993:49 arrives at an estimate of 900 Czech asylum seekers; Poles: Ten Doesschate 1993:134 calculates that in 1981 and 1982 a total of about 250 Poles were granted asylum. Later on larger numbers arrived.

34. Ugandans: Ten Doesschate 1993:72; Chileans: Ten Doesschate 1993:87; Portuguese: Ten Doesschate 1993:64 (in all 584 requests for asylum were received from Portuguese for the period 1968 to 1973 inclusive).

35. This difference with the period after 1975 is also reflected in the policy. Ten Doesschate 1993:32 suggests that up to 1975 the objectives of the policy were primarily directed towards other flows of migrants, such as those of the guest workers and the Surinamese. There was still no regular liaison between the Ministry of Justice and the Dutch Lower House of Parliament about refugees, and questions by members were then often still concerned with individual cases.

36. Rogers 1992 calculated that in the early 1990s there were some 16 million refugees (designated as such by the US Committee for Refugees) and that in addition nearly 4 million lived in 'refugee-like situations'. See also Brink/Pasariboe 1993.

37. 2,500 of them acquired B-status, or in other words, no asylum in the proper sense (A-status) was granted, but they still required a residence permit because there were 'convincing reasons of a humanitarian nature' against return to their country of origin. 700 requests for asylum were refused; see Ten Doesschate 1993:113.

38. The high figures in the table for invited refugees in the years 1979-1983 refer in almost all cases to Vietnamese; see Gooszen 1988:9.

39. These were people who were invited to come to the Netherlands by the Dutch government, for example, at the request of the UN High Commissioner for Refugees. They were by definition recognized refugees.

40. *Asylum seekers* are those who have entered the Netherlands without a previously obtained right of residence and who have submitted an application to be recognized as a refugee. They can stay as long as their application is being dealt with. If the application is approved, then they become recognized *refugees* and are given a residence permit: A-status refugees according to the Geneva Convention, and B-status refugees admitted on humanitarian grounds. If their application is rejected, then they must leave the Netherlands or will be expelled. If this does not happen, they become *illegal immigrants*. Many asylum seekers fail to acquire the official A or B-status of refugee, but the danger to them if returned to their country of origin is thought to be too great; since 1994 they have been able to acquire a temporary and conditional residence permit: they may stay in the Netherlands until the situation in their country of origin is considered to be safe.

41. Gooszen (1988:6ff) estimated the number of refugees and asylum seekers who had entered the Netherlands between 1977 and 1 January 1986, and were officially admitted, at more than 26,000. Muus (1992) also includes in his count the invited refugees and recognized asylum seekers for 1987-1990, and comes to nearly 33,000 by 1 January 1991. This does not, however, include refugees from before 1977, nor those officially admitted in 1991-1994 (49,000).

42. Black domestic servants: Preedy 1984:16ff; German domestic servants: Meulenbroek 1982; Henkes 1993 and 1995. The first study of the history of domestic servants during the Republic based on primary sources is a still unpublished dissertation by Mary Carlson of the University of Dayton, Ohio ('Domestic service in a changing city economy: Rotterdam 1680-1780'). See also Kloek *et al.* 1994.

43. Bruijn/Lucassen 1980; Lucassen 1991a; on foreign soldiers in the Dutch army, the most recent literature is Zwitser 1991; for the Dutch East Indies army, see Bossenbroek 1992.

44. For Armenians: Bekius/Ultee 1985; Curtin 1984:179-206 and 270-272. For Hamburgers: Van

Eeghen 1974:10-11. For the English and Scots: Klein 1984 and Doormont/Vroom 1985. For Italians: Heering 1985 and 1991.

45. Hall 1953:27 and 31.

46. Lucassen 1987b; since then there have been publications on migratory labour from Germany to the Netherlands: see various contributions to Eiynck 1993.

47. Brassé/Van Schelven 1980; Kreukels 1987.

48. Penninx/Van Velzen 1977. For general descriptions see Wentholt 1967; Verwey-Jonker 1971; Marshall 1973; Heijke 1979 and 1986; Penninx 1979; Van Amersfoort/Penninx 1993; Tinnemans 1994.

49. For the Moroccan migrants this approach has been taken from the point of view of households in De Mas 1990 and 1991. For the Turks, Böcker 1994 offers excellent material.

50. Hart 1976; Lucassen 1991a and 1994b.

51. Hart 1976; Noordegraaf 1984; Bruijn/Van Eyck van Heslinga 1984; Nusteling 1985.

52. Satisfactory calculations have been made for the migration balances in the nineteenth century; see Oomens 1989.

53. Meulenbroek 1982; Bovenkerk *et al.* 1983; Van Heek 1936; Dekkers 1981; Benton/Vermeulen 1987; Wubben 1986; Zeven 1987.

54. Penninx 1984; Muus/Penninx 1991.

55. Abadan-Unat *et al.* 1976; Koelstra/Tieleman 1977; Heinemeijer *et al.* 1976; Haffmans/De Mas 1985.

56. Van den Berg-Eldering 1978; Muus *et al.* 1983.

57. De Beer *et al.* 1991; Muus/Penninx 1991.

58. See *Maandstatistiek van de Bevolking (CBS)* (June 1995).

59. Here the wide definition has again been used, based on nationality and/or country of birth, as well as the country of birth of one of the parents. See *Maandstatistiek van de Bevolking (CBS)* (March 1994), 34-37.

60. See Voets/Schoorl 1988.

Notes to Chapter 3

1. For a survey of migration theories see Penninx/Selier 1992; an outstanding recent work on refugees is that by Zolberg *et al.* 1989. The best platform for migration studies, theory, and

methodology is the *International Migration Review*, published by the Center for Migration Studies in New York.

2. Kuyer 1963.

3. Gooszen 1988. The recent survey by Hulshof *et al.* 1992 of 677 asylum seekers of five nationalities confirms selection by sex (many single men), age and education. By far the highest proportion also appear to come from urban areas. See also Brink/Pasariboe 1993.

4. Kuyer 1963.

5. Gwynn 1985:23-24.

6. Cruson 1985:230.

7. Ten Doesschate 1985 and 1993 shows in his analysis of admission policy for Hungarian refugees and of refugees in the period 1968-1972 that economic interests play an important role in official and political considerations.

8. For the South-African situation this means, for example, that potentially people of Dutch nationality can migrate freely to the Netherlands.

9. The Federal Republic of Germany has stretched this claim of belonging to 'the German nation' so far that *Aussiedler*, who in many cases had migrated to the east many generations ago, are free to return to the fatherland. There is no longer any question of legal nationality here, but only of descent.

10. Regarding the Moluccans, this is little known and perhaps least expected. Yet in the period 1951-1984 more than two thousand Moluccans returned home for good. Information on Moluccans from the Moluccan Department of the Ministry of Welfare, Health and Cultural Affairs; on Hungarians, Kuyer 1963. Immigrants sometimes harbour the hope over a long period that they will eventually return to their country of origin: for the example of the Huguenots, see Van Deijk 1989:70ff.

11. Annink 1994; Rijkschroeff 1989.

12. For a survey, see Penninx/Selier 1992. For an early version of a push-pull theory see Lee in Jackson 1968.

13. Two different theoretical trends can be distinguished within this generally formulated framework: the 'equilibrium theory' in Termote 1969, based on liberal-capitalist ideas, and the Marxist-oriented 'historical-structural theories'. The former sees migration as leading to a new balance of the factors of production in both the country of origin and the host country. In the second, migration is rather the consequence of structural economic inequality, and moreover reinforces it. See Penninx/Selier 1992:11ff.

14. Brassé/Van Schelven 1980:209.

15. One example of this is the short-lived economic recession in Western Europe of 1966-1967. Kayser 1972 calculated that within a short period about a third of the 'guest workers' then in Europe returned home: 400,000 of them!

16. Muus *et al.* 1983: Chapter 4; Muus 1986. See also Freeman 1986.

17. See Muus *et al.* 1983; Muus 1986; Van Praag/Frijling 1987; Kubat 1984; Meyer 1987.

18. The data on Turks, Moroccans and Spaniards are based on Statistiek 1981:19-21; those on Dutch emigrants on Elich/Blauw 1981:44 (in the figures for return migration by Dutch emigrants, those emigrating again are counted as return migrants, in order to increase comparability with the CBS figures for foreign workers).

19. Kraak *et al.* 1958:368.

20. See surveys, collected in Muus *et al.* 1983: Chapter 4.

21. See Bovenkerk 1973 and 1978b; Bovenkerk/Verschoor 1983.

22. Elich/Blauw 1981:90.

23. The total number of naturalizations rose from 62,000 in the period 1980-1984 to 132,000 in 1985-1989. In 1991 alone, 29,000 people acquired Dutch nationality; this annual total rose to 49,000 in 1994. In 1994 nearly 24,000 Turks acquired Dutch nationality and around 8,000 Moroccans. See Penninx *et al.* 1993:87; Van den Bedem 1993:12; *Maandstatistiek van de Bevolking* (CBS) (Feb. 1996):43.

24. This always applied to Antilleans and Arubans; it goes a long way towards explaining why the pattern of their migration is different from that of 'foreign' migrants in the Netherlands.

25. Van Geuns 1853:171ff.; for the following see also Leenders 1993:19-27.

26. In this period there is evidence of a pure *jus soli* (a territorial right), which derived citizenship from the place of birth. Later, in the nation-state, the *jus sanguinis* (blood right) was to become dominant: descent (the nationality of the parents) then became decisive, regardless of the place of birth.

27. De Jongste 1985:91-92; Van Geuns 1853:282 (located there in 1722).
28. Van Geuns 1853:258ff.
29. *Ibid.*:269-270.
30. *Ibid.*:282.
31. Prins 1980.
32. Swart 1978; Heijs 1995.
33. Swart 1978:23.
34. Van Geuns 1853:201 (the quotation); for the following see *ibid.*:198ff. and 208-209.
35. For the following: Briels 1978:23ff; Van Geuns 1853:292-294 and V-VI; Swart 1978:24.
36. Cruson 1985; Van Geuns 1853:177ff.; see also the literature cited in note 13 of Chapter 2.
37. For the Constitutions of 1798 and 1815, see Van Geuns 1853:292-294 and V-VI; Swart 1978:24; for the following see also Leenders 1993 and L. Lucassen 1990:31-34.
38. For 1848 and the Aliens Act of 1849: Kossmann 1978:192f.; Giele 1968; Swart 1978:10 (note 54).
39. Swart 1978:11; L. Lucassen 1990:33 shows that the 1849 Aliens Act worked better than Swart believed.
40. For England under the influence of the great immigration of East-European Jews between about 1880 and 1910, see Garrard 1971 and Holmes 1978; cf. also Gans 1971:606.
41. Swart 1978; Leenders 1993; L. Lucassen 1990.
42. The following is based on De Jong 1969:492ff.; see also Weijdeveld 1986 and Berghuis 1990.
43. For persecution of the gypsies, see L. Lucassen 1990:210-225; see also Chapter 6 below.
44. Böhning 1984:29-46.
45. In the period up to 1968 official immigration regulations played an insignificant role. In practice labour migrants were actively recruited through a system set up and supervised by the government, trade unions and employers, but in addition substantial numbers came as 'spontaneous labour migrants', who could regularize their position quite simply once they had found work. See Wentholt 1987:189f. and Van der Staaij 1973:197f. In this period it was thought that the market was the 'regulator', and that interference by an official immigration policy was not necessary. The economic recession of 1967 disrupted this idyll; in a short period many certainly went home (the number of work permits fell from 46,000 in 1966 to 39,000 in 1967), but at the same time it became clear that as unemployment in the Netherlands rose, the majority of the labour migrants were still needed, and that they were staying.
Labour migration had turned out not to be particularly temporary, and moreover has appeared only to be controllable to a limited extent. This last experience led to changes in the legislation and regulations, creating a battery of instruments intended to bring this labour migration, assumed to be temporary, under control again. They were put into effect from 1968: an authorization for temporary residence (MVV) before arriving in the Netherlands, obtained from a representative of the Netherlands in the country of origin, became a requirement. In fact the battery was only effectively deployed after the first oil crisis of 1973; from that time no more authorizations for temporary residence were granted to labour migrants by the Dutch representatives in the countries of origin, and the phenomenon of 'guest workers' came to an end. See also Tinnemans 1994.
46. 'Family reunion' and 'family formation' have in fact developed, via jurisprudence in the Netherlands, from being a privilege to being a right (Swart 1978). This does not, of course, mean that no obstacles can be imposed in their implementation. Thus the requirement for adequate housing before the family arrives, combined with restricted access to the housing list, ensured long delays in the 1970s before many could bring over their families. But the authorities also tried to influence the extent of family reunion in other ways. Lowering the age of majority from twenty-one to eighteen, for instance, officially had a restrictive effect on family reunion in the Netherlands. Restrictive measures were also applied to family formation, such as the '1445 guilders regulation' of 1983, the aim of which was to make it impossible for young people earning less than that amount per month to form families. The regulation was only in force for a short time and its effect is debatable (see Aalberts 1985 and Zijlstra 1988). In 1992 political discussion about new restrictive measures for this form of migration began again in the context of general discussion of the 1993 budget. The Christian Democrats and the Liberals demanded restrictive measures. This led to new instructions being issued on entry permits concerning family formation in September 1993.
47. See Willems/Lucassen 1990.

48. Penninx/Muus 1989.
49. Groenendijk 1989 and 1992a and b.
50. In 1985 the Schengen Accord was agreed between the Federal Republic of Germany, France, Belgium, the Netherlands and Luxembourg. This accord provided for the removal of internal frontiers between the countries party to the agreement. To achieve this, however, a common policy on admission at the external frontiers had to be put into effect.
51. Groenendijk 1989:99.
52. One of the most controversial elements of the Bill for the amendment of the Aliens Act discussed in the Dutch Lower House in September 1993, and passed, was the abolition of the opportunity for asylum seekers to appeal against a negative decision.
53. Kraak 1958:369.
54. Ringeling 1978:84.
55. Van Amersfoort 1987:481; Van Amersfoort/Penninx 1994.
56. Van Amersfoort 1987; Van Amersfoort/Penninx 1994; Van Amersfoort/Surie 1987.

Notes to Chapter 4

1. In this chapter on the Netherlands it is not possible to cite all the relevant literature on the features of Dutch society over the past centuries. We refer the reader to the generally available body of historical literature. Notes are only therefore included in a few specific cases.
2. Van Geuns 1853:245, 252, 274.
3. For the position of various religious minorities in the Republic, see the articles by Zijlstra, Bergsma, Van de Sande and Huusen in Gijswijt-Hofstra 1989.
4. For the franchise see note 37, Chapter 3; also De Vries 1971 and Blok/De Meere 1978.
5. In the 1887 revision of the Constitution it was recognized that in addition to 'social prosperity', other 'tokens of suitability' could qualify someone for entry on the electoral roll. Previously the criteria had been salary, rent, savings, tax, or academic qualifications.
6. Lucassen/Trienekens 1978.
7. Kent/Hekman 1989; Van der Meer 1984, 1989 and 1995.

8. For the discussion on social disturbances and class struggle in the Netherlands see Dekker 1990 and Lucassen 1991b, 1995a and 1995b, and the literature cited there.
9. Lucassen/Trienekens 1978:253.
10. See p. 26.
11. Van Ruller/Ippel 1984.
12. For persecution of gypsies see below, p. 132 ff.; for persecution of homosexuals, see the literature cited in note 7 above (in 1730-32 there were no fewer than seventy death sentences handed down in the Republic (Van der Meer 1984:8)). In this connection n.b. also witch hunts, limited in the Netherlands mainly to the sixteenth century.

Notes to Chapter 5

1. Penninx 1988a:49; see also Penninx *et al.* 1993:104.
2. *Ibid.*:105 defines the ethno-cultural position as 'the extent to which a group is regarded primarily as a different group by the majority of society, and/or the extent to which the group regards itself primarily as such'. See also Penninx 1988a:51.
3. The term refers here only to a specific situation or result, and not to the process leading up to it; see Borrie 1959:58ff.
4. Van Amersfoort 1982; originally published in Dutch in 1974.
5. Ethnic minorities 1979; Advies 1979.
6. This is a paraphrase of Van Amersfoort 1974 and Advies 1979. Penninx 1988a:48 places the emphasis slightly differently in his definition, but in principle bases it on this specific definition of a minority: 'A minority is a group the members of which have for generations given membership of that group priority over other social distinctions, or a group regarded by society, or large sections of it, primarily as a separate group, most of the members of which continually occupy a low social position and who, because of that, coupled with their position as a minority in numerical terms, can exercise little power and influence in society.'
7. Van Amersfoort 1974.
8. Brassé *et al.* 1984. Recent research on the position of the second generation shows an ambivalent position: a distinct improvement of educational

level compared to their parents, but lagging behind their Dutch contemporaries. Their position on the labour market is weak: see Veenman 1994; Vermeulen/Penninx 1994.

9. See Smeets and Veenman in: Vermeulen/Penninx 1994:15-44; see also Steijlen 1996.

10. For a bibliographical summary on caravan dwellers and gypsies, see Hovens/Hovens 1982; for a recent survey, see Cottaar *et al.* 1990. The genesis of this special group in the Netherlands has been analysed in Cottaar 1996.

11. For an account of the minorities policy and its target groups, see the second section of Chapter 6.

12. Definition from Bovenkerk 1978a.

13. Definition from Bovenkerk 1978a.

14. The definition of these terms is taken from L. Lucassen 1990.

15. For a decade or more these concepts have also been used in the Dutch literature on immigrants and their descendants: see Roosens 1982, 1986, 1989; Vermeulen 1984; Tennekes 1990; and Sansone 1992. It marks a reversal of thinking in this field of study about the settlement process of immigrants and their descendants: whereas previously it was particularly centred on the concept of culture and the associated concepts of assimilation and adaptation, in taking a new approach based on the concepts of ethnicity and ethnic movements, it concentrated primarily on subjective location, the criterion being the degree to which people regard themselves as a separate group, and are seen as a separate group by others.

16. See, *inter alia*, Roosens 1982, 1986, 1989.

17. For a systematic examination of the various types of ethnic movement and their relations with nationalism, see Van Amersfoort 1991.

18. Roosens 1982:101ff.

Notes to Chapter 6

1. The most important surveys for the post-war period are: Verwey-Jonker 1971 (1973); Van Amersfoort 1974; Penninx 1979; Entzinger 1984; Van Praag 1986; Penninx 1988a; Allochtonenbeleid 1989; Penninx *et al.* 1993; and Tesser 1993. The most important bibliographies for this period are: Lucassen *et al.* 1974; Ellemers/Vermeulen 1979;

Overzicht 1985; Koulen/Smit 1988; Penninx 1988a; Onderzoek 1989; Onderzoek 1992; Veenman 1994; Vermeulen/Penninx 1994; Roelandt 1994; Penninx *et al.* 1995; Roetman/Van der Tuin-Noordermeer 1996.

2. Faber 1983:235-246.

3. For what follows, see in general Van Geuns 1853:210-241. For recent developments in the study of guilds in the Netherlands, see Prak 1992 and Lucassen 1992.

4. Van Geuns 1853:257.

5. Lourens/Lucassen 1987:38-41.

6. Lucassen 1984:25, 174-175.

7. Van Heek 1936.

8. Van Geuns 1853:292.

9. Cf. Swart 1978:20 and Handboek 1984-, (section Snelle berichtgeving 1985 no 2). In 1986 aliens were once again able to take part in local elections.

10. Reisepredigt, reports by Ludwig Meyeringh 1865 and Gustav Fischer 1869. See also L. Lucassen 1987b.

11. Lucassen 1984:60. For the farces involving Germans see L. Lucassen 1987 and the much less detailed Mertens-Westphalen 1993; for the Amsterdam theatre audience see Ruitenbeek 1993.

12. Van Maurik 1901:15, 65.

13. Hart 1976:132, 180-181; Diederiks (1982:76-85) finds, however, for Amsterdam from 1801 to 1806 that marriage to foreigners was not attractive to the young daughters of citizens, though it was to Amsterdam widows. This would fit in with Hart's comment (1976:132) that the purchase of *poorterschap* increased very strongly between 1776 and 1785 (implying that the opportunity of obtaining it by marriage had diminished considerably). Hart's conclusion, 'The migrants/bridegrooms appear to have had a preference for brides born in Amsterdam', therefore seems to apply less to the period after 1750 (a time when immigration to Amsterdam also seems to have been less then previously).

14. Briels 1978:66 and 79 (bearing in mind that here 'inferior' always means 'simple'). See also Briels 1985.

15. For what follows: Van Maurik 1901:15-67; Ornée 1970 (quote from 1760, p. 12); Reisepredigt, Report Lenhartz 1863; cf. also *Woordenboek der Nederlandse Taal* IX, 1913:990-994, where under *Mof, Hasenkopf*

is also listed as a German term of abuse for the Dutch.

16. Lucassen 1984:211ff.; *Woordenboek der Nederlandse Taal* IX, 1913:990-994.

17. Dekker 1982 (on the participation of foreigners in disturbances, see for example the places of origin listed on pp. 179-188).

18. For anti-gypsy campaigns see p. 132 ff.; for those against homosexuals see Van der Meer 1984 and 1989.

19. Frijhoff 1977; Post 1964.

20. Quoted in Frijhoff 1977:179-180.

21. Wagenaar 1903.

22. De Bruin 1970.

23. Reisepredigt, Report Ludwig Meyeringh 1865; extreme in comparison with average relations: Lucassen 1984:65-71 and Lucassen 1987b.

24. Lucassen 1984:83-90.

25. Faber 1983:246-253.

26. Gans 1971:28.

27. Van Geuns 1853:252 and 245.

28. The standard work on the history of the gypsies in the Netherlands is L. Lucassen 1990, with a discussion of and references to earlier literature, including Van Kappen 1965.

29. Beune/Hessels 1983.

30. Groenendijk 1979.

31. For what follows, see L. Lucassen 1990.

32. L. Lucassen 1990; see also Sijes 1979.

33. Briels 1978:55, 88.

34. Briels 1978:88 ('After 1619 and the next few turbulent years').

35. Berkvens-Stevelinck 1985:33-40.

36. Driessen 1911, bibliography, 1:3-4, 13-14; cf. also Briels 1978:88 and Briels 1985:172-173; J. Lucassen 1992.

37. Bots *et al.* 1985:50 and 121; Berkvens-Stevelinck 1985:40. It is also striking that in the seventeenth and eighteenth centuries ethnic minorities arranged their own mutual insurance: see J. Lucassen 1991b:29.

38. *Inter alia* Von Tschudi 1932.

39. Brassé/Van Schelven 1980.

40. For what follows see J. Lucassen 1994a.

41. For the character of the Jewish quarter in Amsterdam, with a comparison with the Venetian ghetto, see Cohen 1990 and Kistemaker/Levie 1987.

42. Gans 1971:147.

43. Van Cleef-Hiegentlich 1985; Gans 1971:273ff.; note that the assimilation of the Jews in the Netherlands before 1940 was not accompanied by much interest in Zionism. Pre-war Zionism obtained little support in the Netherlands; see Giebels 1975. For a differing view of the significance of Dutch Zionism, see Michman 1989:21.

44. Boon-De Gouw 1984; for anti-Semitism in the Netherlands, see Josephus Jitta-Geertsma/Sanders 1983 and also Faber 1983:250-253 and Gans 1971, e.g. 378-379, 404, 493, 554 and 595-599.

45. For anti-Jewish utterances in the Netherlands in the twentieth century, see Josephus Jitta-Geertsma/Sanders 1983 and Gans 1971:595-599. For a recent review of Catholic anti-Semitism in the Netherlands, see Ramakers 1990.

46. There is now an extensive literature on pre-war right-wing radicalism in the Netherlands. The standard work is De Jonge 1968; for the Black Front and the National Front see Schippers 1986.

47. L. Lucassen 1990:41-42.

48. The history of the gypsies in the Netherlands and neighbouring countries shows that they were in general economically reasonably successful, and that therefore no arguments could be drawn from this to justify the hostile attitude to them; see L. Lucassen 1990 and L. Lucassen 1993.

49. Kommers 1993.

50. Cottaar *et al.* 1990; and Cottaar 1996.

51. The 1970 Policy Statement on foreign workers (Nota Buitenlandse Werknemers, Handelingen Tweede Kamer 1969-1970:10504 p. 9) proposes, for example: 'Finally it should not be forgotten that the demographic situation in the Netherlands is not such as to give any reason to promote immigration, as is done in some other countries. With all sympathy for the human aspects, no other conclusion can be reached than that our country has a need for labour from other countries, but not of new family settlement from abroad.'

52. Van Amersfoort 1983 gives an anecdotal illustration of this: when in 1971 an essay collection about immigrants in the Netherlands, commissioned by the Ministry of Culture, Recreation and Social Affairs, was delivered in manuscript, the Ministry objected to the term 'immigrant' in the title. The collection was later published under the title

Allochtonen in Nederland (Allochthons in the Netherlands). See Verwey-Jonker 1971 and 1973.

53. Van Amersfoort 1974; Surie 1971; Rijsdijk 1985; Willems/Lucassen 1994.

54. Ambonezen 1959.

55. Kraak *et al.* 1958:140-141.

56. Kraak *et al.* 1958:140-141. See also Boon/Van Geleu-ken 1993.

57. For a review of the way in which the first Italian workers were regarded in the Twente textile industry, see Groenendijk 1990.

58. For a survey of references to confrontations of this kind see Groenendijk 1990:55. For a survey with regard to Moluccan youth see Penninx 1979:25ff.

59. This does not mean that there was originally no resistance to the entry of these immigrants either to the Netherlands or to the labour market. The trade union movement in most cases showed reserve, if not actively opposing the arrival and the admission to the labour market of these immigrants.

60. Verwey-Jonker 1971:241ff.

61. See also Gerepatrieerdenvraagstuk 1956; Cottaar/Willems 1984.

62. The only large-scale research is that of the ISONEVO; see Kraak *et al.* 1958. Ex 1966 also contains a small survey among forty families, three years after their arrival; the rest is silence.

63. Surie 1971; Bagley 1973; Van Amersfoort 1974; Rijsdijk 1985.

64. Ellemers/Vaillant 1985 and 1987; Willems/Lucassen 1994.

65. Willems 1990; 1991; 1992; Willems/Lucassen 1994; Willems/De Moor 1995.

66. Filet 1984. Most Eurasians had after all been pressed into forced labour in the Second World War by the Japanese or interned in prison camps.

67. Vriezen 1993.

68. Tinnemans 1991; Lindo/Pennings 1992; Lindo 1996.

69. Van Amersfoort 1974:205. See also Van Amersfoort 1971:67-70; Bartels 1986 and 1990; Steijlen 1996.

70. See also Köbben 1979.

71. Bartels 1986:38. See also Bartels 1989 and Steijlen 1996.

72. Veenman 1990.

73. Problematiek 1978.

74. Muus *et al.* 1983.

75. Haffmans/De Mas 1985.

76. Entzinger used this phrase as early as 1975:327.

77. Entzinger 1975; Penninx 1979; Lucassen/Köbben 1992.

78. Bovenkerk 1973, 1978b; Muus *et al.* 1983; Van Amersfoort/Surie 1987.

79. Penninx 1979:122-126; Groenendijk 1979 and 1981.

80. Entzinger 1984:67.

81. Groenendijk 1981; Van Amersfoort/Surie 1987.

82. Problematiek 1978.

83. Ethnic Minorities 1979; Regeringsreactie 1980; Ontwerp-Minderhedennota 1981; Minderhedennota 1983.

84. To wit: Italy, Spain, Portugal, Greece, Yugoslavia, Turkey, Morocco and Tunisia. Cape Verde was added after it gained its independence from the Portuguese.

85. The inclusion of Dutch caravan dwellers in the target groups on the one hand and the exclusion of large groups of immigrants (such as all immigrants from developed countries, but also, for example, the Chinese) demonstrates that the new minorities policy was not a policy for immigrants in any real sense. It was aimed in essence at groups who were at risk of ending up in a minority situation, and for the same reason at indigenous groups, such as the caravan dwellers. Immigrants from the former Dutch East Indies were not listed as a target group for the policy; from the early 1970s their situation was no longer seen as problematic.

86. From 1986 the Institute for Sociological and Economic Research (ISEO) at Erasmus University Rotterdam has carried out numerous studies, commissioned by the Ministry of Home Affairs as the Ministry co-ordinating minorities policy, under the general label of 'Accessibility and Proportionality'. From 1987 onwards the results of these have been available in the annual publication *Minderheden in Nederland, statistisch vademecum*.

87. In the 1990s the minorities budget has been exempted from the general austerity measures at national government level, and has actually tended to increase. At the same time there has been an almost constant reorganization of services and functions in an attempt to improve efficiency.

88. This fast-growing sector is referred to by some as 'the minorities industry'; see Vuijsje 1986.

89. Minderhedennota 1983:51ff.

90. In 1987 (*Staatscourant* 23-3-1987) the government decided on a target figure of 3 per cent for members of minorities in government employment by 1990. This target was not reached until 1992. The target was then set at 5 per cent for 1995. Furthermore a specific jobs-plan for Moluccans was implemented, providing 1,200 jobs for this group between 1987 and 1992. See Smeets 1989; Tesser 1993:39ff.

91. Penninx 1988a; Allochtonenbeleid 1989; Veenman 1990a; Tesser 1993; Wolff/Penninx 1994; Smeets *et al.* 1996.

92. Bovenkerk 1986.

93. Eerste Interimevaluatie 1992; Stichtingsakkoord 1993.

94. See Overdijk-Francis 1995.

95. Eldering 1989:120.

96. Driessen *et al.* 1988; for an examination of the continuity of the practice and the varying academic arguments, see Lucassen/Köbben 1992.

97. Fase/Van den Berg 1985; Projectgroep ICO 1995.

98. See Van 't Hof/Dronkers 1993 and the subsequent discussion in the journal *Migrantenstudies*. See also the report of the Van Kemenade Committee (Ceders 1992).

99. For a summary see Penninx *et al.* 1993:141ff.

100. See on concentration and segregation Tesser *et al.* 1994.

101. Beune/Hessels 1983.

102. Groenendijk 1987:7; Allochtonenbeleid 1989.

103. Penninx *et al.* 1993:84ff.; Van den Bedem 1993. See also Chapter 1.

104. Since 1986 the LBR (National Bureau against Racism) has also regularly published the results of research into discrimination in various sections of society. The *LBR-Bulletin* has expanded into a bimonthly journal covering every important development in the field of research and practice involving discrimination and the prevention of it.

105. See Buys/Van Donselaar 1994; Witte 1995.

106. Minderhedennota 1983:107ff.

107. De Graaf *et al.* 1988.

108. Both these provisions were discontinued from the early 1990s, and funding for them withdrawn. Only a few remain active. In their place, private initiatives on the part of immigrants have experienced a boom in recent years, and foreign broadcasts have also become available.

109. Hampsink/Roosblad 1992; Landman 1992. See also Rath *et al.* 1996.

110. See also Wagtendonk 1991; Rath *et al.* 1993; Landman 1992; Rath *et al.* 1996.

111. Rath 1991; see also Penninx 1988a: Chapter IX.

112. Penninx 1988a and 1992; TWCM 1995.

113. This argument has been developed extensively in Vermeulen/Penninx 1994, under the title, 'The democratic impatience'.

114. Rath *et al.* 1992.

115. Important sources for developments on the labour market are: Heijke 1979 and 1986; Penninx 1979 and 1988a; Penninx *et al.* 1993; Veenman 1990; Tesser 1993; Veenman 1994; Wolff/Penninx 1994; Veenman 1994; Wolff/Penninx 1994.

116. See Wolff/Penninx 1994.

117. Lindo's study (1996) of the school careers of the second generation of Spanish and Portuguese immigrants showed that their results were as good as and sometimes better than their Dutch contemporaries.

118. The proposal envisaged a recruitment contract for 'guest workers' for a maximum of two years, after which they would have to return home. The regulation was never implemented.

119. Van Donselaar 1991; Elbers/Fennema 1993. NVU and CP were both extreme right-wing political parties.

120. For a survey of studies in these areas see Penninx 1988a:166ff. and Van Praag 1983.

121. This party had already won a seat in the Dutch Lower House in 1982, but lost it again in 1986.

122. For a discussion on the attitude of the Dutch and Belgian governments in these matters, see Penninx/Yar 1993; Rath *et al.* 1996.

123. See Shadid/Van Koningsveld 1992.

124. See Penninx/Muus 1989.

125. Sociaal en Cultureel Rapport 1992:469; Sociale 1993:88.

126. See Buijs 1993 on Moroccan youth; De Vries 1987; Vermeulen/Penninx 1994.

127. Sansone 1992.

128. Buiks 1983; Werdmölder 1990; Sansone 1992.

129. In 1986 twenty-nine non-Dutch candidates were elected as councillors. See Penninx 1988a:181ff. In the 1990 elections forty-five migrants were elected as local councillors (that is to say, they came from

one of the target groups of the minorities policy). In 1993 there were three 'migrants' in the Dutch Lower House; two represented the Labour Party and one the Christian Democrats. For a survey see Rath 1991. In the 1994 national elections no fewer than seven persons of direct migrant descent were elected to the Lower House, distributed over four political parties. The number of councillors of migrant descent elected in the municipal elections of the same year was only slightly higher than in 1990.

Notes to Chapter 7

1. For example, Cornelisse-Koksma 1969. During the last decade efforts to carry out research into immigrants' mastery of the Dutch language and migrants' problems in acquiring a new language have been stepped up. At the Arts Faculties of the Catholic University of Brabant and the University of Amsterdam special research programmes have been instituted in this field: see Roosblad *et al.* 1992. In addition, the availability and quality of Dutch language courses for newcomers has increased significantly as a consequence of the recent integration policy.
2. Becker/Van Kempen 1982; Penninx 1988a; Abell 1994.
3. Penninx 1988a; Opvang 1983. For the 5% rule: Ramakers 1994.
4. Bovenkerk *et al.* 1983; Levie/Zantkuyl 1980:58-59.
5. Van Heek 1936; Kraak *et al.* 1958.
6. Kraak *et al.* 1958.
7. Cruson 1985:230; see also Ten Doesschate 1993.
8. Van Heek 1936.
9. Brassé/Van Schelven 1980:62ff; Penninx/Van Velzen 1977; Muus *et al.* 1983.
10. See Van Tillaart/Reubsaet 1988. Turkish businessmen in the Netherlands have even published their own 'Yellow Pages': *Hollanda Esnaf ve Kurumlar Rehberi* (The Hague, Sila Boekhandel, 1992).
11. Lucassen 1984:116-117.
12. Brassé/Van Schelven 1980:63-64 and 172ff.

13. Penninx 1985.
14. For an excellent analysis of the circumstances which determine whether ethnic organizations are set up or not, in this case applied to the Jewish labour movement in various countries around 1900, see Hofmeester 1990.
15. In the history of the Jews in the Netherlands it should be remembered that in the case of the Portuguese Jews the formation of a minority was not only forced upon them, but was also consciously aimed at by the first generation of refugees from the Iberian peninsula: they were at last able to give expression to their own religious feelings without too many obstacles.
16. Van Heek 1936; Vellinga/Wolters 1966.
17. Cf. Chapter 6 and see the next note.
18. For this comparison see Van Arkel 1984 and 1985; for what follows: Gans 1971:27-28.

Notes to the Epilogue

1. Willems' dissertation (1995) has shown how scholars have contributed over the centuries to disinformation and prejudice against this 'group'; they may even have constructed it.
2. See the famous essays in Park 1950, for example the one entitled 'The etiquette of race relations'.
3. Another striking example of the theory that physical identifiability is not in itself of overriding importance is that of children adopted from abroad. There are more than twenty thousand of them in the Netherlands. Because they come to the Netherlands at a very young age and are raised in a Dutch environment, cultural differences have no role to play for these children. In view of the fact that most of the families adopting them are from a middle or upper-class background, rather than being disadvantaged they tend to have a social advantage. Their position in society, in spite of their physical identifiability, in no way seems to be a problem.

Bibliography

Aalberts, M.M.J.
  1985   *Gezinsvorming door jonge migranten.*
          Verslag van de evaluatiestudie.
          WODC/Ministerie van Justitie. The
          Hague: Staatsuitgeverij.

Abadan-Unat, N., R. Keles, R. Penninx, H. van
Renselaar, L. van Velzen and L. Yenisey
  1976   *Migration and development. A study of*
          the effects of international labor
          migration on Bogazliyan district. The
          Hague/Ankara: NUFFIC/IMWOO.

Abell, J.P.
  1994   *Belemmeringen voor minderheden bij*
          toetreding tot de arbeidsmarkt. Een
          inventariserend onderzoek.
          TWCM-voorstudie 2. The Hague:
          Ministerie van Binnenlandse Zaken.

Advies Onderzoek Minderheden
  1979   *Adviescommissie Onderzoek*
          Minderheden. The Hague:
          Staatsuitgeverij.

Allochtonenbeleid
  1989   *Allochtonenbeleid.* Rapport van de
          Wetenschappelijke Raad voor het
          Regeringsbeleid. The Hague. (A
          slightly abbreviated version was
          published by the Scientific Council
          under the title *Immigrant policy,* 1989).

Ambonezen in Nederland.
  1959   *Rapport van het Ministerie van*
          Maatschappelijk Werk, uitgebracht door
          de Commissie Verwey-Jonker. The
          Hague: Staatsuitgeverij.

Amersfoort, J.M.M. van
  1971   *De sociale positie van de Molukkers in*
          Nederland. The Hague:
          Staatsuitgeverij.
  1974   *Immigratie en minderheidsvorming.*
          Een analyse van de Nederlandse situatie
          1945-1973. Alphen aan den Rijn:
          Samsom.
  1982   *Immigration and the formation of*
          minority groups. The Dutch experience
          1945-1975. Cambridge: CUP.
  1983   'Migratie-onderzoek,
          overheidsfinanciering en beleid.
          Aantekeningen van een participant'.
          In: *Grafiet* 4 (1983) 130-154.
  1987   'Van William Kegge tot Ruud Gullit.
          De Surinaamse migratie naar
          Nederland: realiteit, beeldvorming en
          beleid'. In: *Tijdschrift voor*
          Geschiedenis 100 (1987) 475-490.

Amersfoort, J.M.M. van
1991   'Nationalities, citizens and ethnic conflicts. Towards a theory of ethnicity in the modern state'. In: H. van Amersfoort and H. Knippenberg, *States and nations. The rebirth of the 'nationalities question' in Europe.* Amsterdam: ISG/University of Amsterdam, 12-29.

Amersfoort, J.M.M. van, and R. Penninx
1993   'Migratieontwikkeling en migratiebeheersing'. In: H. van Amersfoort (ed.), *Migratie, bevolking en politiek. Nederland als immigratieland in een Westeuropese context.* Amsterdam: ISG/University of Amsterdam, 57-84.
1994   'Regulating migration in Europe. The Dutch experience, 1960-92'. In: *The Annals of the American Academy of Political and Social Science* 534 (July 1994) 133-146.

Amersfoort, J.M.M. van, and B. Surie
1987   'Immigratieland tegen wil en dank. Nederland 1970-1985'. In: H. van der Wusten (ed.), *Postmoderne aardrijkskunde. De sociografische traditie voortgezet.* Muiderberg: Coutinho, 180-194.

Annink, C.
1994   'Orang Indo en Indonesian-Dutch: Indische Nederlanders in Indonesië en de Verenigde Staten van Amerika'. In: W. Willems and L. Lucassen (ed.), *Het onbekende vaderland. De repatriëring van Indische Nederlanders 1946-1964.* The Hague: SDU, 147-159.

Arkel, D. van
1984   'Historisch racisme-onderzoek. Achtergronden, benaderingen, problemen'. In: *Tijdschrift voor Sociale Geschiedenis* 10 (1984) 438-462.

1985   'Een voorzichtige prognose'. In: D. van Arkel, *et al., Veertig jaar na '45. Visies op het hedendaagse antisemitisme.* Amsterdam: Meulenhoff Informatief, 9-29.

Bade, K. (ed.)
1987   *Population, labour and migration in 19th- and 20th-century Germany.* Leamington Spa: Berg.

Bagley, C.
1973   *The Dutch plural society. A comparative study in race relations.* Oxford: OUP.

Baker, V.J.
1983   *Wooden shoes and baseball bats. A study of socio-cultural integration of Americans in The Hague.* Leiden: ICA/Leiden University.

Bakker, M., *et al.*
1985   *Hugenoten in Groningen. Franse vluchtelingen tussen 1680 en 1720.* Groningen: Wolters Noordhoff/Bouma's Boekhuis.

Bartels, D.
1986   'Can the train ever be stopped again? Developments in the Moluccan community in the Netherlands before and after the hijackings'. In: *Indonesia* (1986) 2.
1989   *Moluccans in exile.* Leiden: COMT.
1990   *Ambon is op Schiphol.* 2 vols. Leiden/Utrecht: COMT/IWM.

Baumann, G. and T. Sunier (ed.)
1995   *Post-migration ethnicity. Cohesion, commitments, comparison.* Amsterdam: Het Spinhuis.

Becker, H.M. and S.J. van Kempen
1982   *Vraag naar migranten op de arbeidsmarkt.* Rotterdam: EUR.

Bedem, R.F.A. van den
1993   *Motieven voor naturalisatie. Waarom
        vreemdelingen uit diverse
        minderheidsgroepen wel of niet kiezen
        voor naturalisatie.* Arnhem:
        WODC/Gouda Quint.

Beer, J. de, H. Kuiper and R. Noordam
1991   'Gezinsherenigende, gezinsvormende
        en retourmigratie van Turken en
        Marokkanen'. In: *Maandstatistiek van
        de Bevolking* (CBS) 39 (1991) 1: 38-49.

Beets, G. and S. Koesoebjono
1991   'Indische Nederlanders: een vergeten
        groep'. In: *Demos* 7 (1991) 8: 60-64.

Bekius, R. and W. Ultee
1985   'De Armeense kolonie in Amsterdam,
        1600-1800'. In: *De Gids* 148 (1985)
        216-224.

Benton, G. and H. Vermeulen (ed.)
1987   *De Chinezen.* Muiderberg: Coutinho.

Berg-Eldering, L. van den
1978   *Marokkaanse gezinnen in Nederland.*
        Alphen aan den Rijn: Samsom.

Berghuis, C.K.
1990   *Joodse vluchtelingen in Nederland
        1938-1940. Documenten betreffende
        toelating, uitleiding en kampopname.*
        Kampen: J.H. Kok.

Berkvens-Stevelinck, C.
1985   'De hugenoten'. In: P. Blom, *et al.*
        (ed.), *La France aux Pays-Bas.
        Invloeden in het verleden.* Vianen:
        Kwadraat, 13-49.

Beune, H.H.M. and A.J.J. Hessels
1983   *Minderheid – minder recht? Een
        inventarisatie van bepalingen in de
        Nederlandse wet- en regelgeving waarin
        onderscheid wordt gemaakt tussen
        allochtonen en autochtonen.* The
        Hague: Staatsuitgeverij.

Bloemberg, L.
1995   *Tussen traditie en verandering.
        Hindostaanse zelforganisaties in
        Nederland.* Utrecht/Amsterdam: NGS.

Blok, L. and J.M.M. de Meere
1978   'Welstand, ongelijkheid in welstand
        en censusrecht in Nederland
        omstreeks het midden van de 19de
        eeuw'. In: *Economisch- en Sociaal
        Historisch Jaarboek* 41 (1978) 175-293.

Böcker, A.
1994   *Turkse migranten en sociale zekerheid.
        Van onderlinge zorg naar overheidszorg?*
        Amsterdam: SUA.

Böhning, W.R.
1984   *Studies in international labour
        migration.* London: Macmillan.

Boon, S. and E. van Geleuken
1993   *Ik wilde eigenlijk niet gaan. De
        repatriëring van Indische Nederlanders
        1946-1964.* The Hague: Tong Tong.

Boon-de Gouw, A.
1984   'Feuilletons in de Rotterdamse pers in
        de jaren 1880-1920'. In: *Tijdschrift
        voor Sociale Geschiedenis* 10 (1984)
        291-314.

Borne, J. van den
1992   'Naturalisaties in Nederland in de
        eerste helft van de negentiende eeuw'.
        In: *Jaarboek van het Centraal Bureau
        voor Genealogie en het Iconografisch
        Bureau* 46 (1992) 208-246.

Borrie, W.D.
1959   *The cultural integration of immigrants.
        A survey based upon the Papers and
        Proceedings of the UNESCO Conference,
        held in Havanna, April 1956.* Paris:
        UNESCO.

Bossenbroek, M.
1992 *Volk voor Indië. De werving van Europese militairen voor de Nederlandse koloniale dienst, 1814-1909.* Amsterdam: Van Soeren.

Bossenbroek, M. and J.B.C. Kruishoop (ed.)
1988 *Vluchten voor de groote Oorlog. Belgen in Nederland 1914-1918.* Amsterdam: De Bataafsche Leeuw.

Bots, J.A.H. and G.H.M. Posthumus Meyjes (ed.)
1986 *La Révocation de l'Edit de Nantes et les Provinces Unies 1685. Colloque international du tricentenaire.* Amsterdam/Maarsen: APA-Holland University Press.

Bots, H., G.H.M. Posthumus Meyjes and F. Wieringa
1985 *Vlucht naar de vrijheid. De hugenoten en de Nederlanden.* Amsterdam/Dieren: De Bataafsche Leeuw.

Bovenkerk, F.
1973 *Terug naar Suriname. Over de opnamecapaciteit van de Surinaamse arbeidsmarkt voor Surinaamse retourmigratie uit Nederland.* Amsterdam: ASC/University of Amsterdam.
1974 *The sociology of return migration. A bibliographic essay.* The Hague: M. Nijhoff.
1978a *Omdat zij anders zijn. Patronen van rasdiscriminatie in Nederland.* Meppel/Amsterdam: Boom.
1978b *Ben je gekomen om te blijven? De terugkeer van Surinamers anno 1977.* Utrecht: Vakgroep KOSES/Utrecht University.
1986 *Een eerlijke kans. Rapport van de Adviescommissie Onderzoek Minderheden.* ACOM-advies. The Hague: Staatsuitgeverij.

Bovenkerk, F., A. Eijken and W. Bovenkerk-Teerink
1983 *Italiaans ijs. De opmerkelijke historie van de Italiaanse ijsbereiders in Nederland.* Amsterdam: Boom.

Bovenkerk, F. and W. Verschoor
1983 'Retourmigratie van Surinamers en Antillianen'. In: P. Muus, *et al., Retourmigratie van Mediterranen, Surinamers en Antillianen uit Nederland.* The Hague: Ministerie van Sociale Zaken en Werkgelegenheid.

Brassé, P. and W. van Schelven
1980 *Assimilatie van vooroorlogse immigranten. Drie generaties Polen, Slovenen, Italianen in Heerlen.* The Hague: Staatsuitgeverij.

Brassé, P., W. van Schelven, L. van der Valk and M. de Vries
1984 *Jonge Turken en Marokkanen op de Nederlandse arbeidsmarkt.* Amsterdam: SGI/University of Amsterdam.

Briels, J.G.C.A.
1976 *De Zuidnederlandse immigratie in Amsterdam en Haarlem omstreeks 1572-1630. Met een keuze van archivalische gegevens betreffende de kunstschilders.* Doctoral dissertation, University of Utrecht.
1978 *De Zuidnederlandse immigratie 1572-1630.* Haarlem: Fibula-Van Dishoeck.
1985 *Zuid-Nederlanders in de Republiek 1572-1630. Een demografische en cultuurhistorische studie.* Sint-Niklaas: Danthe.
1987 'De Zuidnederlandse immigratie 1572-1630'. In: *Tijdschrift voor Geschiedenis* 100 (1987) 331-355.

Brink, M. and M. Pasariboe (ed.)
  1993   *Asylum seekers in the Netherlands.*
          Amsterdam: ISG/University of
          Amsterdam.

Bruijn, J.R. and E.S. van Eyck van Heslinga
  1984   'Seamen's employment in the
          Netherlands (c.1600-c.1800)'. In: *The
          Mariner's Mirror* 70 (1984) 7-20.

Bruijn, J.R. and J. Lucassen (ed.)
  1980   *Op de schepen der Oost-Indische
          Compagnie. Vijf artikelen van J. de
          Hullu, ingeleid, bewerkt en voorzien
          van een studie over de werkgelegenheid
          bij de VOC.* Groningen: Wolters
          Noordhoff/Bouma's Boekhuis.

Bruin, M.P. de
  1970   'Over dijkgraven en polderjongens'.
          In: *Archief van het Koninklijk
          Zeeuwsch Genootschap der
          Wetenschappen* (1970) 100-114.

Buijs, F.
  1993   *Leven in een nieuw land. Marokkaanse
          jongemannen in Nederland.* Utrecht:
          Van Arkel.

Buijs, F.J. and J. van Donselaar
  1994   *Extreem-rechts. Aanhang, geweld en
          onderzoek.* Leiden: RUL/LISWO.

Buiks, P.E.J.
  1983   *Surinaamse jongeren op de Kruiskade.
          Overleven in een etnische randgroep.*
          Deventer: Van Loghum Slaterus.

Buning, E., P. Overbeek and J. Verveer
  1987   'De huisgenoten des geloofs. De
          immigratie van de Hugenoten
          1680-1720'. In: *Tijdschrift voor
          Geschiedenis* 100 (1987) 356-373.

Caestecker, F.
  1993   *Ongewenste gasten. Joodse vluchtelingen
          en migranten in de dertiger jaren.*
          Brussels: VUB Press.

Canny, N. (ed.)
  1994   *Europeans on the move. Studies on
          European migration, 1500-1800.*
          Oxford: OUP.

Cavacciocchi, S. (ed.)
  1994   *Le migrazioni in Europa secc. XIII-XVIII.*
          Prato: Le Monnier.

CBS (Central Bureau of Statistics)
  1994   'Population by country of birth and
          the parents' country of birth, per
          province and in the four big
          municipalities, 1 January 1992'. In:
          Maandstatistiek van de Bevolking (CBS)
          42 (1994) 3: 34ff.

Ceders
  1992   *Ceders in de tuin. Naar een nieuwe
          opzet van het onderwijsbeleid voor
          allochtone leerlingen, deel 1.*
          Rapportage van de Commissie
          Allochtone Leerlingen in het
          Onderwijs. Zoetermeer: Ministerie
          van Onderwijs en Wetenschappen.

Chauvel, R.
  1990   *Nationalists, soldiers and separatists.
          The Ambonese islands from colonialism
          to revolt 1880-1950.* Leiden: KITLV Press.

Chorus, A.
  1964   *De Nederlander uiterlijk en innerlijk.
          Een karakteristiek.* Leiden: A.W.
          Sijthoff.

Cleeff-Hiegentlich, F. van
  1985   'De transformatie van het
          Nederlandse Jodendom in de eerste
          helft van de negentiende eeuw'. In:
          De Gids 148 (1985) 232-242.

Cohen, J.-M.
  1990   *Het getto van Venetië. Ponentini,
          Levantini e Tedeschi 1516-1797.* The
          Hague: SDU.

Cornelisse-Koksma, H.G.Y.
  1969   *Prestaties op verbale en non-verbale tests
           bij Ambonese kinderen.* Amsterdam:
           Laboratorium voor de
           Psychodiagnostische en
           Bedrijfspsychologische Research, Vrije
           Universiteit.

Cottaar, A.
  1996   *Kooplui, kermisklanten en andere
           woonwagenbewoners. Groepsvorming en
           beleid 1870-1945.* Amsterdam: Het
           Spinhuis.

Cottaar, A., L. Lucassen and W. Willems
  1990   'Recht of onrecht? Het 19de en 20e
           eeuwse beleid jegens zigeuners en
           woonwagenbewoners in West-Europa
           nader beschouwd'. In: T. Havinga and
           B. Sloot (ed.), *Recht en emancipatie.
           Bondgenoot of barrière?* The Hague:
           VUGA, 114-140.

Cottaar, A. and W. Willems
  1984   *Indische Nederlanders. Een onderzoek
           naar beeldvorming.* The Hague:
           Moesson.
  1985   'De geassimileerde Indische
           Nederlander. Mythe of
           werkelijkheid?' In: *De Gids* 148 (1985)
           257-270.

Cruson, C.
  1985   'De hugenoten als refugiés'. In: *De
           Gids* 148 (1985) 225-231.
  1987   'Standvastig en frivool. De
           beeldvorming over hugenoten'. In:
           Anne Frank Stichting (ed.), *Vreemd
           gespuis.* Amsterdam: AMBO/NOVIB,
           38-48.

  1990   'Vluchtelingen in de stad. De
           vluchtelingenpolitiek van de
           Amsterdamse magistraat in de periode
           1681-1685'. In: C.I. Cruson and J.
           Dronkers (ed.), *De stad. Beheersing
           van de stedelijke ruimte.* Houten:
           Boon Stafleu & Van Loghum, 89-109.

Cunningham, W.
  1897   *Alien immigrants to England.* London:
           Swann Sonnenschein. New edition,
           New York, 1969.

Curtin, P.D.
  1984   *Cross-cultural trade in world history.*
           Cambridge: CUP.

Daelemans, F.
  1975   'Leiden 1581. Een socio-demografisch
           onderzoek'. In: *A.A.G. Bijdragen* 19
           (1975) 137-215.

Davids, C.A. and J. Lucassen (ed.)
  1995   *A miracle mirrored. The Dutch
           Republic in European perspective.*
           Cambridge: CUP.

Davids, C.A. and L. Noordegraaf (ed.)
  1993   *The Dutch economy in the Golden Age.
           Nine studies.* Amsterdam: NEHA.

De Mas, P.
  1990.   'Overlevingsdynamiek in het
           Marokkaanse Rifgebergte. De
           samenhang tussen circulaire migratie
           en de demografische structuur van
           huishoudens'. In: *K.N.A.G. Geografisch
           Tijdschrift* 24 (1990) 1:73-86.
  1991   'Marokkaanse migratie naar
           Nederland. Perspectief vanuit de
           herkomstgebieden'. In: *Internationale
           Spectator* (45) 3: 110-118.

Deijk, F. van
1989   'Elie Benoist (1640-1728),
         historiographer and politician after
         the revocation of the Edict of Nantes'.
         In: *Nederlands Archief voor
         Kerkgeschiedenis* 69 (1989) 54-92.

Dekker, R.M.
1982   *Holland in beroering. Oproeren in de
         17de en 18de eeuw.* Baarn: Ambo.
1990   'Labour conflicts and working-class
         culture in early modern Holland'. In:
         International Review of Social History
         35 (1990) 377-420.

Dekkers, F.
1981   'Eindhoven 1920-1940. De terreur van
         de Philips Politie'. In: *De Haagse Post*,
         25 July 1981, 18-24.

Deslé, E., R. Lesthaeghe and E. Witte (ed.)
1993   *Denken over migranten in Europa.*
         Brussels:VUBPRESS.

Deursen, A.T. van
1981   *Het kopergeld van de Gouden Eeuw.*
         Assen: Van Gorcum.

Diederiks, H.A.
1982   *Een stad in verval. Amsterdam
         omstreeks 1800: demografisch,
         economisch, ruimtelijk.* Amsterdam:
         Historisch Seminarium van de
         Universiteit van Amsterdam.

Dittrich, K. and H. Würzner (ed.)
1982   *Nederland en het Duitse Exil 1933-1940.*
         Amsterdam: Van Gennep.

Doesschate, J.W. ten
1985   *Het Nederlandse toelatingsbeleid ten
         aanzien van Hongaarse vluchtelingen.*
         Unpublished master thesis, Catholic
         University Nijmegen.
1993   *Asielbeleid en belangen. Het
         Nederlandse toelatingsbeleid ten
         aanzien van vluchtelingen in de jaren
         1968-1982.* Hilversum: Verloren.

Donselaar, J. van
1991   *Fout na de oorlog. Fascistische en
         racistische organisaties in Nederland
         1950-1990.* Amsterdam: Bert Bakker.

Doormont, M.R. and R. Vroom
1985   '"Little London". Engelse kooplieden
         te Rotterdam in de achttiende en het
         begin van de negentiende eeuw'. In:
         Rotterdams Jaarboekje, 197-218.

Driessen, F.
1911   *Het Welvaren van Leiden. Handschrift
         uit het jaar 1659.* The Hague:
         Martinus Nijhoff.

Driessen, G., P. Jungbluth and J. Louvenberg
1988   *Onderwijs in eigen taal en cultuur.
         Doelopvattingen, leerkrachten,
         leermiddelen en omvang.* The Hague:
         SVO.

Dunk, H.W. von der
1979   'Nederland ten tijde van de eerste
         wereldoorlog'. In: *Algemene
         Geschiedenis der Nederlanden*, vol. 14.
         Bussum, 40-52.

Eeghen, I.H. van
1974   *De Gilden. Theorie en praktijk.*
         Bussum: De Haan.

Eerste
1992   *Eerste interim-evaluatie van het
         Stichtingsakkoord 'Meer werk voor
         minderheden'.* The Hague: Stichting
         van de Arbeid.

Eiynck, A. , H. Mertens-Westphalen, H. Kaiser, H.
Saaltink and P. Schonewille (ed.)
1993   *Werken over de grens. 350 jaar geld
         verdienen in het buitenland.* Assen:
         Drents Museum, Museumsdorf
         Cloppenburg-Niedersächsisches
         Freilichtmuseum, Westfries Museum
         Hoorn, Emslandmuseum Lingen.

Elbers, F. and M. Fennema
1993   *Racistische partijen in West-Europa.*
        Tussen nationale traditie en Europese
        samenwerking. Leiden: Stichting
        Burgerschapskunde.

Eldering, L.
1989   'Ethnic minority children in Dutch
        schools. Underachievement and its
        explanations'. In: L. Eldering and
        J. Kloprogge, *Different cultures, same*
        school. Ethnic minority children in
        Europe. Amsterdam/Lisse: Swets and
        Zeitlinger, 107-137.

Elich, J.H.
1987   *Aan de ene kant, aan de andere kant.*
        De emigratie van Nederlanders naar
        Australië 1946-1986. Delft: Eburon.

Elich, J.H. and P.W. Blauw,
1981   *... En toch terug. Een onderzoek naar de*
        retourmigratie van Nederlanders uit
        Australië, Nieuw-Zeeland en Canada.
        Rotterdam: Erasmus University.

Ellemers, J.E. and R.E.F. Vaillant
1985   *Indische Nederlanders en*
        gerepatrieerden. Muiderberg:
        Coutinho.
1987   'Indische Nederlanders en
        gerepatrieerden: de grootste categorie
        naoorlogse immigranten'. In:
        Tijdschrift voor Geschiedenis 100 (1987)
        3: 412-431.

Ellemers, J.E. and J.H.J. Vermeulen
1979   *Geselecteerde bibliografie van*
        sociaal-wetenschappelijke publicaties
        over etnische minderheden in
        Nederland. Groningen: Sociologisch
        Instituut, University of Groningen
        (see also in: *Intermediair* (1980) 1/2).

Engman, M. (ed.)
1992   *Ethnic identity in urban Europe.*
        Comparative studies on governments
        and non-dominant ethnic groups in
        Europe, 1850-1940. Aldershot:
        Dartmonth.

Entzinger, H.B.
1975   'Nederland immigratieland?' In:
        Beleid en Maatschappij 2 (1975) 12:
        326-336.
1984   *Het minderhedenbeleid.*
        Meppel/Amsterdam: Boom.
1985   'The Netherlands'. In: T. Hammar
        (ed.), *European immigration policy. A*
        comparative study. Cambridge: CUP,
        50-88.
1993   'Trage rivieren en het Groen-Linkse
        bootje'. In: *Buitenlanders Bulletin* 18
        (1993) 6: 18-20.

Etnische
1979   *Etnische minderheden.* Rapport 17 van
        de Wetenschappelijke Raad voor het
        Regeringsbeleid. The Hague:
        Staatsuitgeverij. (Also published in
        English by the Scientific Council
        under the title *Ethnic minorities,* 1979.)

Ex, J.
1966·   *Adjustment after migration. A*
        longitudinal study of the process of
        adjustment by refugees to a new
        environment. The Hague: M. Nijhoff.

Faber, S.
1983   *Strafrechtspleging en criminaliteit te*
        Amsterdam, 1680-1811. De nieuwe
        menslievenheid. Arnhem: Gouda
        Quint.

Fafié, T.A. (ed.)
1981   'Nederland en de Evangelische
        Saltzburgers door J.C. Schultz Jacobi
        (1806-1865)'. In: *Bijdragen tot de*
        Geschiedenis van
        West-Zeeuws-Vlaanderen 10 (1981)
        1-221.

Fase, W. and G. van den Berg
1985   *Theorie en praktijk van intercultureel*
        onderwijs. The Hague: SVO.

Filet, B.C.
1984   'Psychotherapeutische hulpverlening
        bij eerste en tweede generatie Indische
        vervolgingsslachtoffers. De invloed
        van sequentiële traumatisering en van
        de wisselwerking tussen "aloes" en
        "kasar"-culturen'. In: J. Dane (ed.),
        Keerzijde van de bevrijding. Deventer:
        Van Loghum Slaterus.

Freeman, G.P.
1986   'Migration and the political economy
        of the welfare state'. In: *Annals of the*
        American Academy of Political and
        Social Science 485 (1986) 51-63.

Frijhoff, W.
1977   'De paniek van juni 1734'. In: *Archief*
        voor de Geschiedenis van de Katholieke
        Kerk in Nederland 19 (1977) 170-233.

Fuks-Mansfeld, R.G.
1989   *De Sefardim in Amsterdam tot 1795.*
        Aspecten van een joodse minderheid in
        een Hollandse stad. Hilversum:
        Historische Vereniging
        Holland/Verloren.

Galard, J.
1985   'Descartes en Nederland'. In: P. Blom,
        et al. (ed.), *La France aux Pays-Bas.*
        Invloeden in het verleden. Vianen:
        Kwadraat, 51-88.

Gallo, B.
1987   *Les italiens au Grand-Duche de*
        Luxembourg. Un siècle d'histoire et de
        chroniques sur l'immigration italienne.
        Luxembourg: Imprimerie Saint-Paul
        S.A.

Gans, M.H.
1971   *Memorboek. Platenatlas van het leven*
        der joden in Nederland van de
        middeleeuwen tot 1940. Baarn: Bosch
        & Keuning.

Garrard, J.A.
1971   *The English and immigration*
        1880-1910. Oxford: OUP.

Gerepatrieerdenvraagstuk
1956   *Het gerepatrieerdenvraagstuk in de*
        Nederlandse pers. Amsterdam:
        Instituut voor
        Perswetenschappen/University of
        Amsterdam.

Geuns, S.J. van
1853   *Proeve eener geschiedenis van de*
        toelating en vestiging van vreemdelingen
        in Nederland, tot het jaar 1795.
        Schoonhoven: S.E. van Nooten.

Giebels, L.
1975   *De Zionistische Beweging in Nederland*
        1899-1941. Assen:Van Gorcum.

Giele, J.J.
1968   *De pen in aanslag. Revolutionairen*
        rond 1848. Bussum: Fibula-Van
        Dishoeck.

Gijswijt-Hofstra, M. (ed.)
1989   *Een schijn van verdraagzaamheid.*
        Afwijking en tolerantie in Nederland
        van de zestiende eeuw tot heden.
        Hilversum: Verloren.

Gooszen, H.
1988   *Vluchtelingen en asielzoekers.*
        Demografische en sociaal-economische
        positie in Nederland. NIDI-rapport no.
        1. The Hague: NIDI.

Graaf, H. de, R. Penninx and E. Stoové
1988   'Minorities policies, social services
        and ethnic organizations in the
        Netherlands'. In: S. Jenkins (ed.),
        Ethnic associations and the welfare
        state. Services to immigrants in five
        countries. New York: Columbia
        University Press, 203-238.

Green, N.L.
1986   *The Pletzl of Paris. Jewish immigrant*
        workers in the 'Belle Epoque'. New
        York: Holmes and Meier.
1997   'The comparative method and
        poststructural structuralism. New
        perspectives for migration studies'. In:
        J. Lucassen and L. Lucassen (ed.),
        Migration, migration history, history.
        Old paradigms and new perspectives.
        Bern: Peter Lang, 57-71

Griffiths, R.T. and J.L. van Zanden
1989   *De economische geschiedenis van*
        Nederland in de twintigste eeuw.
        Utrecht: Aula.

Groenendijk, C.A.
1979   'Van gastarbeider tot medeburger'. In:
        Beleid en Maatschappij 2 (1979) 52-63.
1981   'Minderhedenbeleid in een onwillig
        immigratieland'. In: *Ars Aequi* 30
        (1981) 10: 531-547.
1987   *Migratiebeheersing, controle en*
        discriminatiebestrijding. De
        dubbelzinnigheid van het
        overheidsbeleid. Paper delivered at the
        Conference on Etnische
        Minderheden. The Hague, November.

1989   'Migratiecontrole in Europa. Angsten,
        instrumenten en effecten'. In: B. Top
        and T. Heijmans, *Migranten in het*
        Europa van de burger. Utrecht: NCB,
        41-54.
1990   'Verboden voor Tukkers. Reacties op
        rellen tussen Italianen, Spanjaarden
        en Twentenaren in 1961'. In:
        F. Bovenkerk, *et al., Wetenschap en*
        partijdigheid. Opstellen voor André J.F.
        Köbben. Assen/Maastricht: Van
        Gorcum, 55-95.
1992a   'Europese migratiepolitiek na
        Maastricht. Uitbreiding en beperking
        van vrijheden'. In: *Migrantenrecht*
        (1992) 4: 76-86.
1992b   'Europese migratiepolitiek. Fort
        Europa of het instandhouden van
        denkbeeldige grenzen?' In:
        Migrantenstudies 8 (1992) 4: 44-60.

Guild, E. and J. Niessen
1996   *The developing immigration and*
        asylum policies of the European Union.
        Adopted conventions, resolutions,
        recommendations, decisions and
        conclusions. The
        Hague/London/Boston: Kluwer Law
        International.

Gwynn, R.D.
1985   *Huguenot heritage. The history and*
        contribution of the Huguenots in
        Britain. London: Routledge & Kegan
        Paul.

Haffmans, M.A.F. and P. De Mas
1985   *De gezinshereniging van Marokkanen*
        in Nederland, 1968-1984. The Hague:
        Ministerie van Sociale Zaken en
        Werkgelegenheid.

Hall, J.
1953   *The advancement of learning 1649* (ed.
        A.K. Croston). Liverpool: Liverpool
        UP.

Hampsink, R. and J. Roosblad
1992   *Nederland en de islam.* Nijmegen:
        Catholic University of
        Nijmegen/Instituut voor
        Rechtssociologie.

Handboek
1984   *Handboek minderheden.* Alphen aan
        den Rijn: Samsom; thereafter
        Houten: Bohn, Stafleu, Van
        Loghum/Koninklijke Vermande.

Hart, S.
1976   *Geschrift en getal. Een keuze uit de
        demografisch-, economisch- en
        sociaal-historische studiën op grond van
        Amsterdamse en Zaanse archivalia
        1600-1800.* Dordrecht: Historische
        Vereniging Holland.

Have, W. ten
1983   'De geschiedschrijving over crisis en
        verzuiling'. In: W.W. Mijnhardt (ed.),
        *Kantelend geschiedbeeld. Nederlandse
        historiografie sinds 1945.*
        Utrecht/Antwerp: Aula, 256-288.

Heek, F. van
1936   *Chineesche immigranten in Nederland.*
        Leiden: Brill.

Heering, A.
1985   *Van schoorsteenvegers en pizzabakkers.
        Vier eeuwen Italianen in Groningen.*
        Utrecht: Stichting Matrijs.
1991   'Italianen in Nederland'. In: A.H.
        Huussen jr., *et al.* (ed.), *Vreemdelingen
        ongewenst en bemind.* Groningen:
        Egbert Forsten, 15-19.

Hees, P. van
1987   'Vlaamse activisten als politieke
        vluchtelingen in Nederland tijdens
        het interbellum'. In: *Tijdschrift voor
        Geschiedenis* 100 (1987) 394-411.

Heijdt, J. van der
1995   'Twintig jaar na de Surinaamse
        onafhankelijkheid. Surinamers in
        Nederland'. In: *Maandstatistiek van de
        Bevolking* (CBS) 43 (1995) 10: 19-21.

Heijke, J.A.M.
1979   *Sociaal-economische aspecten van
        gastarbeid.* Rotterdam: NEI.
1986   *Migratie van Mediterranen. Economie
        en arbeidsmarkt.* Leiden: Stenfert
        Kroese.

Heijs, E.
1995   *Van vreemdeling tot Nederlander. De
        verlening van het Nederlanderschap aan
        vreemdelingen 1813-1992.* Amsterdam:
        Het Spinhuis.

Heinemeijer, W.F., J.M.M. van Amersfoort, W.
Ettema, P. De Mas and H.H. van der Wusten
1976   *Weggaan om te blijven. Gevolgen van
        gastarbeid op het Marokkaanse
        platteland.* Amsterdam: SGI/University
        of Amsterdam.

Henkes, B.
1993   'German maids in prosperous
        "Guldenland" (Guilderland) and the
        land of moral threat. Nation images
        and national identity during the
        Interbellum period'. In: A. Galema, *et
        al.*, *Images of the nation. Different
        meanings of Dutchness 1870-1940.*
        Amsterdam/Atlanta: Rodopi, 106-132.
1995   *Heimat in Holland. Duitse
        dienstmeisjes 1920-1950.* Amsterdam:
        Babylon/De Geus.

Herbert, U.
1990   *A history of foreign labor in Germany,
        1880-1980.* Ann Arbor: University of
        Michigan Press.

Heuvel-Strasser, E.A. van den
1986   'Vluchtelingenzorg of
        vreemdelingenbeleid. De Nederlandse
        overheid en de Belgische
        vluchtelingen, 1914-1915'. In:
        Tijdschrift voor Geschiedenis 99 (1986)
        184-204.

Hoerder, D. (ed.)
1985   *Labor migration in the Atlantic
        economies. The European and North
        American working classes during the
        period of industrialization.* Westport,
        Conn.: Greenwood Press.

Hof, L. van 't, and J. Dronkers
1993   'Onderwijsachterstanden van
        allochtonen. Klasse, gezin of etnische
        cultuur?' In: *Migrantenstudies* 9 (1993)
        1: 2-25.

Hofmeester, K.
1990   *Van talmoed tot statuut. Joodse
        arbeiders en arbeidersbewegingen in
        Amsterdam, Londen en Parijs,
        1880-1914.* Amsterdam: Stichting
        Beheer IISG.

Holmes, C.
1978   'J.A. Hobson and the Jews'. In: C.
        Holmes (ed.), *Immigrants and
        minorities in British society.* London:
        Allen & Unwin, 125-157.
1988   *John Bull's island. Immigration and
        British society, 1871-1971.* London:
        Macmillan. New edition 1992.

Hovens, P. and J. Hovens
1982   *Zigeuners, woonwagenbewoners en
        reizenden. Een bibliografie.* Rijswijk:
        Ministerie van CRM.

Hulshof, M., L. de Ridder and P. Krooneman
1992   *Asielzoekers in Nederland.* Amsterdam:
        ISG/University of Amsterdam.

Huussen jr., A.H.
1989   'De joden in Nederland en het
        probleem van de tolerantie'. In: M.
        Gijswijt-Hofstra (ed.), *Een schijn van
        verdraagzaamheid. Afwijking en
        tolerantie in Nederland van de zestiende
        eeuw tot heden.* Hilversum: Verloren,
        107-129.

Israel, J.I.
1989   *European Jewry in the age of
        mercantilism 1550-1750.* Oxford: OUP.
1995   *The Dutch Republic. Its rise, greatness,
        and fall 1477-1806.* Oxford: Clarendon
        Press.

Jaarwerk
1985   *Jaarwerk van de buitenlandse migratie,
        1984.* (Unpublished extended tables
        on international migration at the
        Central Bureau of Statistics.)
        Voorburg.

Jackson, J.A. (ed.)
1968   *Migration.* Cambridge: CUP.

Jansen, J.G.C.M.
1979   'Godsdienstig gedrag van joden en
        zigeuners in de 17de eeuw'. In:
        *Algemene Geschiedenis der
        Nederlanden,* vol. 8. Bussum:
        Fibula-Van Dishoeck, 358-365.

Jong, L. de
1969   *Het Koninkrijk der Nederlanden in de
        Tweede Wereldoorlog,* vol. I. The
        Hague: Nijhoff.

Jonge, A.A. de
1968   *Crisis en critiek der democratie.
        Anti-democratische stromingen en de
        daarin levende denkbeelden over de
        staat in Nederland tussen de
        wereldoorlogen.* Assen: Van Gorcum.

Jongste, J.A.F. de
1985   'Hollandse stadspensionarissen tijdens
        de Republiek. Notities bij een
        onderzoek'. In: S. Groenveld, *et al.*
        (ed.), *Bestuurders en geleerden.*
        Opstellen over onderwerpen uit de
        Nederlandse geschiedenis van de
        zestiende, zeventiende en achttiende
        eeuw, aangeboden aan prof. dr. J.J.
        Woltjer bij zijn afscheid als hoogleraar
        aan de Rijksuniversiteit te Leiden.
        Amsterdam/Dieren: De Bataafsche
        Leeuw, 85-96.

Josephus Jitta-Geertsma, M.T. and J.H. Sanders
1983   *Antisemitisme in Nederland.*
        WVC-literatuurrapport 20. Rijswijk:
        Ministerie van WVC.

Kappen, O. van
1965   *Geschiedenis der zigeuners in*
        Nederland. De ontwikkeling van de
        rechtspositie der Heidens of Egyptenaren
        in de Noordelijke Nederlanden,
        1420-ongeveer 1750. Assen: Van
        Gorcum/Prakke.

Kayser, B.
1972   *Cyclically determined homewards flows*
        of migrant workers. Paris: OECD.

Kent, G. and G. Hekman
1989   *In pursuit of sodomy. Male*
        homosexuality in Renaissance and
        Enlightenment Europe, Research on
        Homosexuality 17. New York:
        Haworth Press.

Kijlstra, R.W.
1960   'Hungarian refugees in Holland.
        Reception, care and integration'. In:
        G. Beijer (ed.), *De vluchtende mens,*
        symbool van de samenleving.
        Wageningen: Veenman, 229-235.

Kistemaker, R. and T. Levie
1987   *Exodo. Portugezen in Amsterdam*
        1600-1800. Amsterdam: Amsterdams
        Historisch Museum/De Bataafsche
        Leeuw.

Klein, P.W.
1984   '"Little London". British merchants
        in Rotterdam during the seventeenth
        and eighteenth centuries'. In: D.C.
        Coleman and P. Mathias (ed.),
        Enterprise and history. Essays in honour
        of Charles Wilson. Cambridge: CUP,
        116-134.

Kloek, E., *et al.* (ed.)
1994   *Women in the golden age.* Hilversum:
        Verloren.

Köbben, A.
1979   'De gijzelingsakties van
        Zuidmolukkers en hun effekten op de
        samenleving'. In: *Transactie* 8 (1979)
        2: 147-154.

Koelstra, R.W. and H.J. Tieleman
1977   *Ontwikkeling of migratie. Een*
        onderzoek naar mogelijkheden ter
        stimulering van de werkgelegenheid in
        minder ontwikkelde regio's in Tunesië.
        The Hague:
        NUFFIC/IMWOO/REMPLOD.

Kommers, J.
1993   *Kinderroof of zigeunerroof? Zigeuners*
        in kinderboeken. Utrecht: Jan van
        Arkel.

Koopmans, J.W.
1991   'Vreemdelingen in Hollandse dienst
        1545-1588. Opmerkingen bij het werk
        van Briels'. In: A.H. Huussen jr., *et al.*
        (ed.), *Vreemdelingen ongewenst en*
        bemind. Groningen: Forsten, 37-45.

Koot, W. and A. van der Wiel
1982   *Op weg naar werk ver van huis.*
        Muiderberg: Coutinho.

Kors, J.W.M. and M.J.G. Kors
1992   'Italiaanse schoorsteenvegers in Den
        Haag'. In: *Jaarboek van het Centraal
        Bureau voor Genealogie en het
        Iconografisch Bureau* 46 (1992) 178-207.

Kossmann, E.H.
1978   *The Low Countries 1780-1940.* Oxford:
        OUP.
1984   *Tolerantie toen en nu.* Coornhertrede
        1984. Gouda: Coornhert Stichting.

Koulen, I. and V. Smit
1988   *Bibliografie etnische groepen. Een
        overzicht van in Nederland verschenen
        publikaties met betrekking tot etnische.
        groepen in de periode 1985-1986.*
        Amsterdam: Noord-Hollandse
        Uitgevers Maatschappij.

Kövi, A.
1987   'Hongaarse immigratie na 1956'. In:
        Tijdschrift voor Geschiedenis 100 (1987)
        446-459.

Kraak, J.H., P. Ploeger and F.O.J. Kho
1958   *De repatriëring uit Indonesië. Een
        onderzoek naar de integratie van de
        gerepatrieerden in de Nederlandse
        samenleving.* The Hague:
        Staatsdrukkerij en Uitgeverijbedrijf.

Kreukels, L.
1987   'Vreemd gespuis en onbedorven
        jongens en mannen'. In: Anne Frank
        Stichting (ed.), *Vreemd gespuis.*
        Amsterdam: AMBO/NOVIB, 66-76.

Kubat, D. (ed.)
1984   *The politics of return. International
        return migration in Europe.*
        Rome/New York: CSI/CMS.

Kuyer, H.J.M.
1963   *Twee jaar na de vlucht. Een onderzoek
        naar aanpassing en persoonlijkheid van
        Hongaarse vluchtelingen.* Nijmegen:
        doctoral dissertation, University of
        Nijmegen.

Landman, N.
1992   *Van mat tot minaret. De
        institutionalisering van de islam in
        Nederland.* Amsterdam: VU-Uitgeverij

Leenders, M.H.C.H.
1993   *Ongenode gasten. Van traditioneel
        asielrecht naar immigratiebeleid,
        1815-1938.* Hilversum: Verloren.

Lequin, Y. (ed.)
1988   *La mosaïque France. Historie des
        étrangers et de l'immigration en France.*
        Paris.

Levie, T. and H. Zantkuyl
1980   *Wonen in Amsterdam in de 17de en
        18de eeuw.* Purmerend: Muusses.

Lijphart, A.
1968   *The politics of accommodation.
        Pluralism and democracy in the
        Netherlands.* Berkeley: University of
        California Press.
1982   *Verzuiling, pacificatie en kentering in
        de Nederlandse politiek.* Amsterdam:
        J.H. de Bussy.

Lindo, F.
1996   *Maakt cultuur verschil? De invloed van
        groepsspecifieke gedragspatronen op de
        onderwijsloopbaan van Turkse en
        Iberische migrantenjongeren.*
        Amsterdam: Het Spinhuis.

Lindo, F. and T. Pennings
1992   *Jeugd met toekomst. De leefsituatie en
        sociale positie van Portugese, Spaanse en
        Joegoslavische jongeren in Nederland.*
        Amsterdam: Het Spinhuis.

Lourens, P. and J. Lucassen
  1987   *Lipsker op de Groninger tichelwerken.*
          Een geschiedenis van de Groningse
          steenindustrie met bijzondere nadruk op
          de Lipper trekarbeiders 1700-1900.
          Groningen: Wolters
          Noordhoff/Forsten.

Lucassen, J.
  1984   *Naar de kusten van de Noordzee.*
          Trekarbeid in Europees perspectief,
          1600-1900. Gouda: doctoral
          dissertation, University of Utrecht.
  1987a   *Migrant labour in Europe 1600-1900.*
          London: Croom Helm.
  1987b   'Hannekemaaiersbrieven 1860-1889.
          Een bijdrage tot de geschiedenis van
          de arbeidsverhoudingen in de Friese
          hooibouw'. In: *It Beaken* 49 (1987)
          200-229.
  1991a   *Dutch long distance migration. A*
          concise history 1600-1900. Amsterdam:
          IISG.
  1991b   *Jan, Jan Salie en diens kinderen.*
          Vergelijkend onderzoek naar
          continuïteit en discontinuïteit in de
          ontwikkeling van arbeidsverhoudingen.
          Amsterdam: Stichting Beheer IISG.
  1992   'Het welvaren van Leiden (1659-1662):
          de wording van een economische
          theorie over gilden en
          ondernemerschap'. In: B. de Vries, *et*
          al. (ed.), *De kracht der zwakken.*
          Studies over arbeid en
          arbeidersbeweging in het verleden.
          Amsterdam: Stichting Beheer IISG,
          13-48.
  1994a   'Joodse Nederlanders 1796-1940. Een
          proces van omgekeerde
          minderheidsvorming'. In: H. Berg, *et*
          al. (ed.), *Joodse ondernemers en*
          ondernemingen, 1796-1940.
          Amsterdam: Joods Historisch
          Museum, 32-46.

  1994b   'The Netherlands, the Dutch, and
          long distance migration, in the late
          sixteenth to early nineteenth
          centuries'. In N. Canny (ed.),
          Europeans on the move. Studies on
          European migration, 1500-1800.
          Oxford: OUP, 153-191.
  1995a   'The other proletarians: seasonal
          labourers, mercenaries and miners'.
          In: C. Lis, J. Lucassen and H. Soly
          (ed.), *Before the unions. Wage-earners*
          and collective action in Europe,
          1300-1850, International Review of
          Social History Supplement 2 (1995).
          Cambridge: CUP, 171-194.
  1995b   'Labour and early modern economic
          development'. In: C.A. Davids and J.
          Lucassen (ed.), *A miracle mirrored.*
          The Dutch Republic in European
          perspective. Cambridge: CUP, 367-409.

Lucassen, J. and L. Lucassen (ed.)
  1997   *Migration, migration history, history.*
          Old paradigms and new perspectives.
          Bern: Peter Lang.

Lucassen, J. and R. Penninx
  1985   *Nieuwkomers. Immigranten en hun*
          nakomelingen in Nederland 1550-1985.
          Amsterdam: Meulenhoff.
  1994   *Nieuwkomers, nakomelingen,*
          Nederlanders. Immigranten in
          Nederland 1550-1993. Amsterdam: Het
          Spinhuis.

Lucassen, J., R. Penninx, L. van Velzen and A.
Zwinkels
  1974   *Trekarbeid van de Middellandse*
          Zeelanden naar West-Europa, een
          bibliografisch overzicht. Nijmegen:
          SUN.

Lucassen, J. and G. Trienekens
1978   'Om de plaats in de kerk. Een
        onderzoek naar maatschappelijke
        ongelijkheid, voornamelijk in de
        negentiende eeuw'. In: *Tijdschrift voor*
        Sociale Geschiedenis 4 (1978) 239-294.

Lucassen, L.
1987   'Poepen, knoeten, mieren en moffen.
        Beeldvorming over Duitse
        immigranten en trekarbeiders in
        zeventiende- en achttiende-eeuwse
        kluchten'. In: Anne Frank Stichting
        (ed.), *Vreemd gespuis*. Amsterdam:
        AMBO/NOVIB, 29-37.
1990   *En men noemde hen zigeuners.*
        Geschiedenis van Kalderasch, Ursari,
        Lowara en Sinti in Nederland,
        1750-1944. Amsterdam/The Hague:
        IISG/SDU.
1993   'Under the cloak of begging? Gypsy
        occupations in western Europe in the
        19th and 20th centuries'. In:
        Ethnologia Europaea 23 (1993) 75-94.

Lucassen, L. and A.J.F. Köbben
1992   *Het partiële gelijk. Controverses over het*
        onderwijs in de eigen taal en cultuur en
        de rol daarbij van beleid en wetenschap
        (1951-1991). Amsterdam/Lisse: Swets
        and Zeitlinger.

Lunn, K. (ed.)
1985   *Race and labour in twentieth-century*
        Britain. London: Cass.

Luykx, P. and N. Bootsma (ed.)
1987   *De laatste tijd. Geschiedschrijving over*
        Nederland in de 20e eeuw. Utrecht:
        Aula.

Manuhutu, W.
1987   'Molukkers in Nederland. Migranten
        tegen wil en dank'. In: *Tijdschrift voor*
        Geschiedenis 100 (1987) 432-445.

Manuhutu, W. and H. Smeets (ed.)
1991   *Tijdelijk verblijf. De opvang van*
        Molukkers in Nederland, 1951.
        Amsterdam: De Bataafsche Leeuw.

Marshall, A.
1973   *The import of labor. The case of the*
        Netherlands. Rotterdam: Universitaire
        Pers Rotterdam.

Maurik, J. van
1901   *Toen ik nog jong was.* Amsterdam: Van
        Holkema & Warendorf.

McNeill, W.H.
1985   'Migratie in historisch perspectief'.
        In: *De Gids* 148 (1985) 191-207.

Meer, T. van der
1984   *De wesentlijke sonde van sodomie en*
        andere vuyligheeden.
        Sodomietenvervolgingen in Amsterdam
        1730-1811. Amsterdam: Tabula.
1989   'De geboorte van de homoseksuele
        minderheid'. In: M. Gijswijt-Hofstra
        (ed.), *Een schijn van*
        verdraagzaamheid. Afwijking en
        tolerantie in Nederland van de zestiende
        eeuw tot heden. Hilversum: Verloren,
        157-194.
1995   *Sodoms zaad in Nederland. Het*
        ontstaan van homoseksualiteit in de
        vroegmoderne tijd. Nijmegen: SUN.

Mertens-Westphalen, H.
1993   'De Duitser en de Hollandganger in
        de kluchten uit de 17e en 18e eeuw'.
        In: A. Eiynck, *et al.* (ed.), *Werken over*
        de grens. 350 jaar geld verdienen in het
        buitenland. Assen: Drents Museum
        Assen/Museumsdorf
        Cloppenburg-Niedersächsisches
        Freilichtmuseum/Westfries Museum
        Hoorn/Emslandmuseum Lingen,
        52-59.

Meulenbroek, H.
1982   'De Duitse dienstmeisjes'. In: *Vrij
        Nederland*, Bijlage 28 (13 November
        1982), 28-47.

Meyer, H.
1987   *SOPEMI-report 1987, Federal Republic of
        Germany*. (Unpublished national
        report for the Continuous Reporting
        System on Migration of the OECD).
        Paris.

Michman, J.
1989   'The Jewish essence of Dutch Jewry'.
        In: J. Michman (ed.), *Dutch Jewish
        history. Proceedings of the Fourth
        Symposium on the History of the Jews in
        the Netherlands 7-10 December Tel
        Aviv-Jerusalem, 1986.*
        Assen/Maastricht: The Institute for
        Research on Dutch Jewry, Hebrew
        University of Jerusalem/Van Gorcum,
        II, 1-22.

Mijnhardt, W.W.
1983   'De geschiedschrijving over de
        ideeëngeschiedenis van de 17e- en
        18e-eeuwse Republiek'. In:
        W.W. Mijnhardt (ed.), *Kantelend
        geschiedbeeld. Nederlandse historiografie
        sinds 1945*. Utrecht/Antwerp: Aula,
        162-205.

Minderheden
1987   *Minderheden in Nederland. Statistisch
        vademecum 1987* [1988 etc.], (T.
        Ankersmit, *et al.*). The
        Hague/Rotterdam: CBS/ISEO, 1987
        (1988 etc. Published annually).

Minderhedennota
1983   *Minderhedennota*. Regeringsnota over
        het minderhedenbeleid. The Hague:
        Staatsuitgeverij (stukken Tweede
        Kamer 1982-83, 16102, no. 21).

Moch, L.P.
1992   *Moving Europeans. Migration in
        Western Europe since 1650.*
        Bloomington/Indianapolis: Indiana
        University Press.

Morelli, A. (ed.)
1992   *Histoire des étrangers et de
        l'immigration en Belgique de la
        prehistoire à nos jours*. Brussels:
        Editions Vie Ouvriere.

Muus, P.J.
1985-   *Migration, minorities and policy in the
etc.   Netherlands. Recent trends and
        developments; report for the OECD,
        SOPEMI – Netherlands – 1985.*
        Amsterdam: Instituut voor Sociale
        Geografie, University of Amsterdam,
        1985 (see also idem 1986; 1987 etc.
        annually).
1986b   *Terugkeren of blijven. Een onderzoek
        onder Turkse werknemers van het
        bedrijf Thomassen en Drijver-Verblifa
        N.V. n.a.v. het instellen van een
        vertrekpremie*. Amsterdam:
        SGI/University of Amsterdam.

Muus, P.J. and R. Penninx
1991   *Immigratie van Turken en Marokkanen
        in Nederland. Een analyse van de
        ontwikkeling tussen 1970-1990, een
        vooruitblik op te verwachten
        immigratie en de consequenties voor
        beleid*. The Hague: Ministerie van
        Binnenlandse Zaken.

Muus, P. J., R. Penninx, J. M. M. van Amersfoort,
F. Bovenkerk and W. Verschoor
1983   *Retourmigratie van Mediterranen,
        Surinamers en Antillianen uit
        Nederland*. The Hague: Ministerie
        van Sociale Zaken en
        Werkgelegenheid.

Niet-Nederlanders
1990-   *Niet-Nederlanders in Nederland, 1*
etc.   *januari 1990 [1991 etc].* The Hague:
         Centraal Bureau voor de Statistiek
         (annual).

Noiriel, G.
1988   *Le creuset francais. Histoire de
         l'immigration, XIXe-XXe siècles.* Paris:
         Seuil.
1991   *La tyrannie du national. Le droit d'asile
         en Europe 1793-1993.* Paris:
         Calmann-Levy.

Noordegraaf, L.
1984   'Buitenlanders in de Republiek'. In: F.
         Wieringa (ed.), *Republiek tussen
         vorsten. Oranje, opstand, vrijheid,
         geloof.* Zutphen: Walburg Pers, 119-128.
1985   *Hollands welvaren? Levensstandaard in
         Holland 1450-1650.* Bergen: Octavo.

Noordegraaf, L. and J.L. van Zanden
1995   'Early modern economic growth and
         the standard of living. Did labour
         benefit from Holland's Golden Age?'
         In: K. Davids and J. Lucassen (ed.), *A
         miracle mirrored. The Dutch Republic
         in European perspective.* Cambridge:
         CUP, 410-437.

Nusteling, H.P.H.
1985   *Welvaart en werkgelegenheid in
         Amsterdam 1540-1860. Een relaas over
         demografie, economie en sociale politiek
         van een wereldstad.*
         Amsterdam/Diemen: De Bataafsche
         Leeuw.

Onderzoek
1989   *Onderzoek etnische minderheden. Een
         geselecteerde bibliografie van onderzoek
         inzake etnische groepen tussen 1984 en
         1989 en samenvattingen van een selectie
         van onderzoeken verricht in opdracht
         van de rijksoverheid.* The Hague:
         ACOM/Ministerie van Binnenlandse
         Zaken.
1992   *Onderzoek etnische minderheden. Een
         geselecteerde bibliografie van onderzoek
         inzake etnische groepen tussen 1989 en
         1992 en samenvattingen van een selectie
         van onderzoeken verricht in opdracht
         van de rijksoverheid.* The Hague:
         ACOM/Ministerie van Binnenlandse
         Zaken.

Ontwerp-Minderhedennota
1981   *Ontwerp-Minderhedennota.* The
         Hague: Ministerie van Binnenlandse
         Zaken.

Oomens, C.A.
1989   *De loop der bevolking van Nederland in
         de negentiende eeuw.* The Hague: CBS.

Oostindië, G. and E. Maduro
1986   *In het land van de overheerser. Deel II:
         Antillianen en Surinamers in
         Nederland 1634/1667-1954.* Dordrecht:
         Foris.

Ornée, W.A.
1970   'De "Mof" in de Nederlandse blij- en
         kluchtspelen uit de 17e en 18e eeuw'.
         In: *Voordrachten, gehouden voor de
         Gelderse Leergangen te Arnhem 27.*
         Groningen: Wolters Noordhoff.

Overdijk-Francis, J.E.
1995   *Wet bevordering evenredige
         arbeidsdeelname allochtonen. Analyse
         en beleidsimplicaties.*
         Houten/Zaventem: BSL/Koninklijke
         Vermande.

Overzicht
  1985   *Overzicht Onderzoek minderheden.*
          Onderzoek minderheden 1980-1985: een
          geselecteerde bibliografie. The Hague:
          ACOM/Ministeries van Binnenlandse
          Zaken en WVC.

Paine, T.
  1791   *Rights of Man, being an answer to Mr*
          Burke's attack on the French Revolution.
          Second edition, London: Watson.

Park, R.E.
  1950   *Race and culture. The collected papers of*
          Robert Ezra Park. Vol. I. Glencoe: The
          Free Press.

Penninx, R.
  1979a   'Naar een algemeen etnisch
          minderhedenbeleid?' In:
          Wetenschappelijke Raad voor het
          Regeringsbeleid, *Etnische*
          minderheden. The Hague:
          Staatsuitgeverij, 1-174.
  1979b   'Towards an overall ethnic minorities
          policy?' In: Scientific Council for
          Government Policy, *Ethnic minorities.*
          Report 17. The Hague:
          Staatsuitgeverij.
  1984   *Immigrant populations and*
          demographic development in the
          member states of the Council of Europe,
          vol. I. Analysis of general trends and
          possible future developments.
          Population Studies 12. Strasbourg:
          Council of Europe.
  1985   'Onderzoek met betrekking tot
          minderheden in Nederland'. In: A.
          Martens and F. Moulaert (ed.),
          Buitenlandse minderheden in
          Vlaanderen-België. Wetenschappelijke
          inzichten en overheidsbeleid.
          Antwerp/Amsterdam: De
          Nederlandse Boekhandel, 233-254.

  1988a   *Minderheidsvorming en emancipatie.*
          Balans van kennisverwerving ten
          aanzien van immigranten en
          woonwagenbewoners 1967-1987. Alphen
          aan den Rijn: Samsom.
  1988b   *Wie betaalt, bepaalt? De ontwikkeling*
          en programmering van onderzoek naar
          migranten, etnische minderheden en
          woonwagenbewoners 1955-1985.
          SGI-reeks. Amsterdam: University of
          Amsterdam.
  1992   *Wie betaalt en wie bepaalt?*
          Onderzoeksbeleid van de overheid
          m.b.t. minderheden en de invloed van
          onderzoek op het beleid. The Hague:
          Ministerie van Binnenlandse Zaken
  1994   'Die niederländische Gesellschaft und
          ihre Einwanderer. Einwanderungs-
          und Minderheitenpolitik, öffentlicher
          Diskurs und Multikulturelles in den
          Niederlanden'. In: M.M. Jansen and
          S. Baringhorst (ed.), *Politik der*
          Multikultur. Vergleichende
          Perspektieven zu Einwanderung und
          Integration. Baden-Baden: Nomos
          Verlag, 105-124.
  1995   'La société néerlandaise et ses
          immigrés. La position des immigrés
          aux Pays-Bas et le multiculturalisme
          dans la société néerlandaise'. In: C.
          Neveu (ed.), *Nations, frontières et*
          immigration en Europe, Paris:
          CIEMI/L'Harmattan, 49-85.

Penninx, R. and P. Muus
  1989a   *Grenzeloos migreren na 1992?*
          Internationale migratie en de Europese
          Gemeenschap in verleden en toekomst.
          The Hague: NIDI, rapport no. 5.
  1989b   'No limits for migration after 1992?
          The lessons of the past and a
          reconnaissance of the future'. In:
          International Migration 27 (1989) 3:
          373-388.

Penninx, R., J. Schoorl and C. van Praag
1993   *The impact of international migration.*
        The case of the Netherlands.
        Amsterdam/Lisse/Berwyn: Swets and
        Zeitlinger.
1994   *The impact of international migration.*
        The case of the Netherlands. NIDI
        Report 37. The Hague: Netherlands
        Interdisciplinary Demographic
        Institute (second edition/reprint of
        the 1993 Swets and Zeitlinger edition).

Penninx, R. and F. Selier
1992   'Theorievorming over internationale
        migratie. Een historisch overzicht en
        een stand van zaken'. In:
        Migrantenstudies 4 (1992) 4-20.

Penninx, R., J. Tillie, H. Vermeulen, M. de Vries
and R. Wolff
1995   *Migratie, minderheden en beleid in de*
        toekomst. Een trendstudie. TWCM
        Voorstudie no. 5. Amsterdam: Het
        Spinhuis.

Penninx, R. and L. van Velzen
1977   *Internationale arbeidsmigratie.*
        Uitstoting uit thuislanden en
        maatschappelijke integratie in
        gastlanden van buitenlandse arbeiders.
        Nijmegen: SUN.

Penninx, R. and H. Yar
1993   *Western European states and the*
        political representation of Islam. The
        cases of Belgium and the Netherlands.
        Paper presented at the Conference on
        The Facelift of Europe. Amsterdam:
        Faculty PSCW/University of
        Amsterdam.

Pieterse, J.N.
1992   *White on black. Images of Africa and*
        blacks in western popular culture. New
        Haven/London: Yale University Press.

Poeze, H.A., *et al.*
1986   *In het land van de overheerser. Deel I:*
        Indonesiërs in Nederland 1600-1950.
        Dordrecht: Foris.

Post, M.J.H.
1964   'De Katholieken op Zuid-Beveland in
        de tweede helft van de zeventiende en
        de eerste helft van de achttiende
        eeuw'. In: *Voor Rogier. Een bundel*
        opstellen van oud-leerlingen de
        hoogleraar bij zijn afscheid aangeboden.
        Hilversum/Antwerp, 111-125.

Potts, L.
1990   *The world labour market. A history of*
        migration. London: Zed Books.

Praag, C.S. van
1983   *Vooroordeel tegenover etnische*
        minderheden. Resultaten van
        Nederlands opinieonderzoek. Rijswijk:
        Sociaal en Cultureel Planbureau.
1986   'Minderheden voor en na de nota'. In:
        Migrantenstudies 2 (1986) 4: 2-53.

Praag, C.S. van, and B.W. Frijling
1987   'De experimentele remigratieregeling.
        Veelbelovend stiefkind van het
        minderhedenbeleid'. In:
        Migrantenstudies 3 (1987) 3: 28-38.

Prak, M.
1992   '"Een verzekerd bestaan".
        Ambachtslieden, winkeliers en hun
        gilden in Den Bosch (ca. 1775)'. In: B.
        de Vries, *et al.* (ed.), *De kracht der*
        zwakken. Studies over arbeid en
        arbeidersbeweging in het verleden.
        Amsterdam: Stichting Beheer IISG,
        49-79.

Preedy, S.E.
1984   *Negers in de Nederlanden, 1500-1863.*
        Nijmegen: Transculturele Uitgeverij
        Masusa.

Prins, W.F.
  1980   'Fugitieven en passanten'. In:
          Mededelingen der Koninklijke
          Nederlandse Akademie van
          Wetenschappen, Afd. Letterkunde,
          Nieuwe Reeks 43 (1980) no. 2.

Problematiek
  1978   *De problematiek van de Molukse*
          minderheid in Nederland. Zitting
          Tweede Kamer 1977/78, 14915, nos
          1-2. The Hague: Staatsuitgeverij.

Projectgroep ICO
  1995   *Intercultureel onderwijs. Impuls voor*
          school en omgeving. Den Bosch: KPC.

Ramakers, J.
  1990   '"Godsmoordenaars en
          adderengebroed". Het antisemitische
          vijandbeeld bij de Nederlandse
          katholieken in de negentiende eeuw'.
          In: H. Righart (ed.), *De zachte kant*
          van de politiek. Opstellen over politiek
          en cultuur. The Hague: SDU, 88-106.
  1994   'Hier is een schuld te voldoen! Het
          huisvestingsbeleid voor repatrianten'.
          In: W. Willems and L. Lucassen (ed.),
          Het onbekende vaderland. De
          repatriëring van Indische Nederlanders
          1946-1964. The Hague: SDU, 108-120.

Rath, J.
  1991   *Minorisering. De sociale constructie van*
          'etnische minderheden'. Amsterdam:
          SUA.

Rath, J., K. Groenendijk and R. Penninx
  1992   'Nederland en de islam. Een
          programma van onderzoek'. In:
          Migrantenstudies 8 (1992) 1: 18-37.
  1993   'De erkenning en institutionalisering
          van de islam in België,
          Groot-Brittannië en Nederland'. In:
          Tijdschrift voor Sociologie 14 (1993) 1:
          53-76.

Rath, J., R. Penninx, K. Groenendijk and A. Meyer
  1996   *Nederland en zijn islam. Een*
          ontzuilende samenleving reageert op het
          ontstaan van een geloofsgemeenschap.
          Amsterdam: Het Spinhuis.

Regeringsreactie
  1980   *Regeringsreactie op het rapport 'Etnische*
          Minderheden' van de WRR.
          Handelingen Tweede Kamer 1980/81,
          16102, no. 6. The Hague:
          Staatsuitgeverij.

Reisepredigt
          Reisepredigt (Working party, which
          includes J. Lucassen, and which is
          preparing for publication the reports
          written by German ministers who
          visited their compatriots in the
          Netherlands between 1849 and 1894).

Rijkschroeff, B.R.
  1989   *Een ervaring rijker. De Indische*
          immigranten in de Verenigde Staten
          van Amerika. Delft: Eburon.

Rijsdijk, A.
  1985   *Repatriëring en opvang van Indische*
          Nederlanders. Departementaal beleid
          1945-1958. Unpublished master thesis.
          Amsterdam: University of Amsterdam.

Ringeling, A.B.
  1978   *Beleidsvrijheid van ambtenaren. Het*
          spijtoptantenprobleem als illustratie van
          de activiteiten van ambtenaren bij de
          uitvoering van beleid. Alphen aan den
          Rijn: Samsom.

Roelandt, T.J.A.
  1994   *Verscheidenheid in ongelijkheid. Een*
          studie naar de etnische stratificatie en
          onderklassevorming in de Nederlandse
          samenleving. Amsterdam: Thesis
          Publishers.

Roelandt, T., H. Smeets and J. Veenman
1993   *Jaarboek minderheden 1993.*
        Houten/Lelystad: Bohn, Stafleu, Van
        Loghum/Kon. Vermande.

Roetman, R. and T. van der Tuin-Noordermeer
1996   *Onderzoek etnische minderheden. Een
        geselecteerde bibliografie van onderzoek
        inzake etnische groepen tussen 1992 en
        1995.* Leiden: LISWO.

Rogers, R.
1992   'The future of refugee flows and
        policies'. In: *International Migration
        Review* 26 (1992) 4: 1112-1143.

Rogier, L.J.
1956   *Katholieke herleving. Geschiedenis van
        katholiek Nederland sinds 1853.* The
        Hague: Pax.

Roosblad, J., R. Penninx and F. Elshof
1992   *Universitair minderhedenonderzoek.
        Lopend onderzoek met betrekking tot
        immigranten en etnische minderheden
        aan Nederlandse universiteiten in het
        najaar van 1991, een inventarisatie.*
        The Hague: Ministerie van
        Binnenlandse Zaken.

Roosens, E.
1982   'Etnische groep of etnische identiteit:
        symbolen of concepten?' In: J.M.M.
        van Amersfoort and H.B. Entzinger
        (ed.), *Immigrant en samenleving.*
        Deventer: Van Loghum Slaterus,
        99-122.
1986   *Micronationalisme. Een antropologie
        van het etnisch réveil.*
        Leuven/Amersfoort: ACCO.
1989   *Creating ethnicity. The process of
        ethnogenesis.* Newbury Park: Sage.

Ruitenbeek, K.
1993   '"Bijna te arm tot
        schouwburgtijdverdrijf". Sociale
        geleding en levensstandaard van het
        publiek in de Amsterdamse
        Stadsschouwburg in de eerste helft
        van de negentiende eeuw'. In:
        *Economisch- en Sociaal-Historisch
        Jaarboek* 65 (1993) 94-149.

Ruller, S. van, and P. Ippel
1984   'Diefstal, doodstraf en lijfsgenade in
        de negentiende eeuw'. In: *Tijdschrift
        voor Sociale Geschiedenis* 10 (1984) 3-33.

Salomon, H.P.
1975   *The 'De Pinto' manuscript. A 17th
        century Marrano family history.* Assen:
        Van Gorcum.

Sande, A. van de
1989   'Roomse buitenbeentjes in een
        protestantse natie? Tolerantie en
        anti-papisme in Nederland in de
        zeventiende, achttiende en
        negentiende eeuw'. In: M.
        Gijswijt-Hofstra (ed.), *Een schijn van
        verdraagzaamheid. Afwijking en
        tolerantie in Nederland van de zestiende
        eeuw tot heden.* Hilversum: Verloren,
        107-129.

Sansone, L.
1992   *Schitteren in de schaduw.
        Overlevingsstrategieën, subcultuur en
        etnische identiteit van Creoolse jongens
        en jonge mannen uit de lagere klasse in
        Amsterdam: 1981-1991.* Amsterdam:
        Het Spinhuis.

Schippers, H.
1986   *Zwart en Nationaal Front. Latijns
        georiënteerd rechts-radicalisme in
        Nederland (1922-1946).* Amsterdam:
        Stichting Beheer IISG.

Schöffer, I.
1981   'The Jews in the Netherlands: the
        position of a minority through three
        centuries'. In: *Studia Rosenthaliana* 15
        (1981) 85-100.

Schoorl, J.J.
1992   *De demografische ontwikkeling van de
        allochtone bevolking in Nederland.
        Trends in migratie, vruchtbaarheid,
        sterfte en naturalisatie.* Paper presented
        at Nederlandse Geografendagen,
        Nijmegen, November.

Scientific Council for Government Policy
1979   *Ethnic minorities.* Report 17. The
        Hague: Staatsuitgeverij.
1989   *Immigrant policy.* Report 36. The
        Hague: SDU.

Shadid, W.A.R. and P.S. van Koningsveld
1992   *De mythe van het islamitische gevaar.*
        Kampen: Kok.

Sijes, B.A.
1979   *Vervolging van zigeuners in Nederland
        1940-1945.* The Hague: Martinus
        Nijhoff.

Smeets, H.M.A.G.
1989   'Het duizendbanenplan Molukkers.
        Proefvaart van het nieuwe
        allochtonenbeleid?' In:
        Migrantenstudies 5 (1989) 4: 13-23.
1992   *Molukkers in Nederland.* Utrecht:
        Moluks Historisch Museum.
1993   *Etnische minderheden bij de overheid.*
        TWCM-voorstudie 3. The Hague:
        Ministerie van Binnenlandse Zaken.

Smeets, H.M.A.G., E.P. Martens and J. Veenman
1996   *Jaarboek Minderheden 1996.*
        Houten/Zaventem: BSL/Koninklijke
        Vermande.

Sociaal
1992   *Sociaal en Cultureel Rapport 1992.*
        Rijswijk: SCP.

Sociale
1993   *Sociale en Culturele Verkenningen 1993.*
        Rijswijk: SCP.

Soly, H. and A.K. Thijs (ed.)
1995   *Minderheden in Westeuropese steden.*
        Brussel: Institut Historique Belge de
        Rome.

Staaij, A.J. van der
1973   'De buitenlandse werknemers'. In: H.
        Verwey-Jonker (ed.), *Allochtonen in
        Nederland.* The Hague:
        Staatsuitgeverij (second revised
        edition), 191-218.

Statistiek
        Statistiek van de buitenlandse migratie.
        Centraal Bureau voor de Statistiek.
        The Hague: Staatsuitgeverij/SDU
        (annually).

Steijlen, F.
1996   *RMS: van ideaal tot symbool. Moluks
        nationalisme in Nederland 1951-1994.*
        Amsterdam: Het Spinhuis.

Stichtingsakkoord
1993   *Het stichtingsakkoord over etnische
        minderheden in de praktijk. Eerste
        vervolgmeting.* The Hague:
        LTD/Ministerie van Sociale Zaken en
        Werkgelegenheid.

Surie, H.G.
1971   'De gerepatrieerden'. In: H.
        Verwey-Jonker (ed.), *Allochtonen in
        Nederland.* The Hague:
        Staatsuitgeverij, 47-110.

Swart, A.H.J.
1978   *De toelating en uitzetting van
        vreemdelingen.* Deventer: Kluwer.

Tanja, J.
  1987   'Brabantse monsieurs, Vlaemsche
          yveraers en Hollantsche botticheyt'.
          In: Anne Frank Stichting (ed.),
          Vreemd gespuis. Amsterdam:
          AMBO/NOVIB, 20-28.

Tas, R.F.J.
  1994   'Surinaamse en Antilliaanse bevolking
          in Nederland, 1 januari 1994'. In:
          Maandstatistiek van de Bevolking (CBS)
          42 (1994) 10: 6-10.

Tennekes, J.
  1990   *De onbekende dimensie. Over cultuur,
          cultuurverschillen en macht.*
          Leuven/Apeldoorn: Garant.

Termote, M.
  1969   *Migration et équilibre économique
          spatial.* Leuven: UCL.

Tesser, P.T.M.
  1993   *Rapportage minderheden 1993.*
          Rijswijk: Sociaal en Cultureel
          Planbureau.

Tesser, P.T.M., F.A. van Dugteren and C.S. van
Praag
  1994   *Ruimtelijke spreiding van allochtonen.
          Ontwikkelingen, achtergronden,
          gevolgen.* Den Haag:
          SCP/Binnenlandse Zaken.

Tillaart, H.J.M. van, and T.J.M. Reubsaet
  1988   *Etnische ondernemers in Nederland.*
          Nijmegen: ITS.

Tilly, C.
  1978   'Migration in modern European
          history'. In: W.H. McNeill and R.S.
          Adams (ed.), *Human migration.
          Patterns and policies.*
          Bloomington/London: Indiana
          University Press, 48-74.

Tinnemans, W.
  1991   *L'Italianita. De Italiaanse gemeenschap
          in Nederland.* Amsterdam: Het
          Spinhuis.
  1994   *Een gouden armband. Een geschiedenis
          van mediterrane immigranten in
          Nederland (1945-1994).* Utrecht: NCB.

Tschudi, P. von
  1932   *Geschichte der deutschen Evangelischen
          Gemeinde im Haag.*
          Göttingen: Vandenhoeck & Ruprecht.

TWCM (Tijdelijke Wetenschappelijke Commissie
Minderhedenbeleid)
  1995   *Eenheid en verscheidenheid: op zoek
          naar de balans. Beschouwingen over
          immigratie- en integratiebeleid.*
          TWCM-Kaderadvies. Amsterdam: Het
          Spinhuis.

Veenman, J. (ed.)
  1990a   *Ver van huis. Achterstand en
          achterstelling bij allochtonen.*
          Rotterdam: ISEO.

Veenman, J.
  1990b   *De arbeidsmarktpositie van allochtonen
          in Nederland, in het bijzonder van
          Molukkers.* Groningen: Wolters
          Noordhoff.
  1994   *Participatie in perspectief.
          Ontwikkelingen in de
          sociaal-economische positie van zes
          allochtone groepen in Nederland.*
          Houten/Zaventem: BSL/Koninklijke
          Vermande.

Vellinga, M.L. and W.G. Wolters
  1971   *De Chinezen van Amsterdam. De
          integratie van een etnische
          minderheidsgroep in de Nederlandse
          samenleving.* Amsterdam:
          ASC/University of Amsterdam.

Vermeulen, H.
1984   *Etnische groepen en grenzen. Chinezen,*
        Surinamers en Turken. Weesp:
        Wereldvenster.

Vermeulen, H., *et al.*
1985   *De Grieken.* Muiderberg: Coutinho.

Vermeulen, H. and A. Böcker
1992   'De studie van migratie in Nederland.
        Een bibliografisch overzicht'. In:
        Migrantenstudies 8 (1992) 4: 21-29.

Vermeulen, H. and C. Govers
1994   *The anthropology of ethnicity. Beyond*
        'ethnic groups and boundaries'.
        Amsterdam: Het Spinhuis.

Vermeulen, H. and R. Penninx (ed.)
1994   *Het democratisch ongeduld. De*
        emancipatie en integratie van zes
        doelgroepen van het minderhedenbeleid.
        Amsterdam: Het Spinhuis.

Verwey-Jonker, H. (ed.)
1971   *Allochtonen in Nederland.* The Hague:
        Staatsuitgeverij (second revised
        edition, 1973).

Verwey-Jonker, H.
1973   'De vluchtelingen'. In: H.
        Verwey-Jonker (ed.), *Allochtonen in*
        Nederland, The Hague:
        Staatsuitgeverij, 234-243.

Verwey-Jonker, H. and P.O.M. Brackel
1957   *The assimilation and integration of pre-*
        and postwar refugees in the Netherlands.
        The Hague: Publications of the
        Research Group for European
        Migration Problems 11.

Vis, S.
1995   *Survey of the archival sources*
        concerning migration and settlement
        held at the IISH. Amsterdam:
        International Institute of Social
        History.

Voets, S.Y. and J.J. Schoorl
1988   'Deelonderzoek demografie'. In: F.N.
        Pieke (ed.), *De positie van de Chinezen*
        in Nederland. Leiden: Sinologisch
        Instituut, Leiden University, 157-191.

Vries, J. de
1971   'Het censuskiesrecht en de welvaart in
        Nederland 1850-1917'. In: *Economisch-*
        en Sociaal-Historisch Jaarboek 34 (1971)
        178-231.

Vries, M. de
1987   *Ogen in je rug. Turkse meisjes en*
        vrouwen in Nederland. Alphen aan
        den Rijn/Brussel: Samsom.

Vriezen, J.
1993   *Rijst of aardappelen? Indische en*
        autochtone ouderen in Nederland.
        Amsterdam: Het Spinhuis.

Vuijsje, H.
1986   *Vermoorde onschuld. Etnisch verschil als*
        Hollands taboe. Amsterdam: Bert
        Bakker.

Wagenaar, L.
1903   'Walcheren in 1778'. In: *Archief*
        Zeeuwsch Genootschap (1903) 27-72.

Wagtendonk, K. (ed.)
1991   *Islam in Nederland. Islam op school.*
        Muiderberg: Coutinho.

Wal, S.L. van der
1979   'Nederland en Nederlandsch-Indië
        1914-1942'. In: *Algemene Geschiedenis*
        der Nederlanden, vol. 14. Bussum:
        Fibula-Van Dishoeck, 379-399.

Weijdeveld, R. (ed.)
1986   *Rode Hulp. De opvang van Duitse*
        vluchtelingen in Groningerland
        (1933-1940). Groningen: Wolters
        Noordhoff/Forsten.

Wentholt, R. (ed.)
  1967   *Buitenlandse arbeiders in Nederland.*
          Een veelzijdige benadering van een
          complex probleem. Leiden: Spruyt, Van
          Mantgem & De Does.

Werdmölder, H.
  1990   *Een generatie op drift. De geschiedenis*
          van een Marokkaanse randgroep.
          Arnhem: Gouda Quint.

Willems, W. (ed.)
  1990   *Indische Nederlanders in de ogen van de*
          wetenschap. Leiden: COMT.

Willems, W.
  1991   *Bronnen van kennis over Indische*
          Nederlanders. Leiden: COMT.
  1992   *Sporen van een Indische verleden*
          1600-1942. Leiden: COMT.
  1995   *Op zoek naar de ware zigeuner.*
          Zigeuners als studieobject tijdens de
          Verlichting, de Romantiek en het
          Nazisme. Utrecht: Jan van Arkel.

Willems, W. and L. Lucassen
  1990   *Ongewenste vreemdelingen.*
          Buitenlandse zigeuners en de
          Nederlandse overheid: 1969-1989. The
          Hague: SDU.
  1994   *Het onbekende vaderland. De*
          repatriëring van Indische Nederlanders
          1946-1964. The Hague: SDU.

Willems, W. and J. de Moor (ed.)
  1995   *Het einde van Indië. Indische*
          Nederlanders tijdens de Japanse
          bezetting en de dekolonisatie. The
          Hague: SDU.

Witte, R.
  1995   *Racist violence and the state. A*
          comparative European analysis.
          Doctoral dissertation, University of
          Utrecht.

Wolff, R. and R. Penninx
  1994   *De ontwikkeling van de positie van*
          minderheden op de Nederlandse
          arbeidsmarkt. TWCM-voorstudie 1.
          The Hague: Ministerie van
          Binnenlandse Zaken.

Woordenboek
  1913, etc. *Woordenboek der Nederlandse Taal.*
          The Hague: Nijhoff.

Wubben, H.J.J.
  1986   '*Chineezen en ander Aziatisch*
          ongedierte'. Lotgevallen van Chinese
          immigranten in Nederland, 1911-1940.
          Zutphen: Walburg Pers.

Zanden, J.L. van
  1985   'De economische ontwikkeling van de
          Nederlandse landbouw in de
          negentiende eeuw, 1800-1914'. In:
          A.A.G. Bijdragen 25, Wageningen.
  1991   *Arbeid tijdens het handelskapitalisme.*
          Opkomst en neergang van de Hollandse
          economie, 1350-1850. Bergen: Octavo.
  1993   *The rise and decline of Holland's*
          economy. Merchant capitalism and the
          labour market. Manchester/New York:
          Manchester University Press.

Zeven, B.
  1987   'Van Chineezenreserves en
          Pindamannen. De kijk van
          Nederlanders op Chinezen in de jaren
          1910-1940'. In: Anne Frank Stichting
          (ed.), *Vreemd gespuis.* Amsterdam:
          AMBO/NOVIB, 77-91.

Zijlstra, B.
  1988   'De fl. 1.445,- maatregel. Sociologisch
          onderzoek en beleidsbepaling'. In:
          Migrantenstudies 4 (1988) 4: 28-33.

Zilverberg, S.B.J.
  1980   'Kerk en Verlichting in
          Noord-Nederland'. In: *Algemene
          Geschiedenis der Nederlanden*, vol. 9.
          Bussum: Fibula-Van Dishoeck,
          318-330.

Zolberg, A.R.
  1981   'International migration in political
          perspective'. In: Kritz, *et al.*, *Global
          trends in migration*. New York: CMS.
  1989   'The next waves. Migration theory for
          a changing world'. In: *International
          Migration Review* 23 (1989) 3: 403-430.

Zolberg, A.R., A. Suhrke and S. Aguayo
  1989   *Escape from violence. Conflict and the
          refugee crisis in the developing world.*
          Oxford: OUP.
  1992   *Vluchten voor geweld. Een analyse van
          het vluchtelingenvraagstuk.*
          Amsterdam: SUA.

Zwitser, H.L.
  1991   *De militie van den staat. Het leger van
          de Republiek der Verenigde
          Nederlanden.* Amsterdam: Van Soeren.

Subject index

Concepts and migrant groups